FLORIDA'S PIONEER NATURALIST

University Press of Florida
Gainesville Tallahassee Tampa Boca Raton Pensacola Orlando Miami Jacksonville

Elizabeth Ogren Rothra

FLORIDA'S PIONEER NATURALIST

The Life of Charles Torrey Simpson

00 99 98 97 96 95 6 5 4 3 2 1

Library of Congress Cataloging-in-Publication Data
Rothra, Elizabeth Ogren.
Florida's pioneer naturalist: the life of Charles Torrey Simpson /
by Elizabeth Ogren Rothra.
p. cm.
Includes bibliographical references (p.) and index.
ISBN 0-8130-1374-7
1. Simpson, Charles Torrey, 1846–1932. 2. Naturalists—Florida—Biography. 3. Conchologists—Florida—Biography. I. Title.
QH31.S5725R68 1995
508.759'092—dc20
[B] 95-9893

The University Press of Florida is the scholarly publishing agency for the State University System of Florida, comprised of Florida A & M University, Florida Atlantic University, Florida International University, Florida State University, University of Central Florida, University of Florida, University of North Florida, University of South Florida, and University of West Florida.

University Press of Florida
15 Northwest 15th Street
Gainesville, FL 32611

For Ellen

CONTENTS

ILLUSTRATIONS

PREFACE

The Goody, Naughty Book was a children's book of manners in an ingenious format. The first half told about a good little girl, but when the book was turned upside down the tale of a naughty child unfolded. Such a double volume seemed a solution to the difficulty of appealing to two widely different audiences: those who wanted to meet C. T. Simpson, conchologist and author of the *Descriptive Catalogue of the Naiades, or Pearly Fresh-Water Mussels,* and those who were looking for Charles Torrey Simpson, Florida's pioneer naturalist. Half of the book would feature Simpson as a specialist in mollusks; turn the book upside down and skip these details, delving only into his life in that southernmost state.

Since this solution is not practical, the author begs the indulgence of the nonscientific reader, noting that Simpson's accomplishments in the field of conchology were integral to his accomplishments as a communicator of Florida's natural history. Additionally, it seems important to call attention to the plight of the naiad mussels, a mute, seldom-observed fauna that was millions of years in evolving and now is declining at an alarming rate.

My great pleasure has been meeting those individuals who have shared with me letters, diaries, photographs, experiences, and other parts of the puzzle that comprise the history of this man's life. I am indebted especially to Mrs. Melvin Dant of the Bureau County (Illinois) Historical Society, Marcia Couch Kenney, and Kenneth Wurdack, who led me to family histories and photographs; to Mary G. McMurria of the Manatee County Historical Society, who gave life to the "Sarasota Gang"; to E. S. Reasoner of Reasoners' Tropical Nurseries, who shared Pliny Reasoner's diary and photograph; to David Honor Stansbery, curator of mollusks of the Museum of Biological Diversity, Ohio State University, who gave me a crash course in uniology and piloted me through the rough shoals of scientific classification; to Ellen Edelen, for her encouragement and for coursing through the manuscript with her blue pencil more than once; to Marjory Stoneman Douglas for her personal remembrances of Simpson and his times; to Joseph Rosewater, Frederick Bayer, and Harald Rehder, Division of Mollusks, and to Robert Read, recently retired curator of botany, all of the National Museum of Natural History at the Smithsonian; and to James Steed, Smithsonian archivist, who provided important clues to Simpson's past.

The Simpson file in Special Collections of the University of Miami Richter Library was especially valuable for letters and papers salvaged from Simpson's abandoned house and for other relevant material. My thanks to George Rosner for his cheerful willingness to give me every assistance, as well to William E. Brown Jr., both of the Richter Library. Significant contributions were also made by Professor Earl Rich of the Biology Department and Gilbert Voss and Kay Hale of the Rosenstiel School of Marine and Atmospheric Science, all of the University of Miami, Florida; and by Rebecca Smith and Dawn Hugh of the Charlton W. Tebeau Research Center of the Historical Association of Southern Florida. Generous assistance also was given by the staff of the Bentley Historical Library of the University of Michigan regarding Simpson's letters to his publisher, Bryant Walker; by the Academy of Natural Sciences of Philadelphia for Simpson's correspondence with Henry Pilsbry; by Vivian Wiser of the Agricultural History Branch of the U.S. Department of Agriculture for details on the Meyer Medal presentation; by the North Carolina State Archives for Helen Simpson's *Early Records of the Simpson Families;* by George K. Small for the letters of his father, John Kunkel Small; and by Bertram Zuckerman of the Fairchild Tropical Garden Research Library.

Other individuals and institutions who have contributed to this biography are Mills Memorial Library of Rollins College; the Putnam Museum of History and Natural Science, Davenport, Iowa; the Hunt Institute for Botanical Documentation; the New York Botanical Garden; the Eaton Florida History Room of the Manatee County (Florida) Public Library System; the Henry Morrison Flagler Museum; the Robert Strozier Library of Florida State University; the P. K. Yonge Library of Florida History at the University of Florida; Samuel Boldrick, librarian of the Florida Collection of the Dade County Public Library; John E. Rawlins of the Carnegie Museum of Natural History; and Kenneth G.

Wood of State University of New York at Fredonia. Also Barbara Fairchild Muller, Graham Bell Fairchild, Isabelle (Mrs. William) Krome, Loy Morrow, Arva Moore Parks, Thelma Peters, Gertrude Peterson, Elsie M. Picot, Alice Mosier Swinson, Charlton Tebeau, and Nicolas Winkleman. Last but not least, I appreciate the help of my brother, Robert Ogren, in providing me with papers on the unios; of the reference desk staff of the James Prendergast Library, Jamestown, New York; and of my daughter, Katie, and my husband, Dann, for their unfailing encouragement and support.

Introduction

After wrestling with the aggravations of a field trip in South Florida's "great southwest wild"—pushing a skiff through the shallow, log-jammed, overgrown channels that meander through the mangrove forests of Madeira Bay, hacking his way through the vine-tangled, thorny thickets of the Keys, torpid from mosquito bites, sweaty, waterlogged, and half-starved—Simpson asked himself, "Why should an old man, past the age when most persons seek adventure, leave a comfortable home and plunge into the wilderness to endure such hardships? . . . I never return utterly worn out from such a trip but I vow it is the last. But in time the hardships are forgotten and recollections of the pleasant features only remain. . . . Personally I cannot resist the call and must respond when I hear it."[1] Even when he was well over seventy Simpson made these grueling treks in Florida's great southwest wild.

To Floridians he was a distinguished personality, revered as the "sage of Biscayne Bay," the "patriarch of the South Florida naturalists," an author of books on tropical horticulture and Florida's natural history, an authority on two branches of science, and the subject of feature stories in the Sunday papers; but in the field he was often mistaken for a tramp and refused hospitality from the humblest homes.

An energetic, muscular man, Simpson was never more himself than when tramping about in woods and thickets and wading in streams and ponds, seeking out the wildlife there. Born in a log cabin on the Illinois prairie, he was following a pattern rooted in childhood, satisfying his perennial curiosity about the origin of natural things, doing what he had always done, what he enjoyed most. "There's nothing like getting out after specimens to make a fellow feel he's really living . . . to feel the wind blowing in your face, to see the clouds scampering and the trees waving," he told a visitor shortly before he died in 1932.[2]

Prior to his retirement to Florida in 1902, Simpson's primary field of science was malacology, the study of shells and the animals that inhabit them. His scientific papers reveal that before he joined the Smithsonian's National Museum in a professional capacity he collected on the rivers of the Southeast when serving in the Union Army; on the shores of foreign ports while in the U.S. Navy; on the ocean beaches, freshwater drains, swamps, and rivers of South Florida; and on the rivers of the Midwest and as far west as eastern Colorado.

Simpson's major contribution to science was his *Descriptive Catalogue of the Naiades, or Pearly Fresh-Water Mussels,* a reference work of vast proportions describing over seventy-five hundred species, compiled when he was an aide in the U.S. National Museum of the Smithsonian but not published until twelve years after his retirement to Florida. Simpson's letters to his patron and publisher, Bryant Walker, begin a new chapter in the history of the classification of these bivalves, while his agony over the professional criticism of his new system adds depth to the personality of this man whose work is seminal to freshwater malacologists. After nearly ninety years, his catalog is still an important reference work and, along with his "Synopsis of the Naiades," is often cited.

But it was for his achievements as tropical Florida's pioneer naturalist that Simpson became widely known. Others came before him, but few ventured beyond the settlements of North Florida. In the eighteenth and early nineteenth centuries, botanist John Bartram, the first native-born naturalist in the New World, and his son, William, explored around St. Augustine and the St. Johns River, but their journeys were limited to that region by the threat of Indian attack and the morass of swamps and trackless wilderness that barred progress to the south. Thomas Say, who published the first American descriptions of New World shells and insects, explored the same region in 1818 and wrote, "On account of the hostility of the Indians it would be the extreme of prudence to venture any further up the river,"[3] and neither Mark Catesby nor André Michaux explored beyond North Florida. John James Audubon explored the St. Augustine area in 1832 and later that year traveled down the East Coast under the protection of a U.S. Revenue Cutter, a small, armored boat, spending five months in the Key West area painting his magnificent portraits of Florida's birds, but he never returned. John Muir, in 1867, on the last leg of his "thousand mile walk" from Indiana to the Gulf of Mexico, found Florida so "watery and vine-tied" that he followed the railroad bed from Fernandina to Cedar Key, where he lingered only long enough to recover from an attack of malaria. Botanists made serious collections in southern Florida beginning in 1830, but their scope was limited to plant collecting.

In Simpson's own time, universities, museums, and academies of natural science sent expeditions to Florida. Specialists such as botanist John Kunkel Small, horticulturalist Henry Nehrling, plant explorer David Fairchild, and malacologist Henry Pilsbry made major contributions to the knowledge of their special branches of science in Florida, but it was Charles Torrey Simpson who settled permanently in South Florida and devoted thirty years to investigating and describing its biota.

Simpson's long acquaintance with Florida gave him a unique perspective. He saw in the Everglades, stretching one hundred miles from Lake Okeechobee to the Gulf of Mexico, a vast, haunting expanse of open land, sky, and water, with towering clouds reflected in shimmering sheets of water studded with tree islands and sawgrass marshes. Waterbirds by the thousands—flamingos, egrets, ibis, wood storks, and herons—roosted, soared, and fed there. He explored virgin hammocks and cruised Florida's rivers when they meandered freely through stands of palms and oaks thickly overhung with vines and air plants. These memories of a swiftly disappearing landscape motivated him to be an environmental spokesman to the settlers and tourists who populated South Florida in the 1920s. They also inspired his determination to preserve some remnants of the Everglades through a national park.

Simpson's lifelong interest in horticulture found full expression in Florida. His botanical garden foreshadowed that of Miami's noted Fairchild Tropical Garden and was a showplace for Miami visitors and residents as well as an outpost of the U.S. Department of Agriculture's tropical experiment station. For bringing more than fifty palms, orchids, ferns, flowering trees, and vines to South Florida he won the Meyer Medal for Plant Introduction. His book *Ornamental Gardening in Florida,* the first comprehensive guide to Florida's tropical plants, changed the way people landscaped their homes. Florida's garden clubs and other nature-related groups met regularly at his home and were inspired by his teaching.

His studies of the Florida tree snails, *Liguus fasciatus,* indigenous only in coastal regions of South Florida, called attention to their diminishing ranks and the threat to their survival posed by overdevelopment. Investigating on foot in the hammocks of the Keys and mainland, he collected and described seventeen of the then-known fifty-two color forms of these arboreal snails.

Simpson has been compared to the noted nature writers of his time, John Muir and John Burroughs. Like them he was country-bred, largely self-educated, and associated with a particular region through his work. All three shared the common denominators of nature writers—a love of nature for its own sake, a sense of loss for what is no longer, and a feeling for man's place in the whole pattern of life. The public careers of Burroughs and Muir were nearly twice the length of Simpson's. Though they were only ten years older than the Florida naturalist, when his books were published their lives had drawn to a close.

David Fairchild liked to call Simpson the "John Muir of Florida," and Muir was much like his Florida counterpart. Both cultivated solitude and ignored human discomforts in their quest to understand the causes of natural things. As Muir studied the mountains, glaciers, and waterfalls of California, so Simpson pondered the ocean currents, island formations, and oolitic and coral limestone surfaces of Florida's shores and Everglades. Though Muir had higher political connections and was more widely identified as an environmental activist than Simpson, both influenced the legislation that established national parks.

Burroughs was less of a scientist than the other two, but, like Simpson, he was a philosopher. Inspired by one of the great American intellectuals of his time, Ralph Waldo Emerson, Burroughs's passages of supreme exaltation in the face of nature have parallels in the writings of both Emerson and Simpson.[4] His essays describing the wild inhabitants around his Hudson River farm attracted a legion of admirers and popularized nature study as a national activity. Many of Simpson's own followers, no doubt, had been touched by Burroughs and were the more eager to embrace the quite different biota of Simpson's own special region.

Simpson's slant on nature differed from that of both Muir and Burroughs; he was less literary than Muir and more intent on teaching than Burroughs. In the theories of Charles Darwin, Simpson found affirmation of his own ideas about the origin of things. He viewed the natural world as dynamic, constantly changing and being changed by water, wind, fire, and "armies" of plant invaders. Not the least of the forces of change, he charged, was human habitation. "Only Florida's climate is safe from vandal man, and, if it were possible to can and export it, we would until Florida would be desolate as Labrador," he wrote.[5]

Simpson's theories on geology have been criticized for their confusion of terms. For example, he described the landmass of lower Florida as being "uplifted" when what probably occurred was a lowering of the sea surface during glacial times. Scientists, too, would be jarred by Simpson's anthropomorphism. He "liked to believe" that plants "think," somewhat as humans do. He knew this was bad form, but many nature writers of his era indulged in it, and it was the only way he could explain such phenomena as the breathing apparatus devised by mangroves or the pollination method evolved by an orchid.

Simpson's ornate writing style reflected his culture and was liberally sprinkled with metaphors of war, biblical analogies, and Victorian hyperbole. Forest succession was a fierce battle for survival, with the live oak "in the very front of the firing line, a determined and courageous fighter." After a hurricane, new leaves on his orchid tree were a sign of hope, "like the dove with the olive branch after the deluge." Archaic words like "anomalies" and "vagaries" were used to describe plants whose behavior deviates from the norm.

Easy to overlook is Simpson's dry sense of humor. A good deal of teasing—what he called "bantering"—went on between him and his companions. Typical was the supreme "put-down," as when Henderson proudly presented his two-foot starfish to the museum, only to be told that ten-foot specimens of the same creature had been found in the Pacific. "Henderson required restoratives," Simpson commented.[6]

Deciphering the broad, open scrawl of Simpson's letters is a challenge, further complicated by his method of "simplified spelling." In a letter to botanist Roland Harper in 1910 he explained, "We leave out all silent letters and use all simple methods of spelling."[7] "Packed" became "packt" and "worked," "workt." Adding to the difficulty of reading his letters was his haphazard way of splitting words whenever they reached the margin, not on the syllable. In later years, however, he typed his letters. They are quoted as written. All underlining for emphasis is his. No attempt has been made to update nomenclature in excerpts from his letters and books, though current terminology has been used in the biographer's narrative.

Simpson's career in Florida bloomed late in his life, yet it spanned thirty years. Today he is little remembered except by old-timers and by those Florida gardeners and nature lovers who treasure his books; by professional botanists (some of whom still confuse him with his brother, Joseph H. Simpson); and by both amateur and professional students of mollusks. Yet he has won a place with his contemporaries, John Muir and

John Burroughs, in the galaxy of twentieth-century nature writers who, in a particular time and place, brought the natural world into sharp focus and spoke in its defense. The late Dr. Gilbert Voss, a University of Miami marine scientist, commented, "He was the only one who set down the natural history of this unique American region before its rare plants and animals began to disappear. More than any other, he wrote about the plants and animals and geological formations of South Florida and the Florida Keys at a time when new settlers were surging into that once under-populated state."[8]

In 1937, Orator F. Cook, onetime chief of the USDA's Office of Foreign Seed and Plant Introduction, dedicated a new palm to "the late Charles Torrey Simpson, whom future times may recognize as a great pioneer naturalist of tropical Florida."[9] This biography restores Simpson's long-silent voice, illumines the hidden years of his youth when he distinguished himself as an American field naturalist and conchologist, and reveals to a new generation of nature lovers the events that led to his distinguished career.

CHAPTER ONE

The Shaping of a Naturalist, 1846–1881

No man will see again the long-grass prairie where a sea of prairie flowers lapped at the stirrups of the pioneer.

Aldos Leopold, "Wilderness"

CHILDHOOD DISCOVERIES

The craving for the wild, the compulsion to sift and study the stuff of nature, was always a part of Charles Torrey Simpson's life. He believed this curiosity about the natural world was innate, like intuitive knowledge, physical dexterity, or artistic talent. Other noted naturalists confirm his experience. As a toddler, Linnaeus, the great Swedish systematist, was content for hours if placed on a grassy spot with a flower in his hand.[1] Thomas Nuttall, an early nineteenth-century naturalist, wrote in his journal, "To converse with nature, to admire the wisdom and beauty of creation has ever been . . . to me a favorite pursuit."[2] A more recent naturalist, ornithologist-artist Roger Tory Peterson, was inspired as a child by the sudden flight of a flicker he had thought to be dead.

By his own account, one of Simpson's earliest memories was finding thousands of tiny river snails washed up after a storm: "I was probably not more than four years old when I found those shells, a freckled, barefoot child with a ragged homemade straw hat, and one of those old-fashioned denim aprons which covered the entire body to the knees. I eagerly gathered hundreds of specimens and carried them home."[3]

Soon he discovered the live, algae-backed mollusks that inhabited the stream, plowing furrows in the sandy shoals or laying half-buried, apertures open, drawing food and oxygen from the water. By the time he was seven he had begun his collection: "I went with my parents to Hennepin, on the Illinois River, where they did their trading, and we had to wait on the banks of the stream for the ferry. While there I wandered along the shore and to my joy I found a number of large mussel shells and periwinkles, all of which were totally different from those near my home. When the boat came I pleaded to be allowed to stay and consent was finally but reluctantly given. . . . I can never forget the unalloyed delight of that day as I wandered and gathered the treasures so profusely scattered along the shore, all of which I insisted on having brought home."[4]

These anecdotes are excerpts from "Incidents in the Life of a Naturalist," a chapter in Simpson's book *Out of Doors in Florida,* published in 1923 when Simpson was seventy-three. Confirmation of his recollections is found in his land and freshwater shell collection now in the Zoology Department at the University of Miami (Florida). Among the specimens are two large naiad mussels—one identified in handwritten notations as "*Quadrulla solida* Lea, Hennepin, Ill. Collected as a child. Simpson" and the other as "*Unio gibbosus* Bar. Collected at seven years of age. Hennepin, Ill. Illinois River. Simpson." The shells in this collection—tiny river snails, fat muckets marked with green rays, ponderous "washboards" lined with opalescent nacre—were the boy's playthings that became the man's collection numbering some twenty thousand species. The large shells bulge from their boxes, threatening to jam the shallow drawers, while others are so small they lodge comfortably in thin, hollow bamboo stems. Without doubt, this is Simpson's original collection, formed in his boyhood and youth, before he became an aide at the U.S. National Museum. When he was hired he agreed to store his collection and not add to it during his employment, and after leaving the museum he did not unpack his shells for nearly ten years. It is apparent, too, that the collection was made before he was trained in scientific notation, for the shells are rather informally identified on precisely torn scraps of paper resting under each specimen or nested in a box of specimens.

A FORTUNATE TIME

Simpson's youth, in the mid- to late nineteenth century, was a time when everything in the natural storehouse of North America was being discovered and named. Wealthy patrons in Europe vied for natural history specimens from the New World and paid well those who could supply them. Collecting specimens was for many a slender means of support as well as an opportunity to pursue one's greatest delight. Naturalists accompanied U.S. military expeditions to make topographical observations and examine the flora, fauna, and minerals of unknown regions. Others joined fur-trapping parties or set off on solitary explorations in quest of new discoveries. Careless of personal comfort or safety, they scrambled through the undergrowth of virgin forests, clambered up glacial moraines, and faced the vast, inhospitable, open prairies of the Midwest and the arid deserts of the Southwest. Following the rivers, they penetrated deep into the newly opened land, cataloging its plants and animals, preserving specimens as best they could, and shipping them back to their sponsors. It was a harsh life; some suffered fatal accidents in remote areas, and others were killed in Indian warfare or died of disease aggravated by hunger and neglect.

Among those pioneer collectors who are remembered today were the two Bartrams: John, botanist to the king of England, who described and collected the wild flowers of the Shenandoah Valley; and his son, William, who, in 1791, published his *Travels,* the first widely circulated account of the "soil and natural productions of East and West Florida." Others included Alexander Wilson, ornithologist and bird artist, who journeyed from Maine to North Florida in the first decades of the nineteenth century; Thomas Say, the first zoologist to explore the American West, who returned from a military expedition with the pelts of deer, fox, brown shrews, and coyotes and the skins of eight new Western birds as well as hundreds of specimens of insects and freshwater shells; Thomas Nuttall, scholar and collector, whose scientific explorations in wilderness America have never been equaled in extent and productivity; and John James Audubon, perhaps the most universally known of the naturalists, whose portraits of the American flamingo, the Key West pigeon, the great blue heron, and hundreds of other birds and animals have kept his memory bright nearly 150 years after his death.

History records the substantial contribution to the knowledge of wild America made by these men and other noted specialists, but for every Audubon there were many lesser-known collectors driven by the excitement of discovering new species or just insatiable curiosity. Often these early American pioneer naturalists were doctors, chemists, clergymen, or engineers. Sometimes, like the young Simpson, they were self-taught farmers or unlettered persons imbued since early childhood with a love of nature. Women, too, were drawn to natural history, but, with few exceptions, their demanding lives as homemakers on the frontier left little time for pursuing birds or naming wildflowers. Nor were they free, socially, to join expeditions or embark on solitary tramps. Women did play a part, not to be diminished, in bonding their offspring to nature. Simpson, for example, records that his mother taught him the names of flowers and cleared a plot in her garden for his wild transplants.

As vast numbers of shells, pelts, fossils, minerals, sheets of dried plant specimens, and other natural materials accumulated from every corner of America, organizations were formed to name, classify, study, and curate them. In 1846 the last will and testament of an Englishman, James Smithson, bequeathed half a million dollars to the young American nation for the "increase and diffusion of knowledge among men." Soon the red sandstone towers of the Smithsonian Institution rose on the greensward in Washington.

People thronged into its lofty rooms to view rocks, shells, mounted birds, mammals, fishes, beetles, butterflies, and other natural history collections displayed in glass cases. The public education system was just being formed, and people were eager for knowledge. Washington's Smithsonian was an attraction high on every visitor's list and the inspiration for an upsurge of amateur nature study. Adding force to the movement were the startling theories of Charles Darwin, which challenged the cherished concept of creation by divine intervention and suggested that humans had evolved from some apelike ancestor.

In Philadelphia, the Academy of Natural Sciences was formed by a group of men who met periodically in the shop of pharmacist John Speakman. In New York, botanist John Torrey and his fellows laid the ground rules for the Lyceum of Natural History, forerunner of the New York Academy of Sciences. Robert Owen brought his "Boatload of Knowledge," literally a flat-bottomed ark floated down the Ohio River and poled up the Wabash bearing artists, teachers, zoologists, botanists, geologists, printers, and artisans—the human nucleus of an experimental communal society—to New Harmony, Indiana, not more than two hundred miles from Charles Simpson's birthplace.

Davenport, Iowa, a frontier city of twenty-five thousand inhabitants, established its own Academy of Natural Sciences in 1867. Simpson read his first paper on conchology to this group,[5] and it was published in their *Proceedings,* a journal that dealt with such diverse subjects as butterflies, skulls, bones, Indian mounds, and even the habits of a singing mouse.

Urbanization also played a part in Victorian America's interest in the natural world. Rural villages had expanded into crowded cities, and large farms had been divided into fifty-foot housing lots. Country people, drawn to cities to earn a living, looked back on their rural roots with nostalgia and responded by enthusiastically embracing ornithology clubs, botany study groups, garden clubs, and the lectures offered by local scientific societies. Teachers' training schools included ornithology and botany in their curriculum, and mail-order home study courses such as the Chautauqua Institution's Literary and Scientific book club offered astronomy, mineralogy, and other life sciences for those unable to attend classes in person. The Sabbath was "the Lord's Day" and tongues clicked in conservative communities when a farmer worked on Sunday, but birdwatching, shell collecting, and similar pursuits were approved recreation, edifying to the mind and invigorating to the body.

When family members traveled to foreign places through military or missionary service or in search of fortune, they brought back from foreign lands objects of strange beauty or exotic character. These appeared in the parlors of even the humblest homes: an abalone shell from the Orient; a length of the heaviest wood in the world from South America; a parrot from the West Indies; or a leopard skin from Africa. "Curiosity cabinets" where these and more indigenous oddities were displayed were a source of family pride. It was in this expansive age of discovery of the natural wonders of America that Charles Simpson grew up.

AN INDELIBLE IMPRINT

If his times were fortunate, so also was his birthplace—not the subtropical state of Florida where he would find renown, but mid-continent, near the north-central Illinois village of Tiskilwa. He was born on June 3, 1846, in a pioneer's cabin on the prairie, a seventh-generation American and the sixth child of a landowning farmer. The Senachwine, a little "mill race" named for an Indian chief, ran near the eighty-acre farm where he grew up, and prairie sloughs and ponds were common features of the landscape. Just a few miles distant flowed the broad Illinois River, and the Mississippi, Wabash, and Ohio rivers bordered his home state. These broad watercourses are part of the vast Mississippi drainage system, which nurtures the richest fauna of freshwater mollusks in the world, particularly the pearly freshwater mussels, or naiads.

Simpson found the whole of nature challenging. As a boy, with the enthusiasm that marked him throughout his life, he observed and sought those wonders of the plant world that grew near his home. To the south of the farm he could see an enormous cottonwood. Simpson remembered it as being eight feet in diameter and eighty or ninety feet high and divided into two immense horizontal branches that curved up like a lily petal: "I had a great desire to explore the ground on which it stood, to stand by it and touch it, but everywhere around it an almost impenetrable scrub made this impossible. Finally, after several unsuccessful attempts, I went up the prairie along the north side of the stream, . . . waded across and fought my way towards it. . . . In a few moments I stood by it. I patted it, extended my arms around it, talked foolishly to it and was as happy as it was possible for a child explorer to be."[6]

Wildflowers abounded in the warm, scented summers of his childhood: hepatica, spring beauties, bloodroot, columbine, meadow rue, bellwort, Solomon's seal, and two varieties of lady slippers. The clear, sparkling brooks were edged with dogtooth violets, hyacinth-like scillas, marsh marigolds, and bluebells. "The plants of the prairies, the sloughs, the wooded stream, and 'the barrens' differed in each locality; . . . I was learning my first lessons in distribution of life, a subject that has had a great fascination for me ever since."[7]

The natural features of his native state also made their mark. During early geological ages, Illinois had been covered with an inland sea, home to many ancient life-forms. Thick seams of coal are found throughout Illinois, and in the associated sandstone, shale, and limestone are many fossils. Low river bluffs with their rocky outcrops and a gravel pit near the Simpson's homestead were sources of great delight to the boy naturalist, for many curious fossil-bearing rocks could be gathered there.

The broad, open prairies of his childhood, interrupted by the streambed's long fingers of dense foliage, were rooted in his memory. These retinal images of sunlight and shade and the contrasting textures of grass and leaf may have influenced Simpson's landscaping plans for his Florida home, where shady, green islands of palms and bamboos pointed into bright, sunlit lawns.

A LITTLE FAMILY HISTORY

Charles's paternal ancestors were Alexander Simpson, a Scotchman, and Magdaline Chine, of French nationality, who emigrated to America with the early colonists. One of their descendants, Stephen Simpson, was born in 1718, settled in Washington County, Pennsylvania, near Ten Mile Creek, and married Sarah Conger. A yeoman farmer, Stephen fought in the American Revolution and lived to be 107. His son, David Conger Simpson, was Charles's grandfather.

David Simpson was born in the Year of Independence in a military fort where his family had taken refuge from Indian warfare. By coincidence, the woman who was to be his bride, Elizabeth Baldwin, was born the same year, and in a military fort as well. Elizabeth's parents, neighbors of the Simpsons, were educated, enterprising people of substance. Members of the family founded the Baldwin Locomotive Works in Philadelphia, and another relative, Caleb Baldwin, became chief justice of the Supreme Court of Iowa.

Jabez, Charles's father, born in Ten Mile, Pennsylvania, in 1804, was the eldest of David and Elizabeth Simpson's six children. When he came of age at twenty-one, he set out on foot for the Midwest, where land in the public domain could be bought for $1.25 an acre. In Lexington, Ohio, he married Matilda Hubbard Cook, presumably a hometown girl, since Matilda's family also had lived in Ten Mile. The Cooks were descended from Francis Cook, one of the 102 passengers on the Mayflower, but like most pioneers, Charles was little impressed. "Each individual must stand on his own record. . . . I don't feel especially proud of the Mayflower business for there must have been some useless or worse people aboard if I may believe the hundreds who claim it carried their ancestors."[8]

In 1839, Jabez and Matilda, with their daughters, Anna Harriet and Mary Elizabeth, moved from Ohio to Arispie County, Illinois, in a horse-drawn wagon. Five more children were born into the family, but only three—Mary Elizabeth, Joseph Herman, and Charles Torrey—lived to maturity. Headstones in old graveyards are grim evidence of the high mortality rate for children. Cholera, typhoid, pneumonia, and childbirth took a heavy toll.

The names of the Simpson children hint of the family's personal convictions. Abolition of slavery was not a popular cause in Illinois—even the churches were divided on the issue—but the Simpsons christened their sixth son "Owen Lovejoy" for an ardent abolitionist, the brother of Elijah Lovejoy, a martyr for the antislavery cause. Charles's middle name, "Torrey," proved to be prophetic, since John Torrey was a noted professor of botany at Princeton University, a founding member of the New York Academy of Science, and coauthor with Asa Gray of *Flora of North America.* As a boy and young man, Simpson answered to "Charley," while his older brother was "Jo" or "Brother Jo."

At first the Simpsons settled in the timberland because the early settlers regarded the treeless prairies as worthless. Land that could not support trees would hardly grow crops, they reasoned. The timberland proved too expensive, however, and Jabez gambled on the prairie where he bought eighty acres for about a hundred dollars. "My family was the first in the neighborhood who dared to leave the woods. When they built their house, no land or roads had been surveyed."[9] The idea that the prairie was sterile proved false. On the contrary, the thick, virgin topsoil that fostered the head-high blue-stem grass had been formed by glacial drift and was some of the most fertile land in the country.

Jabez planted pear, peach, and apple trees, and his orchards were famous for miles around. Joseph, who recorded the family history in a handwritten journal, recalled that his father harvested one thousand bushels of peaches in 1855. Joseph's journal, written in a style that leans heavily on exaggeration and parallels, described his father as "the best drummer, basket-maker, rail-splitter, splint-bottom chair bottomer, and the greatest expert with an axe and drawing knife of any man in the county."[10] Joseph's picture of his energetic, skillful father conflicts with his statement that his father was ill for sixty-two years, suggesting that Jabez suffered from spells of "the ague," the form of malaria that was common in swampy areas where mosquitoes found ample breeding places.

In 1852 Jabez opened a nursery, offering seedlings he had propagated. From his father, Charles learned not only the skill but also the joy of growing things. "Only the true plant lover feels the pleasure of digging up a cutting and finding at its base the heavy white callus or the delicate, young, soft roots pushing out. In his hand he holds the possibility of a noble tree which may live for generations to cheer and bless mankind long after he has passed away."[11]

Simpson attributed his love for the out-of-doors to his mother. Matilda Simpson taught him the names of wildflowers and made room in her garden for the things he dug up in the woods. "When they did well, I rejoiced, but I cried over them if they did not."[12] His first wages were spent on a basket of greenhouse plants.

Like many pioneer women, Matilda was either pregnant or nurturing an infant for most of her married life. The loss of four of her seven children added to the burden of pioneer life. She made the family's clothing of hand-loomed cloth made of rough linen, or a durable fabric called "Hard Times" because it would hold so many patches. Shoes were homemade from tanned skins of deer or cattle. There never were enough of them. "My sister went barefoot one whole winter," recalled Joseph Simpson.[13]

The Simpsons and most of their neighbors in this close-knit community were Protestants, members of the Baptist congregation. "My father and mother out-orthodoxed the orthodox. On the Sabbath we drove nine miles to a meeting held in a ramshackle building where they would allow no fire because we must 'crucify the flesh.' My mother wouldn't season her food, and she dressed her children so they looked like hobgoblins, all to keep down ungodly pride. As a result of this dreadful Puritanism, all three of the children, Elizabeth, Joseph, and I, at maturity, left the church forever."[14]

Despite the optimistic, buoyant nature that marked him as a man, he never forgot the jeers and taunts of childhood. "I belonged to the under stratum of society such as there was in the little town of Tiskilwa. There were boys who always wore good clothes and never worked. . . . I wore the denham and the ragged straw hats while I went barefoot in summer. Several of these boys would on no account associate with me. . . . I have lived to see nearly every one of them run out. One or two even went to the penitentiary."[15]

When Simpson was a youngster, his paternal grandparents, David and Betsy Simpson, lived nearby. Grandfather Simpson was a "walking dictionary": "He could give the definition of every word in 'Walker's dictionary' and spell them correctly," said Simpson, "but he hadn't an atom of business sense."[16]

Simpson described his Grandmother Simpson as an imposing, intelligent woman. "If she could have had a chance, I believe she would have made her mark . . . a strongly intellectual woman who, notwithstanding her poverty, was a sort of landmark in the neighborhood. She wrote very good poetry."[17]

The steady influence of his grandparents and of his sister Elizabeth kept the young Simpson on an even keel during the difficult days of his youth. His memoirs and letters contain little mention of his parents or other family members, but he reserved his deepest words of affection for Elizabeth: "My dear sister Elizabeth came nearer to me than anyone I ever knew. She might have made a naturalist if the soul hadn't been worked out of her. From the time I left home as a boy we always lovingly corresponded; . . . I never triumphed or was shown marked favor but what she was happier over it than I was; she always helped me up. . . . Since she died, the very light of day seems to have faded out and I miss her continually."[18]

Elizabeth had begun school when she was four years old and learned to read before leaving Ohio. Later the Simpsons, with three other families, hired a teacher who kept school in a nearby log cabin. Reading, writing, and arithmetic were the only subjects, but on the frontier they were all that was necessary. Joseph says with some bitterness that, though his father owned land and livestock and held mortgages, "the entire amount he spent on my education was three dollars and fifty cents."[19] The sum Joseph mentioned could have covered one school year. The elder Simpson seemed penurious, but, like many farmers, he may have felt that his sons' survival rested on their ability to win a living from the land.

Simpson confessed that beyond the rudiments of reading and writing, he made little progress. "Parsing a sentence was a task beyond me and fractions and mathematics I just hated. The fields and woods were my school. We had no Boy Scout movement in those days, but I did my own scouting and beat the game by nearly fifty years."[20]

Charles read geology and paleontology from his father's books: Edward Hitchcock's *Geology,* Gideon Mantell's *Medals of Creation,* and Hugh Miller's *Testimony of the Rocks.* It is difficult to imagine more stimulating reading than *Testimony of the Rocks* for an imaginative, scientifically inclined youngster. Miller's book was well illustrated with intriguing steel engravings of the skeletons of mammoths and other prehistoric mammals and birds, as well as fossils of extinct life-forms. In lucid, entertaining prose, the noted Scottish writer described the geological ages and the first appearance of life on earth. *Testimony of the Rocks* introduced Charles to the concept of evolution and the systematic classification of plants and animals.

Upon reading about the cabinets collectors used to display their specimens, Charles constructed a crude box with shelves where he arranged his shell collection. A distinguished professor of mineralogy came to see Mr. Simpson's orchards one day, and when the various fruits had been inspected and sampled Charles asked the gentleman if he would like to see his "cabinet." Mr. Simpson was somewhat embarrassed by his son's boldness, but the visitor went along, and when he saw Charles's collection he was interested. "I told him that the Physa shells turned one way and the Lymnaeas the other, that the Planorbis were rolled on themselves, and that the Unios from the Senachwine were unlike those I found in Illinois. When we got through he turned to my father with considerable emotion and said very impressively: 'Mr. Simpson, that boy will make a naturalist, if he isn't one already.' "[21]

Habits of thrift, temperance, honesty, self-reliance, charity, and industry ingrained during his boyhood days on the prairie were what Simpson called his "log cabin manners," and they were marks of his character throughout his life.

His boyhood ended abruptly in 1860 when his brother Owen died, his parents divorced, and his father sold his farm and nursery and moved away. Charles, then fourteen, had to leave school and go to work, taking odd jobs to help support his mother. Divorce was a family disgrace in Victorian America, and his father's subsequent remarriage and move to Missouri added to the isolation felt by this teenager. No longer constrained by parental ties, Charles adopted the stance of an agnostic. This, he admitted, "hurt me dreadfully in the eyes of the pious," and on one occasion the editor of the local newspaper denounced him as a "reprobate."[22]

NEW HORIZONS

When the Civil War broke out Charles was eager to join up, and he twice tried to enlist but was turned down because he was too young. Finally, though three months short of the mark, he convinced the recruiters he was eighteen, and in March 1864 he was mustered into service in Chicago as a private in Company F, Fifty-seventh Illinois Infantry. His service record describes him as five feet, four inches tall, with a fair complexion, auburn hair, and hazel eyes. His occupation was listed as "florist," perhaps because he had worked for a nursery.

Charles marched from Atlanta to the sea and through the Carolinas with Sherman and came within earshot of cannon fire. Except for minor skirmishes, he was never on the front line. The young Simpson's skills would have been valuable in the construction of barracks, bridges, and rifle pits. He also may have been detailed to guard and move prisoners. On one assignment, Charles's company was captured, but it was paroled in two days. Railroads followed rivers, and whenever possible, the army followed the railroads, finding their tracks a convenient highway through the countryside. Often the army camped for the night by a river, and the avid young naturalist could gather specimens in the Chattahoochie, the Ocmulgee, and the Ogeechee in Georgia as well as the Congarie in South Carolina and the Peedee and Neuse in North Carolina and other smaller streams.[23] All had large populations of unionids, the foundation of Simpson's youthful collection. "I took more interest in the world of new plants, the geology, and shells than I did in soldiering, though I did my duty faithfully. I diligently collected whenever an opportunity offered, putting my material into the sutler's wagon when we were on the march and sending it home from time to time."[24]

Brother Joseph records that Charles was in "six different hospitals in six different states" during his Civil War service. Most likely he had contracted malaria, either in Illinois where it was a common complaint or in the southern swamps. Simpson suffered from "chills and fever" throughout his adult life, and the quinine he took to control them may

Simpson as a young man, ca. 1875. The reverse of this photo is inscribed, "To Norman, with best regards of his long time friend, Charlie." Courtesy of the Estate of Marcia Couch Kenney.

have caused his deafness in later life. Not until thirty years later would mosquitoes be identified as transmitters of this debilitating infection.

Mustered out with an honorable discharge in July 1865, Charles returned to Tiskilwa. What was this nineteen-year-old like? Though he had not attained his full height, he was well built and muscular. With penetrating eyes and a sensual mouth, he would have been appealing to young women. Glimpses of his emotional nature can be caught in his self-descriptions. His vivid imagination is revealed in a passage from *Lower Florida Wilds.* While drifting along a remote, mangrove-lined river in the moonlight, he comments, "I never visit one of these estuaries without half expecting to see Plesiosauri crawling about in the mud or Pterodactyls hanging from the branches."[25] On one occasion he is terrified by a raging hurricane and on another overcome with claustrophobia when shut off from the sun under the dense canopy of the jungle trees. He writes of the "spirit of the forest" sweeping over him, and in the quiet of the hammock he gives way to euphoria and makes his confession to "the Great Power of the Universe."[26]

The teasing, bantering quips that marked his dialogue with fellow naturalists and the self-assertive, jaunty style of his letters to close friends suggest that these were traits carried over from his youth. Abundant evidence in his letters and writings suggests that he was generous-hearted but quick-tempered, easily offended, and impatient with obstacles that interfered with his goals. He burst into events not counting the cost—

falling off a cliff in his eagerness to capture a rare land snail, stuffing the pockets of his white linen suit with quantities of sea snails that exuded purple ink, breasting an ocean tide in a shark-infested channel to reach a tempting beach. Not one to hide his feelings, he "stomped up and down" when thieves entered his hammock and stole his plants. In his own words, he "yelled and pawed the ground" when he solved one of nature's elusive secrets. All these qualities in the mature Simpson would have been magnified in the youth.

In 1870 he signed on for a three-year hitch in the U.S. Navy. His departure was rumored to have been motivated by a "muss" with a young woman. The story agrees with Simpson's other romantic encounters, but he would have been equally motivated by the promise of adventure and travel. During the six years between his army enlistment and his service in the Navy he had a growth spurt, gaining six additional inches.

He sailed aboard the USS *Shenandoah* and the USS *Brooklyn* as a landsman, carpenter, and carpenter's mate. In the navy he became acquainted with astronomy and learned to tell time by the stars. While serving on the *Brooklyn,* a wooden-screw sloop-of-war, he cruised in European waters, visiting more than twenty countries and sending mementos back to Elizabeth for her curio cabinet: an olivewood cane from Jerusalem, shells from the Mediterranean, rocks, minerals, bits of petrified bones, and fossils. He recalls, "That army and navy experience made a man of me. I learned to stand and walk erect and to obey orders."[27]

After completing his tour of duty, Charles came home sporting a moustache and wearing his thick hair in duck-tail sideburns. Soon he would add a thin beard and, like many men of his day, would seldom again be clean-shaven. "Nothing contributes so much emphasis to character or to manly strength as a full, natural beard," he claimed.[28]

Little is known about Simpson's activities during the period following his service in the navy. Official records testify to his marriage, in 1875, to Cornelia Ann Couch from Tiskilwa, but no letters, diaries, or other written records hint of their courtship. Joseph's journal says that prior to Charles' position at the U.S. National Museum, he made his living as a farm laborer, construction worker, and coal miner. Charles confirms this, describing his youthful work experience as "jack-of-all-trades, farming, carpentering and . . . for nine years I worked in an Illinois coal mine."[29] It is apparent that his employment was never more than a means to an end. "In those days I learned much about shells, plants, and rocks. While following the plow it was my custom to carry a little box on the plow handles and when a shell or fossil stone turned up I put it in the box and looked up the subject in a book or sent the specimen to the state geological survey. A friend from New England lent me Alfonso Wood's book on botany. Later, I read Gray on botany, and with these books worked out a list of the plants in my native county."[30]

During this period Samuel P. Woodward's *Manual on Mollusks* started Simpson on the study of conchology, and as he added to his boyhood collection of local shells he sent some of them to the U.S. National Museum in Washington for identification.

CHAPTER TWO

Paradise Won, 1881–1885

I loved Florida on sight. I have loved it ever since, and it is, today, dearer to me than any spot on earth.

Charles Torrey Simpson

THE MOVE TO MANATEE

Winter with its naked trees, snow, sleet, and biting winds, the earth entombed in snow, was anathema to Simpson. "There are those, even naturalists, who claim to love a northern winter but I never did. The snow which has such an appeal to childhood never had any for me; it meant cold, wet feet, dreariness and discomfort. I am a child of the sun and as I grow older I dread even such cold as comes to us in lower Florida. . . . Humboldt was right when he said, 'Man lives in the tropics; he only exists elsewhere.' "[1] As he labored in a coal mine or tended his farm, he longed for the sunlight and warmth he had found in the South as a soldier in the Civil War and the brilliant skies and towering clouds of the Mediterranean he had known in the navy. These brief experiences led him to consider relocation to a more hospitable climate where the progression of life could be observed without interruption. He eagerly read the alluring ads in Northern newspapers extolling Florida as the "place where summer spends the winter" and dreamed of moving to this last American frontier, which sounded to him like paradise on earth.

The population of Florida had lagged behind that of other American regions, but with the conclusion of the Seminole Wars and the Civil War the prospect of peace came to this southernmost state, and small communities began to spring up along the Gulf Coast. Even though its population was less than a thousand, Tampa was considered a metropolis. Its Orange Grove Hotel was open for business, as were other inns in seashore towns as far south as Sarasota.

Simpson devoured everything written about tropical life, finding references to its West Indian flora in Torrey and Gray's *Flora of North America* and in Alvin Wentworth Chapman's *Southern Flora*. Though South Florida was less surveyed than other parts of the country, significant botanical collecting had been done there since the 1830s. This led to the inclusion of some subtropical species in the manuals available to Simpson. From Sidney Lanier's handbook, *Florida: Its Scenery, Climate, and History,* he learned about living conditions in this newly developing state and considered the prospects of resettling there.

In December 1881 Simpson had the opportunity to join two friends on a fishing trip to Florida. The party "ran by rail" to Cedar Key on the Gulf Coast, where they continued by steamer to Bradenton. As they disembarked a crowd gathered on the wharf to look over the passengers and escort them into town. One of Simpson's companions scooped up some of the sandy soil, ran it through his fingers, and commented that it was too poor to even sprout beans. A rough-looking man in the group spoke up. "If you could see my little place, maybe you'd change your mind."

> He had a small house embowered in trees and vines, an orange grove that was a picture of health, and was loaded with ripe fruit. There was a wonder of a vegetable garden, and in the border, his wife had beds of flowers. . . . Back of the house were some ridges, but there seemed to be nothing growing among them. When we asked if the soil there was too poor to raise stuff he went to one of the ridges and dug away revealing a hill of fine sweet potatoes which were fairly crowding each other out of the ground.
>
> Then he struck an attitude and said, "Ladies and gentlemen. I have been here nine years. All this stuff I have raised and never bought a pound of fertilizer. What you see is because of the wonderful climate; there is lots of land here for sale just as good as mine, and at prices that anyone can afford to pay.[2]

Simpson was impressed and considered the possibility of buying land in Florida. This could wait, however, for plans had been made to charter a boat for a week's fishing trip along the Gulf Coast. While the others were casting, the skipper had agreed to take Simpson ashore in the skiff to collect marine shells. On Mullet, Anna Maria, and Long Keys as well as at several points on the mainland, Simpson reveled in the thousands of beautiful shells to be found on the beaches, noting that entirely different species populated the muddy tidal flats. He gathered shells by the quart, for they were a medium of exchange for him. He traded them or sold them to other collectors. Also, for the purpose of classification, large groups of shells are needed to rule out variables.

> Going down Sarasota Bay we met a sailboat coming north and to my delight found in it Dr. John Velie, who was collecting shells and other marine stuff for the Chicago Academy of Sciences. I knew the names of only a few of the shells, but the Doctor was well posted so he got into our boat and Johnnie gave me an old chart for a slate. The Doctor gave me the name of each species. . . . I had a few things he had not found, and he had some I had not obtained, so we exchanged. It was probably the first floating academy of science founded in Florida.[3]

Before returning to the still-frozen north, Simpson had a fateful encounter with a wily land agent who offered to show him his vegetable garden.

> I confess I never saw a finer growth and it evidently had not been injured by a frost that had visited the area shortly before our arrival. The owner, whose face was as bland as that of the Heathen Chinee said he had lived where he was many years. No, there had never been any frost at his place, partly because of its high elevation and because of the warm air that blew up from the Gulf. True, they had frost all around him, but his land was wholly free from it. Yes, he had a little land which he would sell. It belonged in the tract he had gotten from the government, but it was mostly sold, only a little was left.[4]

Simpson, hopelessly enamored of the Florida dream, bought some lots from the man, afraid they would be snapped up before he could return. He would never regret his move to Florida, but as for the frost-free climate of his property, he was in for a surprise. On the rare occasions when Manatee County had a freeze, his vegetables always suffered, while those of the man who sold him the land came through unscathed.

> I had to get up very early one cold morning and passed by the old man's place . . . there was frost beside the road, but I saw, to my astonishment, that his garden was covered with canvas! Just then the old man came out, and I dodged behind a big pine tree. He looked care-

fully around to see that the coast was clear, then began to pull off the canvas. He carried it in and hid it under the house. The great climatic mystery was solved![5]

The other remarkable garden proved a hoax as well. Simpson discovered that a land speculator supplied the owner with all the fertilizer he could use in exchange for showing off his garden to prospective settlers.

Simpson's older brother, Joseph, then a bachelor of forty, moved to Manatee in April 1882. He would distinguish himself as a botanist and also be remembered as a teacher and historian. Unlike Charles, who had loved nature from childhood, Joseph claimed that he "detested botany" until he was thirty years old. Then it became his passion. "As soon as the flowers bloomed in the spring I borrowed Wood's Class Book of Botany, and Sunday mornings I would take a lunch and the book and tramp 12 or 15 miles alone with dear old nature," he noted in an autobiographical sketch.[6] Laboriously teaching himself the Latin names and the family identification key, he had compiled a list of Illinois plants to be found in Bureau County.

Within a month after Joseph's arrival, Charles and Cornelia made their move to Manatee County. The railroad ended at Cedar Key, so their goods had to be shipped there, then reloaded onto a steamer for Bradenton, and finally carted by oxen over the sandy trails that led to the community. Added to the household goods were Simpson's "camel load of shells," boxes and boxes of books and collecting equipment, as well as dried botanical material for comparison with tropical species. One wonders what household comforts Cornelia left behind to accommodate the unwieldy gear of a collector-naturalist.

Simpson, a skilled carpenter, built a house on one of his lots in the Fogartyville area of Bradenton, near the mouth of the broad Manatee River. In this bustling frontier town with newcomers arriving on every steamer, a man could make a living in construction, so he hung out his shingle as a builder-contractor and became so widely known as "Charley Carpenter" that some folks forgot his surname. As his workload increased, he went into partnership with a Mr. Wadham.

EMERGING CONCEPTS AND NEW GOALS

At thirty-five, though intelligent, personable, and energetic, Simpson had met with little material success. His attention was too divided, his thoughts too absorbed with questions that had plagued him since his youth. "Where did things come from?" "How do living forms evolve?"

Charles Torrey Simpson at about forty years of age, ca. 1887. Courtesy of the Estate of Marcia Couch Kenney.

He had discarded the biblical view of creation, as well as geologist Hugh Miller's attempt to reconcile what he found in the fossil record with the explanation of separate creations. His voting record described his religious affiliation as an "infidel" or, in less pejorative terms, a "nonbeliever."[7]

An inveterate reader, Simpson was acquainted with Darwin's theories on evolution, which were still hotly debated in scientific circles. He was enamored with these new concepts and embraced them with great enthusiasm, finding in them confirmation for his own emerging concepts. "The old idea that species were formed by an act of creation, fixed and unchangeable as coins stamped out in a mint, is fast becoming obsolete," he stated in one of his early papers in *Nautilus*.[8] This idea that all life was in a process of becoming, rather than fixed at the moment of creation, energized Simpson's drive to probe his new environment.

When time permitted, Simpson explored around Bradenton, sometimes joining a friend on a sail out to Terraceia Island or to Snead's Island at the mouth of the Manatee River. Often Cornelia or Joseph accompanied him on these jaunts. Joseph had found the flora of Terraceia Island astounding in its variety. Jutting out into the Gulf and surrounded by its warm waters, the island escaped the chilling finger of frost that periodically killed off tropical growth on the mainland. Charles visited the island in 1883 with Cornelia and a young friend, who piloted them in his sailboat, named the *Judas Iscariot.* In a letter to the editor of the *Bureau County Republican* (Illinois), he describes the orange grove and tropical vegetation they found there and, in this excerpt, their voyage home.

> The sun was dropping low, and we took our way over the old wharf for home, bidding our guide adieu; but we found the "Judas" true to her instincts, hard and fast aground and the power of twenty men would not have moved her. So there was nothing to do but wait for tide. . . . We hunted among the mangrove flats for shells. . . . One of our party caught a magnificent specimen of a spotted salt water trout with a cast-net, a beautiful fish with greenish silvery sides and dark brown spots.
>
> Darkness came, and if we had been in any other boat but the "Judas" the tide would undoubtedly have floated us, but she sat there glued to the bottom as stubborn and unyielding as a mule. . . . As we had provisions aboard, one of us started a fire while another went ashore and brought an arm load of mangrove wood which, when dry burns splendidly. But he had forgotten that dead mangrove wood is always full of ants, and when he began to break it the savage fellows issued out from their chambers, biting right and left. We made a slaw of cabbage, and cooked the trout and a more delicious meal I never ate, for there is something about such a way of cooking and camping that gives me a relish for food that nothing else will.
>
> Nine o'clock came before the boat condescended to float and at last we were under way with a good stiff breeze and making good time towards home. When we got out into open water the sea was a sheet of pale phosphorescent light and the wake left by the boat was dazzling beyond description. This light on the sea is produced by a microscopic animal . . . which exists in countless millions on all warm and tropical seas. Then there was a jelly-like animal an inch or more in diameter, which was very brilliant. It is astonishing the vast quantity and variety of life found in these Florida waters.
>
> We arrived at the mouth of the river by 10 o'clock, and here the trouble began. . . . [A]fter sailing the better part of the night against wind and tide, we found ourselves more than a mile from home, so we lowered our sails in disgust, got out the poles and poled the boat

Cornelia Couch Simpson. Courtesy of the Estate of Marcia Couch Kenney.

up to the wharf, tired and sleepy, and as we walked home I reflected that one generally pays for pleasure in one way or another.[9]

This passage, the earliest published example of Simpson's writing, is easily recognized as the style of the man who became "the patriarch of the South Florida naturalists." It is a fair guess that the unfortunate fellow who was attacked by fire ants when he broke up the firewood was Simpson himself.

The *Judas Iscariot* was not the first stubborn boat Simpson had encountered. Since boyhood he had spent much of his life in or near water. He was a river rat, beachcomber, seaman, oarsman, and sailor of small boats. He was probably more often wet than dry, whether from falling overboard, stumbling across watery prairies, groping for mussels in riverbeds, or simply being caught in the rain far from shelter. Now he was a familiar figure on the wharfs, meeting the fishing boats to see what marine oddities might be dumped from their nets. After a storm, lean, lanky "Charley Carpenter" could be seen on the beach stooped over the sea rick in search of shells cast up by high tides. In a little catboat he probed the bays and estuaries in search of the mollusks that burrowed in muddy banks and anchored themselves on rocks. His feet were sometimes cut and bloody from treading out clams.

When Simpson found material he could not classify, he sent it to the National Museum in Washington, where it landed on the desk of William Healey Dall. Dall had been a student of Louis Agassiz in zoology and anatomy at Harvard University. As a young man he had joined the Western Union International Telegraph Expedition to Alaska, charged with collecting scientific data. Later he commanded the expedition, accumulating valuable collections in natural history, chiefly of mollusks, in which he specialized. He published hundreds of papers, many on these invertebrates, and was honored at home and abroad by scientific institutions as well as his fellow scientists, who conferred his name on many newly discovered species of plants and animals. When his path crossed Simpson's, he was honorary curator in the National Museum's Department of Mollusks, working in an office in the north towers of the Smithsonian with his scientific aides, classifying specimens the museum received from collectors around the globe. Dall examined with some curiosity the specimens Simpson sent from Florida, for the marine fauna of Florida's coastline was little known.

Gradually Simpson began to work toward a dimly perceived goal—to make a living as a shell specialist. More clearly defined was his plan to publish a catalog of Florida marine shells, for he knew that collectors everywhere were eager for material from South Florida.

Simpson's arrival in Florida coincided with the push by railroaders, ranchers, and land developers to open the state to commerce and settlement. Several million acres in the Everglades, under water for much of the year, were being drained and sold to farmers for truck gardens and sugar plantations. The giant maws of Hamilton Disston's dredges were already biting into rock, mud, and sand, deepening rivers and straightening their graceful bends. Channels were dug to connect the shallow lakes of Central Florida and provide waterways for commerce and boating. The rocky rim of the Everglades that contained its freshwater was dynamited, and the water flowed out into the bay, bringing with it tons of black muck from the Everglades, sullying the pristine sandy bottom and choking marine life. When the tides changed, seawater infiltrated the freshwater ground table.

In this push for progress, the "reclamation of the Everglades" proceeded without the benefit of environmental studies to determine the effect of drainage on water control, the food chain, or how long the seemingly rich soil would sustain agriculture. No one knew that the vast sheets of warm, shallow water flowing slowly through the Everglades alleviated cold fronts and provided a barrier against fire. Nor did ecologists understand the role meandering rivers and overflowing marshes played in purifying water. The words "ecology" and "environment" were not yet part of the general vocabulary.

From the standpoint of land developers, the Everglades were a vast, useless wasteland. Simpson, however, felt otherwise and described what he saw there in 1882: "Wild life fairly swarmed . . . bear, deer, otter, mink, raccoons, various wild cats and the opossum were abundant, while every swamp and stream was full of alligators. Vast numbers of roseate spoonbills, snowy herons, American egrets, and the great white heron . . . winged their way over the pineland as they visited the swamps in search of food. And food was everywhere abundant, for all the waters were swarming with small fish and the lowlands contained unnumbered millions of pond snails."[10] During this early sojourn, from 1881 to 1886, before Florida's natural features were reshaped to accommodate a growing population, Simpson gained a perspective of its ecosystems that would later energize his words as a spokesman for their preservation.

PLINY REASONER

Not long after Simpson's arrival in Manatee County he met Pliny Ward Reasoner, who was just seventeen when he came to the area in 1881. The two men were a generation apart, but both were raised on nearby farms in Bureau County, Illinois, and from the gist of letters the younger man wrote to his mother, it would seem the families were known to each other. Clearly, the two men shared a love for plants as well as a distaste for Illinois's bleak winters, but the bonds of their friendship were forged of sterner stuff.

Pliny had studied Latin, Greek, Dutch, and German, as well as philosophy and geometry. A gifted writer, his letters, diaries, and the articles he wrote for the *Bureau County Republican* were a significant contribution to the history of Manatee County. Simpson described him as "almost a giant in stature . . . [although] a mere boy, kindly and unselfish, fairly bubbling over with glorious young life and energy, an excellent botanist and plant lover."[11]

This precocious young man came to Florida looking for land suitable for a nursery and orange grove. He bought forty acres of pineland for $250 and, as he explained to his mother in a letter, "it takes time and money to start an orange grove, but I don't think there is any surer way

The young pioneer plantsman, Pliny Reasoner, ca. 1886. Courtesy of E. S. "Bud" Reasoner.

to make a fortune."[12] By July of 1882 he had cleared his land and planted four varieties of oranges, as well as lemons, limes, figs, bananas, papaya, avocados, and other things he thought might do well.

A LUNATIC FOR SHELLS

In the winter of 1884, Simpson signed on as a "sort of super cargo sailor and carpenter" aboard the schooner *Asa Eldridge,* sailing for the Bay Islands of Honduras for a load of seed coconuts to bring back to Florida.[13] When the ship was in port, Simpson hoped to explore the island, mingle with the inhabitants, and collect shells and plants, some of the latter of which he promised to bring back for Pliny's nursery.

Key West was their first anchorage. As a major coaling station, an official U.S. port of entry, and the center for the ship salvage business, Key West, with its population of eighteen thousand, was then the largest city in Florida. It was also the pivotal point of embarkation between the east and west coasts of Florida and the Caribbean. The *Asa Eldridge* would have shared its berth with three-masted schooners, sloops, and barkentines as well as U.S. naval ships.

One Sunday morning, decked out in a white linen suit and his straw bowler, Simpson went sightseeing. This bilingual, multiethnic city was full of strangeness and delight to him. The streets resounded with strumming guitars and voices chattering in foreign languages and dialects, while everywhere flowering shrubs and trees were a feast to his eyes. As he strolled along the waterfront, he spotted a broad band of violet color on the beach. A huge colony of violet snails, or *Janthinas,* had blown ashore during the night. These pelagic mollusks eject a purplish fluid as a defense when disturbed and had stained the sand with their bright color for some distance. "It was the most astounding sight . . . of molluscan life I had ever seen and when I recovered from my surprise, I proceeded to collect specimens. . . . I used my handkerchief, then my new straw hat, then one pocket after another of my fresh white linen suit, and when fully loaded, I started for the schooner."[14]

His enthusiasm faded as he looked down to see his white suit streaked with the snails' violet ink. Feeling ludicrous, he took the back alleys and side streets back to the ship, only to be greeted with shouts and laughter by the crew. "My smart suit was ruined, nor could I even wear it around the vessel without being derided,—but I had the satisfaction of cleaning up over two thousand fine Janthina shells."[15] Only a confirmed naturalist would have called such a tedious, malodorous task a "satisfaction," but to Simpson the shells were a treasure.

The *Asa Eldridge* was an unseaworthy old vessel and began to leak as soon as they reached the rough water of the Caribbean. With four feet of water in the hold and the hand pumps going continually, Simpson was advised to be ready to launch the lifeboats in case an alarm was given in the night. They arrived in Utilla, however, without incident. The ship anchored there for six weeks while the cargo was taken aboard. Simpson made good use of his free time, investigating the shell-strewn beaches, searching for land snails, and studying the flora.

One morning, carrying a lunch of green coconuts and bananas, he set out across the island to find a coral reef that he had been warned by his host was treacherous and difficult to approach. When he reached it he found it full of jagged potholes but not impossible for a determined man to negotiate. On the far end of the reef was a deep channel, perhaps fifty feet wide, and beyond it beckoned a sandy cove covered with shells. This promised good collecting, so he tied his basket to a length of bamboo and paddled across the channel aboard this makeshift raft. For hours he was lost in the pleasure of examining what the sea had cast up. When it came time to return, however, he found the channel in a riptide.

> I was simply dazed and realized how foolish I had been. There was neither house nor boat anywhere near. In fact, this part of the island was rarely visited by anyone.

Finally, however, my wits came to me, and I remembered that I must have crossed at about half past nine at the time of high tide. Consequently there would be low tide at about half past three. Even . . . now the current became less rapid so I got my bamboo, hunted up a piece of sea fan which I tied securely over my shells and lashed the basket firmly to my float. Finally I became impatient, and pushed out from the head of the channel. But I found, though I tried to swim upstream . . . I was being rapidly carried out into the rough sea. I struggled on, and at last found that the current was not so swift. Then I began to swim upstream, . . . and soon got ashore with nothing worse than a few bruises.[16]

When Simpson returned to his lodgings, he found his host and his family waiting for him on the piazza. When Simpson told him about his adventures, he looked aghast and questioned him.

"How in the worl' yo git dere?"

"I swam across the channel," said I.

When I said this I thought the entire family would fall over in a fit. As soon as the old man could speak he said:

". . . Man, doan' you know dat's de wusses place for caymans an' man eatin' sharks in de hole worl'? Dey's bin half a dozen people killed and eated by dem critters in de souf channel. . . . Prammis me yo won't nebber do no sich foolish ting agen long's yo in dis ilan."

"I promised."[17]

Simpson always had trouble explaining his activities to the natives he encountered on his collecting trips, but his adventure on the reef turned to his benefit.

Heretofore I had been regarded . . . as a semi-lunatic. . . . No man in his right mind would leave his home and come a thousand miles to wander around the woods and along the shores to pull leaves from the trees . . . or crawl around picking up utterly worthless shells. Even the children followed me and sometimes threw stones from behind the bushes. . . . Of course . . . the story of my wonderful adventure . . . went all over the island. Everyone not only became civil but was anxious to be my friend. A man who could go swimming on terms of perfect equality with caymans and man-eating sharks must be a superior being—perhaps a conjuring man. . . . I might bewitch the entire community. . . . In addition to my former name, "De shell mans," they began to call me, "De miracle mans." Houses, bags, odd corners, and old boxes were searched and many fine shells were brought out to be sold or even given to me.[18]

Questions regarding the dispersal of the West Indian flora to southern Florida intrigued Simpson. Some scientists contended that birds carry most seeds across oceans. Simpson wrestled with this theory but discarded it, reasoning that the time of bird migration and fruiting did not coincide. Instead, he believed that most seeds had been borne on ocean currents. An observation he made in Utilla helped him form this theory: "In little bays along the coast of Utilla Island, Honduras I have seen acres of seeds of every conceivable description densely crowded together and floating—held, as one might say, in these great warehouses awaiting shipment to Mexico, Jamaica, Cuba or to Lower Florida."[19]

When the *Asa Eldridge* trimmed her sails for home, Simpson's duffel bags were filled with shells; below deck he stowed plants, cuttings, and seeds for Pliny's nursery, many of them never before planted on North American soil. Mid-voyage, Simpson confessed, he robbed the ship's drinking water to keep his green cargo alive.

THE SARASOTA VIGILANCE COMMITTEE

Simpson had been a resident of Manatee County for just over two years when his community became polarized by fear and suspicion. Though most settlers were peaceful and law-abiding, some harbored petty jealousies, hatreds, and the desire for vengeance. Others were desperate because the state of Florida, in an effort to free itself from debt, had enacted legislation that deeded vast tracts of land to developers, railroaders, and cattlemen for sums as small as twenty-five cents an acre. In effect, this wiped out the homesteading option for pioneers after 1883 and, in some cases, when coupled with the Swamp Lands Act of 1850, threatened to confiscate land from settlers who had farmed it but had never applied for a deed.

In June 1884 a man was found shot with his throat slashed on a sandy trail near the neighboring community of Sarasota, and on Christmas Day, six months after this murder, Charles Abbe, the postmaster of Sarasota, was fatally shot in broad daylight. A young man had witnessed the crime, but the killers had so little fear of the law that he was threatened, but not harmed. The sheriff of Sarasota suspected that the crimes had been instigated by a group known as the Sarasota Vigilance Committee, which was known to be plotting against persons suspected of dealing with land agents.

Rounding up the perpetrators posed a problem, however, because many Sarasotans sympathized with or were intimidated by the vigilantes. For this reason, a posse was formed of twenty-six men from the Manatee River section to the north of Sarasota to track down the alleged murderer and his accomplices. Among the posse members were Pliny Reasoner and Charley "Carpenter." Reasoner, writing to his mother, described the posse as "quite a Yankee brigade—I guess it is a good thing we had no guns or we might have done some lynching before we got back."[20]

A week after the second murder, the manhunt was nearly over and Pliny wrote home, "We have got several of the gang, and possibly will get them all. Everything according to law. We have Sheriff Watson and Justice of the Peace Adams along. Fred and Sam and Lansing and Simpson and a big crowd of good men are here . . . there has never been such an excitement here in the history of Manatee, not even in the Indian war."[21]

Charles Willard, Abbe's murderer, was still at large, however. During the first week of January 1885, Pliny and "Charlie C.," armed with pistols and shotguns, took part in an exhausting hunt for Willard through the Florida swamps and thick brush. Though they did not capture him, their dogged tracking led to his surrender.

When the case came to trial, the activities of the Sarasota Vigilance Committee, which was led by several prominent members of the community, were revealed. Under the pretext of a popular, democratic club, the vigilantes had recruited impressionable young men, bound them with fear and intimidation, and pledged them to carry out assassinations of troublesome persons. The case, scarcely surpassed in modern times for its wanton, vicious brutality, was a national sensation in the press.[22] Historians disagree on the motive for the murders. Some blamed resentments smoldering since the Civil War, while others laid the cause to land confiscation, pointing out that both northerners and southerners were members of the vigilante group.[23] Reasoner and Simpson, however, regarded it as a personal vendetta between "crackers" and "yankees."[24]

But the feud was not over. Resentments festering against the men who took part in the posse would break out and have far-reaching consequences in Simpson's life, leading to his retreat from Florida and, ironically, bringing him one step closer to becoming a full-time specialist in the study of mollusks.

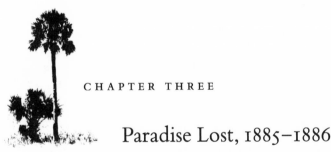

CHAPTER THREE

Paradise Lost, 1885–1886

No time was lost; we hurried across the prairie, up to our ankles in mud and water, . . . cutting a passage through the intervening jungle with a machete. Finally we stood, awestricken, at the foot of a gigantic, gleaming shaft; truly the "King of the Palms."

Pliny Reasoner

SAILING DOWN THE COAST

Simpson had befriended a fisherman, Hugh Culbert, who brought him shells he took in his nets, and sometimes fish. On occasion he would eat with the Simpsons. "He was a bachelor and a woman hater, but, somehow, soon took a liking to Mrs. Simpson and later declared to me that she was the only 'wommern' he ever seen that had any sense." In *Out of Doors in Florida* Simpson described Culbert as

> a native of the coast of North Carolina who proudly boasted of being a "Tar heel." As a boy he had taken to the water as readily as a duck and had followed it all his life. He might have been fifty or a little more, with sharp features, high cheek bones, and a shock of curly, grizzled hair, was little given to talk and made few friends. He had a certain crustiness of manner and speech which sometimes amounted to irascibility when aggravated, but, as a general thing, was kindly and good-natured. . . .
>
> I am quite sure that he could neither read nor write, though he took great pains to conceal his lack of knowledge. Ordinarily his only oath was "By juckies," which he used on all occasions, but the few

times I have seen him fully wrought up his profanity was as vivid and complicated as that of any old seafarer I ever knew. In short, he was an out and out sailor, a man whose every act and utterance smacked of the sea.[1]

Culbert had been building a boat—a seven-ton sharpie—and in the spring of 1885 Simpson, Pliny, and Cornelia were invited on a shake-down cruise for the new vessel. This flat-bottomed craft, christened the *Permit* after a food fish of the southwest coast of Florida, had two masts, each with a long, gaff-rigged, triangular sail, and also carried a rowboat.

As Culbert put the finishing touches on the *Permit,* Simpson built a dredge for hauling up material from deep water and waited "on thorns" to cast anchor. His shell collection at this time numbered some 2,500 to 3,000 species, and he hoped the voyage would net him many new discoveries. His shell exchanges were growing, and his correspondents now included a collector in France who had told him that two of the landshells he sent from Honduras were probably new.

Reasoner eagerly anticipated adding to the stock of his nursery and seeing for the first time Florida's native royal palms, which had been reported by other botanists. Describing the financial arrangements for the excursion, he wrote, "This trip is not going to cost so much as I was afraid it would—$20 for him and Mrs. Simp & $10 for me. . . . We furnish the grub, me one third and Simp two thirds. I presume Culbert would have gone for a good deal less than that, for he thinks a good deal of Simp."[2]

Culbert delayed the sailing repeatedly, fiddling with the rigging and making last-minute alterations, wanting everything shipshape, but finally, on May 1, 1885, the party boarded at Fogartyville where a large group of friends gathered on the dock for the send-off. Culbert was the captain, Reasoner the cook and sailor, and Simpson the general roustabout. Cornelia, well along in her first pregnancy, was their passenger. As they cruised down the Manatee River and entered Tampa Bay, an enormous manta ray came alongside and, raising its wing, threw several barrels of water into the boat, completely dousing Cornelia. Seasick at the outset, "Mrs. Simp" was so surprised by the incident that she completely forgot her nausea.

Early the next morning they dropped anchor at Sanibel Island, and all but the captain went ashore in the rowboat to collect shells. "I have been about the world somewhat as a collector, but in no other spot have I seen such a wealth, such an overwhelming magnificence of marine shells as is to be found along the inner shore of this island," commented Simpson. "We were simply crazy with delight, overpowered by the extravagance of marine life before us."[3]

Near disasters beset them daily. Once, only Culbert's quick thinking saved the party from being carried into the open sea by a strong tide, and on another occasion the rowboat was swamped by a large breaker, casting Cornelia into the water. Reasoner wrote to his mother,

> I have been ashore after Simp & the Madam—My sides ache from laughing yet. I landed all right—shells were put aboard, also Mrs. Simpson. Then we undertook to push her [the boat] off—. . . . Just as I piled in, a whopping big breaker came along and filled the boat. I tried to bail her out, but she went down a whooping. [Mrs. Simpson] grabbed my arm—and I stepped out, water up to the middle. She stepped out and waded ashore and Simp and I gathered up the boat & boards & floating paddles. . . . We were so full of laugh we didn't know what to do, and Culbert was fairly splitting he was so tickled. . . . And Mrs. Simpson had on a mother hubbard. She said Charles wouldn't let her wear it before except nights. . . . Simp says it was all on account of that mother hubbard.[4]

Writing of the incident, Simpson recalls, "I heard a loud, derisive laugh from the sharpie and something like, 'Them fool land lubbers'll mandige to git drownded yit.'"[5]

The party continued down the coast, stopping along the uninhabited shoreline to collect and botanize. On the third day they entered the northern extreme of lower Florida's subtropical zone. Many of the plant and animal communities were entirely new to Reasoner and Simpson. Dropping anchor at Marco Island, they went ashore at W. D. ("Captain Bill") Collier's place, where fifty acres were planted with coconuts and other tropical fruits, including avocados, sapodillas, lime trees, and sugar apples.

The visit to Collier's marked the beginning of a quest that Simpson pursued for the remainder of his days. In a nearby hammock he encountered for the first time *Liguus fasciatus,* the colorful Florida tree snails. As he put it, "I was overjoyed to find them and from that day to the present time I have been completely daft about them."[6]

When they parted, Collier gave them some good advice. "If you meet anyone, tell them your name, what your business is and where you are going. And don't ask them their names nor what they are doing."[7] Simpson tucked this tip away, and it served him well on his explorations into isolated areas.

From Marco Island they went to Goodland Point, where they stayed for several days, finding abundant tree snails in a large hammock. Unfortunately, it was also overgrown with the "half sprawling, half climbing *Cereus pentagonus* [cactus], perhaps the most dreadful plant torment found growing in Florida." Mosquitoes and sand flies interfered somewhat with their enjoyment, "so much so that people carried smudge pots about with them," wrote Simpson facetiously, but the natives assured them that "the few which were about were not worth mentioning, only a sort of vanguard, the advance agents, as it were, that had come to arrange for the main body."[8]

Simpson does not say what color form of *Liguus* he found that day, but on other trips to Goodland Point he reported finding *Lineolatus simpsonii* (*Liguus faciatus form lineolatus* Simpson 1920), a large, porcelaneous, cream-colored shell threaded with green along its spirals, with a pink tip and columella.

Setting sail again, the *Permit* cruised along the Ten Thousand Islands and visited Rabbit and Pavillion keys. Pliny's twenty-second birthday proved to be a historic occasion for the young plantsman, for, on a side trip up the Rodgers River, they saw for the first time the royal palms of the West Indies growing in the wild. This was a sensational discovery, since botanists had only recently recognized that these tropical palms grew on the mainland of the United States.

Stopping on Cape Sable, Simpson noted a white *Liguus* finely marked with green spiral lines living on Jamaica dogwood, a tropical tree unrelated to the northern species. "At the time of our visit the trees were so loaded with *Liguus* that they appeared as if full of glossy whitish fruit," Simpson observed.[9] Sailing on, they visited the Content Keys and from there set course for Key West.

Pliny's delight was "unbounded" at the sight of Key West's tropical foliage—West Indian silk cotton trees, East Indian laurels, tamarinds, tropical almonds, royal poincianas, and a variety of other trees that had not been introduced to Manatee County. Chinese hibiscus with pendulant scarlet blossoms, golden allamandas, and other flowering vines covered arbors and the walls of the houses. "Whenever Pliny saw a plant that was new to him, he would rush in to the place of the owner and ask if he could get seed, cuttings, or suckers. There was something so bright and winsome about him that no one could refuse him, and in no time the proprietor would be out with him helping him to get whatever he wanted," recalled Simpson.[10]

As was too often his fate when on an excursion, Simpson suffered an acute attack of malaria and was "sick abed" all of one day. However, he was sufficiently recovered the next morning to show Pliny the plants and trees he had noted on his earlier trip to Key West. Leaving this southernmost Florida city, the party continued on to the Marquesas Keys.

> We ran in through a channel at the southeast part of the archipelago and came to anchor. . . . Then we all got into the skiff and landed on the shoal which we found well stocked with mollusks, great pink strombs, . . . beautifully marked Olivas, cones, and a variety of lovely Tellinas, the large, orbicular Codakia whose white shell was elegantly marked with red. . . . I collected the smaller stuff, but Pliny raved over the big pink conchs and filled a gunnysack with them. . . . Culbert told him to chuck them down by a stake which stood in the shallow water and get them when we came back. So he emptied the bag and we wandered delightedly on over the flat and an hour later came back to the stake. Not a conch was to be seen, all having crawled away or buried themselves in the sand. Then Culbert laughed until he nearly fell into the water, for he had all along known exactly what would happen. . . . We left the lovely islands with regret and steered for the Tortugas, about thirty-five miles to the westward. This group is a sort of atoll consisting of eleven keys and fine assortment of rocks and shoals, the whole arranged somewhat in the shape of an irregular horseshoe with an open lagoon in which the water reaches in places a depth of ten fathoms. At the time of our visit, Fort Jefferson, a great hexagonal brick structure, was peacefully rotting away. Great Columbian guns of the date of the Civil War rested on tottering wooden carriages; in places the walls were crumbling and falling. . . . Our first afternoon was spent on an extensive reef near the fort which, owing to an unusually low tide, was almost bare. . . . [W]e were astonished at the variety and richness of life . . . marine worms with calcareous tubes, sea anemones of wonderful beauty, great warty star fishes and the "corn pone," Metalia, sometimes eight inches across. In the pools among the rocks were beds of hydroids which looked almost exactly like seaweeds, but when examined, the former have little cups along their stems, and the latter have not.[11]

Simpson suffered another attack of chills and fever, which prevented him from walking out on the reef, but between intervals of shaking he got out of the boat, laid down on the beach, and found it full of interesting, finely colored things. "Although tortured with malaria, I was able to collect about three hundred species of small tropical shells."[12]

Returning from the Tortugas, the party encountered a severe gale:

> The wind from the northeast probably reaching fifty miles an hour. . . . Mrs. Simpson became dreadfully seasick and could not remain in the hot stuffy hold, but, when I got her on deck the motion of the boat was so violent it was hard for her to hold on. . . . Finally, perhaps from fright, Mrs. Simpson's nausea left her and Pliny and I got her below. I noticed that Culbert was very pale and apparently agitated; in fact, Pliny was the only one who seemed unmoved. Finally the storm abated and towards evening we ran into our old channel in the Marquesas. After supper Pliny in an aggravating spirit, said he believed Culbert was scared, at which the old smuggler became angry.
>
> "By juckies," said the latter, "Ye don't know whut ye'r talkin' about. That wuzzent nawthin' but jist a capful of win', not enuff to blow a settin' hen offen her nest."[13]

Pushing on, the party cruised homeward. Pliny's hoard of plants were stored in the cabin to protect them from high seas, and bags and boxes of shells were crammed into every corner above and below deck.

> In the hurry of collecting, many shells were taken with the animal, and as the weather was warm, they began to announce their presence by a perfectly hair-lifting odor. Culbert fussed about these "stinkers" as he called them and from fussing he came to growling, and finally to an open outbreak. A boat came along side and the man aboard asked if someone was dead and others had shied off when they came near.
>
> "See hyer," said Culbert. "This boat is gittin to be a regular outlaw all on account of these infernal stinkers. By juckies, it's got so that all the craft about these parts gives us a wide berth, an' even the people ashore is movin' away on account of 'em. Now you understan' you got to do sumpin' or I'll heave the hull kit an' calabash overboard."
>
> Then Pliny and I . . . went into executive session. We sorted over all our shells, putting those that had bad breath into certain sacks which, with Culbert's permission, we towed overboard.[14]

Simpson and Reasoner had one more important stop to make. Botanist Allan Hiram Curtiss had written about his discovery, in 1880, of a large stand of royal palms six or seven miles from the coast in the watery wilderness around Caxambas and the Ten Thousand Islands.[15] Pliny, tingling with excitement, was determined to find them. At Goodland Point they hired a Mr. Johnson as guide and boatman, and early the next morning Pliny and Simpson set out with him in a rowboat through the labyrinth of channels that wove through the islets.

> [They] were everywhere clothed with a dense growth of mangroves standing high out of the mud on their long, stilted, curved roots, reminding one of some strange kind of spider. . . . [W]e came to and entered one of the canals common to that region which are, no doubt, the work of a prehistoric race. They were perfectly straight, only a few feet in width, and still showed the earth on either bank that had been excavated.[16]

After laboriously working their way through overgrown, tortuous waterways, they finally found a place that appeared to have been a landing. Johnson tied the boat to a stake—perhaps the very mooring used by Curtiss. Following traces of an old path, they emerged into a wide, swampy prairie. Pliny gave a shout and pointed to the shiny black-green crowns of dozens of royals rising above a large hammock in the distance. Pliny recalled,

> No time was lost; we hurried across the prairie, up to our ankles in mud and water; . . . cutting a passage through the intervening jungle with a machete. . . . A little further on . . . we stood, awestricken, at the foot of a gigantic, gleaming shaft, towering far above us, over the tops of immense live oaks . . . truly the 'King of the Palms.' . . . Nearby was the fallen trunk of the tree cut by Mr. Curtis . . . a great many of the trees are, no doubt, 150 feet high. After a long and careful search underneath the big trees, we began to despair of getting any young plants, but finally closer to the edge of the forest, . . . we found fifteen or twenty. . . . Glad was the heart of the cook [Pliny] as he labored back across the prairie in mud and slush up to his sides for his heart's desire was accomplished—the Royal Palms were his.[17]

The light was fading from the sky when the party, loaded down with seedling palms, poled their boat back through the twisting channels to the *Permit*'s mooring. Culbert set sail for home that night, and the next day, weary but elated with their treasures, the adventurers entered the Manatee River and landed at the Fogartyville wharf.

Their delight was to be short-lived. Six weeks after returning from their cruise Cornelia gave birth to a daughter, but the infant lived only four days. To add to the emotional scene, Simpson became involved with Mrs. Wadham, his business partner's wife, who had attended Cornelia during her pregnancy. He begged her not to come to the house, but to no avail. Finally, he considered moving to Tampa.

Simpson's indiscretion became known, and local gossip embroidered the facts with slander against both Simpson and Cornelia. Wadham, who once claimed to "love Simpson like a brother," now was in a fury and vowed to "shoot the villain if he ever crossed his threshold again." Gossip about the Simpsons even traveled to Bureau County, causing Pliny's mother to chide her son about the company he was keeping. In a letter home, Pliny loyally defended his friend.

> There is not a shadow of truth to any of it except to the yarn about Mrs. Wadham and him, and that is as much (or more) her fault as his. You know he is very passionate. He has always been very fond of Mrs. Wadham—(He acknowledged to me that he was a *fool,* but he couldn't help it). . . . I think Wadham was jealous of Simp—as Simp was a better carpenter than he and thought that if Simp would clear out he would have more jobs.
>
> *And I really think that there is considerable of the old rebel spirit left.* They hate a Yankee, especially if he is a prosperous Yankee. . . . I don't think there is any real danger as far as Simp is concerned; Simp is very excitable, and has imagined all sorts of things . . . a more generous, straight-forward chap never lived. He has his faults, as we all have, and some of them are bad ones. I know lots of little things that he has done—many a poor man or woman to whom he has given $10.00 when they were in a tight place.[18]

THE REMOVAL

Simpson's affair of the heart followed hard on the heels of the trial of the vigilantes, and both were contributing factors to his move from Bradenton. Resentment flared high in some quarters against the members of the Manatee posse that arrested the vigilantes. Threats were made to burn Simpson's house and destroy his shell collection, and messages bearing a skull and crossbones and ordering him to leave town were nailed to his door. Though he wanted to explore around Lake Okeechobee and Florida's southeast coast, he didn't dare leave his wife and home. The hostility between Simpson and his former partner soured their business and made it difficult for him to make a living.[19]

As the harassment continued, Simpson imagined the worst and began to break under the strain. Though not lacking in courage when it came to exploring in the wilderness or tracking down a murderer, Simpson shied from personal confrontation. To add to his depression, on January 10, 1886, Florida was struck by the worst freeze of the century. Snow fell and the temperature hovered between twenty-five and thirty-eight degrees. Oranges froze on the branch, and Pliny lost all his guava and mango trees. Simpson sailed down the coast to survey the frost damage to the forests of giant mangroves and other tropical life.

"Billions of fish of a great many species" died and covered the surface of the ocean, clogging the entrance to the Manatee River. After mooring his sailboat, Simpson tried to row ashore in his skiff, but he could make little progress because the oars simply skidded on the fish. Tons of dead fish washed ashore, and, although the odor was powerful, Reasoner hauled up what he could to use as fertilizer for his groves.[20]

With his business failing and his wife in poor health, Simpson could hold out no longer. Rather than stand and fight, he chose to retreat. "I attempted to sell out, but they blocked me and at last I almost gave away part of my property and abandoned the rest. I had a little property in Ogalalla and hither I went to a free country to build anew a home and with great difficulty I succeeded in getting away my collections."[21]

Pliny too had been under fire, quite literally, for his orange groves had been set ablaze to harass him into leaving, but when "Simp" unveiled his plans for retreat the younger man dug in his heels and said, "I'd rather live in a house on stilts in the delta of the Orinoco, than in Nebraska."[22]

By the end of January the Simpsons had packed up and moved out. Pliny's mother wrote suggesting he must be glad to be rid of the man, to which Pliny replied, "I am *not* glad Mr. Simpson has gone away, & he is *not* crazy. . . . To tell the solemn truth . . . I haven't a better friend in the world."[23]

Pliny held his ground and, with his brother, Egbert, established the first nursery for tropical plants in Manatee County, christened "Reasoners' Royal Palm Nurseries" for the palms he brought back from the Ten Thousand Islands. His prolific pen and enterprising spirit gained him a reputation as an authority on tropical fruit. His one-hundred-page report on tropical and semitropical fruit in 1887 was Bulletin #1 of the U.S. Department of Agriculture's new Division of Pomology. This ambitious young plantsman had already begun plant exchanges with major botanical gardens throughout the world and had propagated many ornamental plants native to South Florida.

CHAPTER FOUR

The Midwestern Years, 1886–1889

Your welcome letter came a day or two ago and still finds me on the plains of Ogalalla. I have never been more at sea than this spring.

C. T. Simpson to W. H. Pratt

BECOMING A CONCHOLOGIST

When Simpson resettled in Nebraska, the era of the open range was drawing to an end. The Union Pacific railhead in Ogalalla had been shipping headquarters for the longhorns driven from Texas up the grassy corridor of the Great Western Trail. Within a few years of his arrival, the once-booming cattle industry crashed after more than five million head of cattle perished throughout the Great Plains in the terrible winter of 1886–87. Range wars between cattlemen and homesteaders diminished, and once-free pastures of the open range were closed, the land fenced and plowed by farmers. Hunters with single-bore rifles had virtually exterminated the vast herds of buffalo that had once dominated the prairie. Now the hapless animals' bones were stacked in glistening, white piles by the railroad tracks awaiting shipment to eastern factories. Surely the sight indelibly marked the naturalist's memory and would contribute to his determination to save some remnant of the wildlife of another region.

How Simpson acquired the four-hundred-acre farm in Nebraska is not known, but it is certain he made the move out of necessity rather than by choice. Nebraska was a world apart from Florida, where Simpson had found and reveled in what he called "paradise"—the warm, humid climate, the vast, watery wilderness of the Everglades, the pinelands carpeted with wildflowers, and the jungly hammocks. The sparkling Gulf of Mexico and wide mouth of the Manatee River beckoned a few blocks from home, and down the coast stretched long, slender islands, deep bays, and estuaries where he could poke the prow of a little boat and explore areas largely unknown to naturalists.

In contrast, the vast plains of Nebraska stretched to the horizon, flat, treeless, and frequently arid. The cold front that had devastated Florida's west coast that year was a rare occurrence, but long, cold winters were the rule in Nebraska. Blizzards were so intense that a man could be lost five feet from his front door. In spring, when the Platte River overflowed its banks with snow melted from the Rockies, it spread over the land for two or three miles, and homesteaders compared it to an inland sea. Muddy with silt and so shallow that the prairie schooners heading west drove right through it, this broad expanse of river was unlike any sea Simpson had known.

Despite these drawbacks, the Midwest was rich in lakes and free-flowing watercourses teeming with freshwater mollusks. Simpson's correspondence and publications from this period indicate that he was an active shell collector and student of conchology. His father-in-law, B. C. Couch, in a family history, describes him at forty as "a man of more than ordinary intelligence, and is especially gifted in the science of conchology. He has traveled and seen much of the world. . . . He has given the science of botany a good deal of thought, but conchology is his favorite. It is a pity his usefulness in this direction cannot be fully utilized. Had he an official position, where such knowledge is wanted, . . . I am satisfied his success would be of no mean importance."[1]

When sending a packet of shells to Dr. Dall in June 1886, Simpson explained his move from Florida:

> Since writing to you from Bradenton, Florida, I have been compelled to change my residence. I took an active part . . . in helping ferret out and bring to justice the notorious "Sarasota Gang" . . . that was terrifying the country. Public sentiment which at first wavered finally set in favor of the ex-rebels. . . . For this and for being an independent Northern man I was persecuted. My wife and I were ostracized from all society. . . . I could not obtain a day's work. I dared not leave home to collect lest on my return I should find it in ruins and kept my shells

packed to be ready to move in a minute. . . . Pardon the recital of my troubles. It was necessary say something to explain my being here. . . . and had hoped to make a life study of the Florida shells. I still desire to publish a list, but under the circumstances I had better confine it to the species in the collection.[2]

Simpson spent three frustrating years in Nebraska. The pressures of making a living warred against his longing to go tramping or to arrange his shells. His Florida collection alone now numbered nearly one thousand species, but without access to the literature found in scientific libraries and institutions he found it difficult to classify them. To W. H. Pratt, curator at the Davenport Academy of Sciences, he wrote, "At last I have made out, by working on it a few minutes at a time, the box of Florida shells long ago promised to the Academy. It should have been sent long ago, but I have been too greatly hurried with work to attend to the shells."[3]

HENRY PILSBRY

On a more positive note, in the Midwest he would find men whose intellectual curiosity matched his own. One of these was Henry A. ("Harry") Pilsbry (1862–1957). The son of an Iowa farmer, Pilsbry received his Bachelor of Science degree in 1882 from Iowa State University and was supporting himself in the printer's trade while acting as librarian and curator of mollusks at the Davenport Academy of Natural Sciences when he became acquainted with Simpson. Pilsbry would become one of the giants of malacology, writing more than nine hundred papers. For over seventy years he was associated with the Academy of Natural Sciences of Philadelphia as curator of mollusks, lecturing, writing, studying, and conducting research. He succeeded to the editorship and authorship of *The Manual of Conchology,* published by the Academy of Natural Sciences in thirty-one volumes between 1888 and 1935. Pilsbry and Simpson became friends and, in July 1886, Simpson became a corresponding member of the Davenport Academy.

William D. Averell, editor and publisher, of Chestnut Hill, Philadelphia, launched the *Conchologist's Exchange* in August 1886. The first issue, printed on a penny postcard, described the publication as a "medium of exchange of those most beautiful productions of nature, 'the mollusks,'" to be printed monthly with subscriptions offered at twenty-five cents a year. The publication soon expanded, becoming *Nautilus,* the distinguished journal of malacology, and Simpson was one of its faithful contributors. In 1887 alone, seven of his articles appeared on subjects such as dredging in Tampa Bay, distribution of land and freshwater shells in the tropics, and new species.

History records the winter of 1886–87 as one of the most severe in the annals of the Great Plains. The snow began falling in November. Time and again, blizzards swept out of the north and continued for days, followed by weeks of bone-chilling cold and snow. Cornelia became pregnant, and this, along with her already frail health, created additional burdens for Simpson. Doggedly, he worked by lamplight to identify, classify, and describe several new taxa of Florida shells. Finally, in December, he was able to write to curator Pratt, "My Catalogue of Fla. Shells is finished and ready to have something done with it. Mr. Pilsbry told me that you would publish it in the Academy's Proceedings."[4]

Pratt replied, inviting him to send the paper on, and "Contributions to the Mollusca of Florida," was read at a meeting of the Davenport Academy on December 31, 1886. The catalog listed 650 varieties of Florida marine, freshwater, and land shells. Four species were described as new; William Dall, and John Ford of the Philadelphia Academy, aided in the identification and description of these new species. Simpson confessed that only after the synonymy was thoroughly worked out would it be known if the names would stand. In his conclusion the Nebraska farmer begged the indulgence of his readers: "I have no doubt there are errors in this catalogue. It has been prepared in haste in odd moments of a very busy life. I have but little literature on the subject and have never had opportunity to examine extensive libraries or collections. . . . I thought it better, however, to do something than to wait for leisure which might never come. I therefore ask the kindly consideration of all into whose hands it may fall."[5]

On January 28, 1887, temperatures hit new lows, and some five million head of cattle on the open range were lost throughout the Great Plains, changing forever the economy of the Midwest. Nothing could hold back the spring, however, and the sandhill cranes gathered in the Platte River by the thousands as they had for generations. Simpson marveled at the noisy spectacle as the sociable birds fed, rested, and performed their ritual dances before moving on to nesting grounds in the northern tundra.

In August Cornelia gave birth to a son, who was named "Pliny Ford" to honor Pliny Reasoner and John Ford. Ford was one of Simpson's treasured correspondents, a link with the academic world where answers could be found to the puzzles of nature.

Pilsbry left Davenport that summer for the East to tour the science museums and find work. His ebullient letters home were full of descriptions of shell collections and museums he had seen. While visiting the Philadelphia Academy he met Professor George Tyron, conservator of the academy's conchological section, who hired him in December 1887 to assist in compiling a manual on conchology.

Inexperienced as a contributor to scientific journals, Simpson found interminable the time lag between the reading of his Florida shell paper and its publication. Delays followed delays. Galleys sent to Dall for editing were lost in the mail. A misprint in the title had to be corrected. A year passed, and Simpson wrote in despair to Dall: "I am sorry for the delay for I do not know if the new species you described have been published elsewhere and, of course, it will be stale when it is ready for distribution."[6]

Dall, however, was accustomed to the snail's pace of academic presses, and in his reply he suggested that Simpson might submit a more complete catalog to the *Proceedings* of the National Museum. Simpson, however, responded with characteristic caution that this would have to wait until he made a more comprehensive study of Florida's mollusks.

PLUNDERING THE MIDWESTERN RIVERS

In the spring of 1888, Simpson wrote to Dall to gain his support for a collecting trip he was planning through eastern Kansas, "Indian Territory" (Oklahoma), western Arkansas, Missouri, and north Texas. "It is a region rich in conchological treasures and I think not at all thoroughly worked up," he commented. Inquiring about localities that might be of special interest, he offered to make collections and report on matters of distribution that might prove useful to the museum. "I can run down the Missouri Pacific railroad through the eastern portion of the Territory, and then work over westward on my return. I presume the rivers will be high at present, but I am likely to remain on the river all summer and hope to do a little dredging. . . . There may be a little difficulty in collecting in Indian Territory as I have been told that the authorities do not like to have white men running loose here."[7]

To ease his passage, he requested an endorsement from Dall stating that he was collecting and making notes for the U.S. National Museum. The signed statement was forthcoming, and later that month Simpson packed up his camping and collecting gear and set out. Matches were stored high and dry in his hatband, for he knew this was wet work.

The object of his trip was not only collecting. Simpson was looking for a new place to live. After the terrible winter of 1886–87, he had put his farm up for sale in hopes he could relocate in a softer climate, perhaps Oklahoma or even Texas. How did Cornelia, ailing and caring for her eight-month-old baby, cope when her naturalist-husband was off on tramps? Presumably she had hired help, as she did in Bradenton, and the household may have included extended family as well as visitors and farmhands.

The trip Simpson described followed the Platte, Missouri, and Red rivers and their tributaries. His restless feet ranged well over a thousand miles one way on this ambitious field expedition. Modern-day malacologists might envy his opportunity to mine the riches of virgin beds of naiad mussels in America's wild rivers before their waters were channeled and impounded to serve the needs of industry and a growing population. Simpson's enthusiasm for what he found shines through in the following passage: "It is here, where the streams flow over vast beds of limestone and where food is abundant, that the conditions for *Unio* life are most favorable and nature has fairly reveled in the creation of the beautiful, the ponderous, and the grotesque. Here the genera *Unio* and *Margaritana* assume a variety of forms that are odd and strange; here are developed species with winged hinges, strong corrugations, knobs, and sinuses."[8]

One might wonder how he traveled. The Union Pacific Railroad cut through Nebraska east and west, intersecting with the Missouri Pacific, which ran south along the border between Oklahoma and Arkansas. Did Simpson buy a railroad ticket and travel like a respectable citizen, or did he, like a hobo, "ride the rails"? Did he hop a slow-moving freight, travel to the next town, and jump off to explore the nearby watercourses, moving on again by rail to a new collecting site? By his own definition, he was an "old tramp," a "knight of the road." In the distant future, another railroad, still to be surveyed, would open up for him the humid, cactus-tangled, mosquito-ridden hammocks of the Florida Keys.

Though he was on the move most of April and May, Simpson termed the trip a "failure." Heavy rains caused the streams to overflow, making collecting difficult. His efforts to find land snails were hampered as well. A three-year dry period and forest fires had destroyed many trees, and with them the snails. He complained that in some places he could not find a living specimen, though dead shells were everywhere.

After working Muddy Boggy Creek in southeast Oklahoma, he received word at the railway station at Stringtown that Cornelia was critically ill. He cut his trip short and hurried home. There he found her condition alarming, and when she failed to rally, he took her home to Illinois to recuperate with her family.

More bad news arrived in a letter from brother Joseph. Yellow fever had broken out in Bradenton. Some forty residents of Manatee County had contracted the disease. Several had died, among them Simpson's young friend, Pliny Reasoner. Pliny had been in Cincinnati supervising the Florida Exhibit for the Cotton States' Centennial when the epidemic began. As soon as the exposition closed its doors, and against the advice of his family, Pliny dashed home, where he contracted the fever shortly after his arrival. He died on September 17, 1888, the last fatality of the disease in Manatee County. His death deeply saddened Simpson, who would remember the exuberant young plantsman as one of his three most loyal friends and cherished companions.

FAILURE AND BANKRUPTCY

Although Simpson gained ground as a specialist in conchology, he was going bankrupt as a farmer. The harsh winters were followed by successive hot, dry summers. Crops withered. The price of wheat plummeted, and with it the value of farmland. Simpson was threatened with foreclosure. To "Friend Pratt" he moaned:

> Your welcome letter came a day or two ago and still finds me on the plains of Ogalalla. I have never been more at sea than this spring. Supposed I had sold, but the party backed out. . . . Since she has gone I have been baching—my brother-in-law and I—and I am in charge of the cooking and housework. With wife and baby gone I am lonesome beyond anything I can describe. . . . I want to get somewhere with a little milder climate for my wife's sake at least—and somewhere where I can study nature and collect a little. This lonely desert of endless prairie was always disgusting to me.[9]

The following year, after a series of crop failures, Simpson lost his farm and moved on to rent another in Taggert, Missouri. Despite these setbacks, he continued to seek recognition as a conchologist. In January 1889 he wrote to Dall, "I would like to publish a few notes on the shells I obtained this spring in Indian territory and to describe the new species of Helix (*Mesodon*) and, what is probably new, the little zonites. Could I do this in the Proceedings of the National Museum? Would it be possible to have something figured?"[10] The museum accepted his paper and published it later that year as "Notes on Some Indian Territory Land and Freshwater Shells."

When volume 3 of *Nautilus* came out in 1889, Pilsbry had joined Averell as coeditor. Later the journal was edited jointly by Pilsbry and Charles W. Johnson, director of the Boston Natural History Museum. Simpson contributed a paper on taxonomy to the first number of volume 3. Written with confidence and gusto, it was titled "Genus Making."

> Genus making is the fashion now-a-days with a certain school of conchologists. . . . [A] few species are found having a certain peculiar pattern of sculpture or coloring or some little singularity in the fold of the columnella or hinge teeth, and presto, a genus is formed and science is burdened with another name. . . .
>
> I think that the classification should be founded on nature or in other words that nature should do the classifying, and that our efforts should be directed to deciphering the Old Dame's work.
>
> I think the time has come when a healthful reaction from this fever of creating genera and species should set in. . . . No one but an expert, a closet naturalist, who sits in his snug alcove surrounded by scientific books and collections, and who devotes his entire time to the study, can keep track of the names introduced by this mania.[11]

The term "closet naturalist" stood for all Simpson abhorred in the natural scientist. Whether in botany or malacology, it was his pet peeve, his bête noire. Time and again he wrote of the "pale, anemic specialist" sequestered from the stuff of nature, the antithesis of the field-worker. "They have no idea of the great out-of-doors. Their work scares and discourages those who would learn about animals and plants. . . . They dig in a tunnel and see nature through a pinhole," he said.[12] In science, as in his private life, Simpson was an egalitarian. He championed the rights of the part-time collector for simplified nomenclature, for he knew the feeling of being an amateur, groping for knowledge amid the shifting sands of science.

Another paper Simpson wrote in 1889 was published in two parts in *Nautilus.* Titled "What Is a Species?" it was written in the same brisk style and suggested this definition for separating a species or a variety: "A mollusk which differs from all allied forms by certain distinct constant characters is entitled to specific rank. As a friend remarked to me: 'It is not so necessary that the differences be great, as that they be constant.' " After expanding on his topic and citing one member of the "new school of conchologists" who claimed to know 162 species of *Helix* of the group *Pomatia,* he wisecracked, "Of these he possesses 151! And he classifies them in two grand sections and nineteen series! One feels like using the language of the happy father who, when the nurse presented him with triplets, exclaimed, "Great Scott! Did any get away?"[13]

By summer he sent Dall one of his "Florida pamphlets" published in the Davenport Academy's *Proceedings.* He apologized for the printer's errors. To his embarrassment, the tree snails came out as *Ligums* rather than *Liguus.* Flushed with confidence, he proposed a survey of the distribution of Florida mollusks: "I would like to make a survey of the coast of Florida putting in a few weeks in November and December along the western coast. . . . There are many Atlantic land species found in that region. I could collect freshwater species from the rivers as at that time of year they would not be swollen by rains. . . .

I would like to thoroughly search the southern and southeast keys and go up the East coast to observe where the West Indian forms ran out on the state. Do you suppose it would ever be possible to make such a trip in the employ of the Smithsonian?"[14]

AN OFFICIAL POSITION

Dall, impressed by Simpson's published papers, his careful attention to detail as to location of specimens, and his cautious approach to systematics, replied on October 15, 1889, with an astonishing offer—the "official position" Simpson's father-in-law had envisioned.

> My dear sir,
>
> I am in need of an assistant in the Department of Mollusks and . . . it occurred to me that perhaps the opportunity might offer some attraction for you. I must say frankly, the position does not offer too much in the way of salary. To begin with our aides have seventy-five dollars a month which, in the case of our department, if the appropriations continue as liberal as we have good reason to hope, could probably be increased in the second or third year to 1200 per year and in the course of time to 1500 which is the limit for an assistant curator. . . . The only restriction I remember which would affect you would be that which prohibits anyone permanently connected with the museum from forming a collection or conducting exchanges on his own account. Of course, your collection formed before joining the museum would be at your disposal. . . .

As an opportunity for the right man to become a thorough conchologist, I do not believe it can be excelled in the world . . . and, from time to time, there are opportunities for field work.[15]

Simpson could hardly believe his good fortune—to be a scientific aide with the nation's most prestigious museum far exceeded his expectations. He wasted no time in replying.

My dear sir,

I can hardly tell you how greatly I feel honored that you should offer me this situation. I must tell you frankly that I am a little dubious of my ability to come up to the mark. I have but a very limited education. I know absolutely nothing of any language but the one I speak and very little of that. I have never had any access to scientific libraries or large collections. I know nothing of the anatomy of the mollusks or how to dissect them. I fear I haven't much genius or taste in that way. What knowledge I have is merely of shells and very little of the habits of the animals, and distribution gained from a somewhat extensive experience in collecting.[16]

In his letter he went on to request time to settle his business without "pecuniary loss," explaining that his wife is an invalid and he would need to arrange for her and "the child" to stay in Illinois until he was settled in Washington. His only reservation concerned his shell collection.

I don't quite understand . . . would I be allowed to keep [the shell collection] and mount it at my home, providing I made no additions to it? Or would I have to sell or give it away. I should be sorry to have to dispose of it as it represents many years of collecting in many lands, and the gifts of friends and exchanges . . . yet, of course, . . . I will do so. . . . The chance to collect would be delightful and I have always been used to an active outdoor life. . . . I hope you will not expect me to be much advanced. My studies have been done during odd moments caught from my daily labor, . . . but I love nature and have from childhood.[17]

Simpson wasted no time spreading the good news to Pratt, who immediately relayed the news to Pilsbry at the Philadelphia Academy.

I had a letter from [Simpson] yesterday saying that he is to start for Washington D. C. 'as soon as he can make arrangements'. . . to take a position with Dr. Dall at the Drs. office at $75.00 a month—to be advanced later to $1,500 per annum, seven hours a day, one month vacation *with* pay.

Isn't that fine? Think of a man like him drudging on a farm all his life (or you in a printing office).[18]

Simpson impatiently awaited further word from Dall. Finally an envelope arrived bearing the Smithsonian logo, but it proved to be only a copy of Dall's most recent scientific paper. Thanking him for his paper, Simpson politely inquired, "I wrote you a few days ago accepting your kind offer of a position at the Museum. I speak of it merely because of the possibility that my reply might have been miscarried in the mails."[19]

Within a week, just two weeks after his initial offer, Dall reassured him. "I am glad you decided to try the work. I understand, of course, what you say about your qualifications. To my mind, the most important qualifications of all are that a man should be really interested in the work and that he should be willing to take pains and not too conceited to learn. These qualifications, I believe, you possess. . . .

Make no sacrifices. We can wait until January, if that would enable you to settle up your affairs."

Regarding Simpson's shell collection, Dall declined to give a positive answer because the question had never arisen with other assistants. "I know that most of the private collections of persons permanently connected with the museum have been given or purchased by the museum sooner or later," he explained. "I do not know that they would insist on your getting rid of your collections, providing it was agreed that nothing would be added to it."[20]

Simpson replied on a postcard. "I trust in a very few days I will be there, by the middle of December at the farthest."

CHAPTER FIVE

Smithsonian Towers, 1890–1902

When we squeeze our feet into shiny black shoes we throw away the moccasin of freedom; as they gall and pinch the unaccustomed foot, so does the dread of our friend's opinion gall and pinch our minds.

Warburton Pike

THE DEVOTED UNIOLOGIST

Stepping from the train in Washington in mid-December 1889, forty-three year old Charles Torrey Simpson looked the part of a proper Victorian gentleman. Walking with an erect, military carriage, he was respectably attired in a starched, high-collared shirt, waistcoat complete with watch and chain, and black leather shoes. He wore a full, natural mustache, and his dark, slicked-down hair emphasized his large, oval head, deep-set eyes, broad forehead, and prominent cheekbones.

The historic buildings of the nation's capital, seen for the first time by this country man, were overwhelming. With great excitement he climbed the steep, granite steps and entered the doors of the Smithsonian red sandstone "castle on the mall," where his attention would have been caught by the natural history collections displayed in glass cases among the marble pillars of the Great Hall. The U.S. National Museum, a branch of the Smithsonian, was housed there, and Simpson was given an office in the north-central tower. His position was that of a museum aide in Dr. Dall's Department of Mollusks, where he was assigned the work of classifying, labeling, and arranging the museum's shell collections. For a

The Smithsonian's "red castle on the mall," designed by James Renwick. Simpson's office was in the north tower. Courtesy of the Smithsonian Institution. Photo no. 32913.

Natural history exhibits in the great hall of the Smithsonian Institution, ca. 1890. Courtesy of the Smithsonian Institution. Photo no. 16847.

An aide in the National Museum's Department of Mollusks, ca. 1886. Courtesy of the Smithsonian Institution. Photo no. 3669.

man who repeatedly lamented the lack of "literature" and difficulties of identifying his specimens, the museum library and immense collection of specimens was beyond belief—box after box, tray after tray of shells of every size and description.

He was unsure of his ability to come up to the mark. Though he used Latin names with ease, he claimed to speak no foreign languages. He could have identified hundreds of shells blindfolded, but he knew very little about their owners' anatomy. Though well-read in the natural sciences, geology, and paleontology, he could claim only a grammar school education. To his credit, in citing his "somewhat extensive experience in collection" he understated the case, since his travels had taken him to the countries of the Mediterranean, Honduras, the southern states, and most of the area served by the Mississippi drainage system, as well as the Florida west coast and Keys, where little serious collecting had been done. However, after a successful six-month probationary period, Simpson's salary was raised to eighty dollars per month, enabling him to buy a house and send for Cornelia and Pliny.

In April 1890, shortly after Simpson joined the staff of the museum, the American Association of Conchologists was founded in the office of John Campbell of Philadelphia. Its charter members included Campbell, president; John Ford, vice president, Charles W. Johnson, secretary; and Henry A. Pilsbry, the Rev. A. Dean, Uselma Smith, John Shallcross, F. C. Baker, William J. McGinty, Theodore G. Brinton, Joseph Willcox, S. Raymond Roberts, and C. T. Simpson. This short-lived association was a brotherhood of scientists pledged to cooperative study. Each member selected a subject for specialization. Most chose a particular family of mollusks, but the comprehensive nature of Simpson's inquiries led him to select "geographical distribution" and "nomenclature."

CARIBBEAN ADVENTURES WITH HENDERSON

Before the year was out Simpson had become acquainted with John Brooks Henderson Jr., the son of a regent of the museum. Though John was only twenty and still a student at Harvard, the two men hit it off at once. John's father was a U.S. senator from Missouri, author of the Thirteenth Amendment, which abolished slavery. Perhaps John saw qualities in Simpson that he admired in his father. What is certain is that both men were "completely daft" about mollusks, and the gap in years was easily bridged by this mutual interest. "Born to the purple" was how Simpson described John, for the Hendersons had ample funds at their disposal and often used them to the benefit of the museum. Between 1891 and 1915 Simpson and Henderson made more than a dozen expeditions to Florida, Cuba, Jamaica, and Haiti, exploring on land and dredging at sea. While Henderson financed the expeditions, Simpson's assets included both broad experience in collecting and practical skills such as repairing a dredge or strapping a barrel with iron hoops.

In December 1891 Henderson and Simpson took their first voyage, a "flying visit" to the Gulf coast of Florida. For the trip, Henderson hired a six-ton sailboat with a skipper and cook for crew and obtained two weeks' provisions. Reporting the trip in *Nautilus,* Simpson tells how they cast the dredge overboard and eagerly awaited its contents.

> There is a kind of excitement about the operation; the jar and tremble of the rope as the implement—far out of sight—scrapes over the bottom, gathering in the treasures of the deep—produces a sensation

John Brooks Henderson, Jr., ca. 1895. Courtesy of Division of Mollusks, National Museum of Natural History, Smithsonian Institution.

> akin to which an angler feels when he gets a bite. . . . This feeling reaches a fever heat when the dredge is hoisted slowly, leaving a cloudy wake in the water and its contents are dumped in the screen.
>
> Starfishes, . . . a big horseshoe crab or two and mingled with living mollusks and fishes, . . . dead shells inhabited by hermit crabs, fish, sea-worms, and a dozen other kinds of life, many of which may be puzzling even to an experienced naturalist. . . .
>
> But dredging though very delightful at first, when followed for eight or ten hours consecutively gets to be a good deal like work, and hard, heavy, wet work too.[1]

Henderson's special study of the West Indian land snails dovetailed with Simpson's interest in Florida's tropical tree snails, and the two men searched isolated mogotes and mountainsides, and lush, green valleys and caves in Cuba and other islands in pursuit of these shelled animals. Their enthusiasm was boundless. As Simpson put it, "The sight of large, handsome arboreal snails clinging to the trunks or branches of trees is startling, but to the enthusiastic conchologist it is simply thrilling; it fairly turns his head."[2]

Often their zeal led them into tight spots. Simpson tells of Henderson's predicament when exploring in Jamaica:

> Henderson, wild with excitement and regardless of bats, centipedes, and scorpions, and poisonous vines wedged himself into a dark cave whose mouth was at least two feet too small for his body. He, stuck fast, alone, and far from help, could get neither forward or backward; he pushed on to be rewarded by finding quantities of *Helix peracutissima* and the great purple *H. jamaiccensis* clinging to the roof like stalactites, a snail which we had been told was extinct.[3]

The two ardent naturalists skirted disaster on occasion, like when Simpson blundered into a sacred voodoo shrine while collecting in the hills of Haiti. The Haitians, misunderstanding his intrusion, were about to attack him with clubs and stones when a village official intervened.[4]

BOTANIST JOSEPH H. SIMPSON

While Charles Simpson was gaining a reputation in Washington, his brother, Joseph, still a resident of Bradenton, Florida, had become a botanical collector, and his services were contracted for by botanists such as Allan Hiram Curtiss, John Kunkel Small, Charles Sargent, and Alvan Wentworth Chapman, as well as the U.S. Department of Agriculture. In 1891 he was appointed a field agent for the USDA and paid fifteen hundred dollars to make a coastal botanical survey from Bradenton to Key West. He later extended his range southeast to the Florida Keys and Biscayne Bay, describing many plants new to science and sending thousands of specimens back to the USDA's Division of Botany. In a letter to Dr. George Vasey in Washington accompanying a six-hundred-page report on his four-month expedition, he wrote, "I have at last finished my report on the two trips taken down the coast. It has simply been a monstrous job and has taken an untold amount of study to write it. I found many of the plants were but little known in the extreme south part of the State. Many of the descriptions were at fault, having been taken from the plants as they grew in the West Indies.[5]

Although he was relatively young—only fifty when he made his botanical survey—Joseph complained bitterly, "A good deal of the work is hard enough to kill a mule, but I guess I shall weather it through," he had written to Vasey several years earlier.[6] Arthritis and weak kidneys were among his ailments, and ill health continued to plague him after his 1892 survey.

At the museum, Charles Simpson focused on the naiads, or pearly freshwater mussels, the largest group of freshwater bivalves in terms of both

numbers of species and individual size. In the course of his work he described eight new genera, a number surpassed only by the nineteenth-century French naturalist Rafinesque. Naiads are commonly called "mussels" or "clams." Simpson himself often used these terms, but many modern scientists prefer to call freshwater mussels "naiads" or "unionids," or "unios," because most mussels and clams are marine animals. Their lifestyles differ as well. Naiads, though sedentary, are free-moving, while mussels usually live attached to rocks and pilings by fine byssal threads, an apparatus that is absent or degenerate in the naiads.[7] The zebra mussels, an exotic freshwater species, as well as some marine mussels, use these byssal threads to colonize in cooling-system pipes and water-intake tubes of ships and waterside industrial plants, causing considerable damage.

Naiads are found in lakes and ponds, but they are especially numerous in rivers. These stream-dwelling animals abound in greatest numbers and varieties in central and eastern North America, where conditions for their development have been ideal for many millions of years. Among the several dictionary definitions of *naiad* is "a freshwater mussel of the family Unionidae." Its first meaning, however, is "one of the nymphs in ancient mythology living in and giving life to rivers, springs, lakes and fountains," not unlike a naiad, which is capable of purifying enormous quantities of water. While the modest, algae-backed outer skeleton or shell is hardly nymphlike, the parts of the living animal—its fringed apertures emerging from its valves, its rippling mantle, and freeform, prehensile foot—are indeed graceful, while its inner chamber, jeweled with iridescent nacre, would be a fitting home for a mystical creature.

Naiads may contain pearls, which explains the ambiguous family name of Unionidae, or, more familiarly, "unio," for a shell with two valves. The ancient Greeks named the shell "unio" for its pearl because each was "unique." In modern times other names have been bestowed by the river people who made their living harvesting them by dragging rivers with crowfoot bars. At first they sought pearls, but as the number of older mussels bearing gem-sized pearls dwindled, they marketed the shell to button factories. They dubbed them "spectacle case," "snuffbox," "washboard," and "pocketbook" for articles in daily use, or "wartyback," "three ridge," and "papershell" for the shell's sculpture, strength, or lack thereof. "Heelsplitter" describes the painful encounter between flesh and the shell's sharp dorsal "wing," while the bulging "Higgins eye" depicts the doleful eye of a drowned sailor.

To understand Simpson's method of sorting the naiads, it helps to know a smattering of their life history. This varies widely among the members of the order, but in general terms, naiads are sedentary filter feeders, dependent on moving water to bring them food and oxygen, which are drawn in through their apertures from the water outside. The gills function as a brood pouch for the near-microscopic larvae, which are known as glochidia. This marsupial function is a unique feature of the naiads, distinguishing them from marine mussels and clams. Hundreds of thousands of glochidia may be nurtured within one gravid female. After a period, the glochidia are cast into the water in prodigious quantities, where a very few successfully attach to an appropriate fish and are nourished by the flesh or fluids of their host until they are sufficiently mature to drop to the stream bottom. There they become a valuable part of the food chain or survive to live many years.

When Simpson came to the museum, few details were known of the life history of naiads. Rafinesque made some basic studies of their anatomy as early as 1820, and other investigators published accounts of various aspects of their reproductive processes, but they were primarily sorted by shell characteristics. Specialists such as Victor Sterki (1846–1933), a Swiss physician who became an honorary assistant at the Carnegie Museum of Natural History in Pittsburgh, studied the soft parts and anatomy of these mollusks early on, but few animals (the "wets") were available in the museums. Hooks and threads had been observed on the young naiad mussels, but only in Europe had the glochidia been noted as attached by these structures to the host fish.[8]

The mollusk's life history is etched on its shell. The beak, or "umbo," is the original bivalve; a gap between the valves indicates where the apertures opened and the foot was extended; the sharp, wrinkled edge marks where the half-buried unio projected from the bottom; and its size, shape, and weight reveal its habitat—turbulent, fast-moving river currents or the quiet waters of ponds, for example. The shell collector, stroking the mussel's satiny inner surface, encounters indentations where the adductor and retractor muscles and the mantle were attached, as well as its hinge "teeth"—slender, bladelike "laterals" and stubby, toothlike "cardinals." These are not teeth in the sense of food grinders; rather, they function as guides, aiding the muscles in aligning the two valves and stabilizing the animal in strong currents.

Malacologists question whether the life history of all or even most species of the naiads will ever be perfectly known, because the fauna is declining rapidly. The numbers of individuals living in North American streams has dwindled to less than 10 percent of those that existed in the late nineteenth century.[9] David Honor Stansbery, curator of bivalve mollusks for the Museum of Zoology at Ohio State University and a specialist in endangered mollusks, states, "We are gradually destroying nearly a thousand endemic species of freshwater mollusks. This fauna was millions of years in coming into being and is in the process of being eliminated in only a century or two—and all this before we have even begun to seriously investigate their potential value."[10]

Concern for the survival of the naiads is of long standing. As early as 1858, Frank Higgins, a collector in Ohio, commented on "this remarkable decrease and extinction among the mollusca," laying its cause to "the change of the wilderness into a highly cultivated country, the immense area of forest which has yielded to the plow; the decrease in the volume of the water in our rivers and creeks."[11]

Topsoil from agriculture and building excavations washes into watersheds, enters rivers and lakes, and reduces their oxygen content, severely impacting living conditions for mollusks. Pollutants from paper mills, petroleum brine, pesticides, and other industrial waste have further destroyed naiad habitats. Perhaps the most significant cause of their decline has been the channeling of rivers for barge traffic and impounding of their waters for hydroelectric power. On a four-hundred-mile stretch of the Mississippi River, once home to large populations of naiad mussels, twenty-six navigation dams have been built. The once free-flowing river has become a chain of lakes, a far less suitable habitat for the unio beds that once studded the river bottom. Commercial fishing for both the pearls and their shells made deep inroads in the mussel populations as well. Hundreds of thousands of tons of shells were harvested for the pearl button trade. In 1898 forty-nine button factories were operating on the upper Mississippi alone. The introduction of plastic and glass buttons reduced demand for natural shell, but a new market developed when was it was discovered that it could be used as the nucleus of cultured pearls.[12]

Naiad mussels are a valuable resource both to commerce and as food for humans and other animals. They contribute to the purity of rivers, filtering silt and detritus from the water and depositing it on the stream bottom, where it becomes food for other riverine animals. Scientists also mark the value of mollusks as stream monitors, warning of pesticide and metal pollutants. Now they are being snuffed out, one by one, and each loss leaves an irreversible gap in the broad spectrum of biota that binds all life together.

UNTANGLING THE "UNIO MUDDLE"

In 1890 much was being written about the need for a new classification of the freshwater bivalves. The best-known researcher in this field had been Isaac Lea, who made his living as a publisher but devoted much of his leisure to science, principally the study of the unios. Born in Philadelphia in 1792, he lived to the age of ninety-five and published some 157 papers on these shelled animals. His major work was *Observations on the Genus Unio,* thirteen quarto volumes illustrated with hundreds of plates. Lea recognized over twelve hundred species in the family Unionidae, most of which he himself had named, almost entirely on the criterion of shell sculpture. Simpson commented candidly to Pilsbry, "The fact is Lea was a hog, and he hated Conrad so that he pumped his species indiscriminately and didn't even trouble to refer them to species which they most nearly resembled."[13]

In December 1891, Simpson's paper "Notes on *Unionidae*" was published in *Nautilus.* Calling Lea's classification "almost wholly an artificial one," he wrote, "I believe he instituted it for convenience in working, just as Linnaeus founded the artificial system of classification in botany. Both these great pioneers in science recognized the natural systems, and probably used them as makeshifts. . . . To some capable student of the future is reserved the task of determining these groups and assigning species to them."[14]

An undertone of longing can be heard here as the ardent uniologist found himself engaged in the very task he described. Six months later he followed up "Notes" with another paper in *Nautilus,* on the classification of the American *Unionidae,* explaining the need: "In the first place most of the literature on the subject is out of print, and much of it, such as the 'New Harmony Disseminator,' *Nicholson's Encyclopedia* and the like, is so rare as to be practically out of reach of the average student. It is scattered in a very large number of publications and it will take a considerable amount of careful research to hunt up what has been written on the subject."[15]

Later that year he made another foray into the "unio muddle" when the museum's *Proceedings* published "Notes on the *Unionidae* of Florida and the Southeastern States." This major paper, with thirty-two pages and twenty-six plates, foreshadowed his future works, such as the "Synopsis of the Naiades." In its "Introduction" he stated his objectives:

> Much confusion exists among collectors and students regarding the material in their collections, a considerable proportion of the shells from this region having been sent out under wrong names. Fully one-half these species are not understood and the cabinets of conchologists in general exhibit the most deplorable confusion in this matter.
>
> It is my desire in this list to considerably reduce the number of so-called species by showing that they vary into each other, or that many of them have without proper study simply been assumed to be new and renamed.[16]

"Notes" discussed the distribution of these regional unios and divided the species into natural groups, "doing as little violence as possible to Mr. Lea's general arrangement." Here Simpson was discarding tradition and blazing a new trail, a process that was bound to be controversial. In a few cases identical shells had been given different names by different authors. Simpson sorted out these synonyms and authenticated the name with the earliest date, since the law of priority dictates that the first published name is the valid one. Any name given that shell later becomes a synonym unless the earlier name is officially suppressed by an international commission.[17] Scientific names can be a highly personal affair. Many include the latinized name of a person the author wished to honor, such as *Lampsilis higginsi* Lea, 1857 (Higgins Eye), which was first described by Isaac Lea in 1857 and named to honor Frank Higgins.

Further controversy arose because, when the mollusks of North America were first being discovered, described, and named, the law of priority was not yet established. Even after it was firmly in place, it was not always followed. And disagreements arose over the law's meaning. What constituted a "publication," for example? "Lea read the descriptions of most of his species before scientific societies, claiming that such reading was a *bona fide* publication and dated them from that time; Conrad held that no species could be considered published until a description had been printed and circulated."[18]

Other disputes centered on the validity of the names credited to Rafinesque, the eccentric and controversial French naturalist who collected in the early nineteenth century and was the author of a remarkable number of mollusks. Rafinesque's publications of his mussel discoveries were accompanied only by crude drawings, and the type shells—those that authenticated his newly named species—were not deposited with a museum until ten years after the descriptions were published.[19] Rafinesque had, and still has, his supporters, but Simpson's opined, "His work, like a tax-title deed, will always leave a cloud on what it was intended to cover."[20]

Reviewing Simpson's controversial article, Henry Pilsbry commented, "In this critical study of the mussels of the southeast drainage we find much to commend. . . . Lea's well-known *classification* of Unio is criticized and designated as 'artificial and not in accordance with all the facts of nature'; and in this conclusion we heartily join Mr. Simpson." He warned, however, that "some of his conclusions may cause our Unio-specialists to hurl (verbal) missiles at Mr. S.'s devoted head, 'just to show there's no ill feeling'; but the Uniologist must learn to dodge these little things or take them in good part, as they are all incident to the pursuit of a noble science."[21] No question about it. It was a touchy matter, one that might have been handled with more diplomacy, but the plain-speaking Simpson plunged in feet first, optimistic that his colleagues would willingly sacrifice tradition for accuracy.

The museum underwent a period of growth in the early 1890s, and working conditions were not always ideal. Interruptions caused by remodeling were irritating to Simpson and were probably magnified by his poor health. Dall was on expedition in the West when his aide wrote:

> The crowd is simply immense. Monday there were more than 10,000 visitors in the Smithsonian, and today there will be more. . . . Orders have been issued closing off the department and everything is locked up. Dust is an inch thick in the gallery . . . and the noise is deafening. I have been sick abed with chills and fever. Have crawled over this morning to send your mail. . . . I closed the door Monday leading into the [illegible] and tied it with a string, but they constantly untied it, and came up. . . . I am going back home too weak to sit up.[22]

Scarcely an issue of *Nautilus* came out without some mention of the classification of the unios. Conchologists agreed that a revision was needed but disagreed on methods. It was suggested that a "Congress of American conchologists" be appointed to settle contested points of nomenclature. Simpson squelched this idea.

> I believe that an expert, a specialist, who has devoted years to the loving study of a family or genus is better qualified to judge on these

> points than any body of students, no matter how capable they may be otherwise, but who probably have only a mere smattering of the matter in question. . . .
>
> A specialist who works on a difficult or puzzling group, goes over his work again and again, putting it aside when he tires of it, and taking it up when the mind is rested. . . . As a rule, his collecting is done in the direction of his hobby, and he, therefore, has more material to work on than one slightly interested. He eagerly reads all literature, relating to his work, and in time, if his judgment is well balanced, he becomes an authority.

Conceding the pitfalls that lay in wait for such a specialist, he continued: "And even when such a specialist publishes his studies they must stand the test of criticism, merciless and searching; they must be subject to all the modifications that will be caused by future discoveries and enlarged discoveries, for it is the naked truth alone that will stand.[23]

A reclassification of so large a group of mollusks would be impossible for a museum to undertake without special funds. At this time the Rev. and Mrs. L. T. Chamberlain, son-in-law and daughter of Isaac Lea, offered to underwrite the purchase of material, literature, and other supplies needed to complete the work. Happily, since Simpson was the museum's unio specialist, the assignment was laid on his desk. He would have at his command Lea's superb collection, as well as the Smithsonian's material, which included unios from foreign countries on every continent except Antarctica. At the Philadelphia Academy were the historic collections of Say, Rafinesque, and Conrad. Specimens would be loaned from many other museums and private collections. Though a rich lode of shells was available, Simpson had the soft parts of only four hundred species to work with. He would bring to his task his zest for collecting and his field observations, which dated from childhood.

Simpson had won his prize—the opportunity to author a new classification of the naiads. The prize was not without cost. By nature an outdoorsman, he now found himself much like his despised "closet naturalist," bent over a desk in a stuffy room. His health would suffer, and the poor lighting in the museum rooms, along with the quinine he took to control his malaria, would damage his eyesight. For many years he would harvest only disappointment and criticism for this demanding work.

Field trips were welcome relief to the desk-bound Simpson, as well as to Henderson, who was in his last year of Georgetown law school when the two collectors took a break in December 1893 and sailed off to Jamaica for two months to collect fossil, land, and marine shells. Reporting back to Dall, Simpson said they had been well received by the president of the Boston Fruit Company, who allowed them to collect on his company's property and assigned two of his workers to assist them. "We filled three pretty good-sized boxes. The marl seems quite rich. We could not obtain a pick, but had to work it out with a crow bar and a spading fork. Impossible to obtain barrels. Only flour barrels, poor at that. Boxes were one inch stuff and I built them over and strapped them with hoop iron."[24]

When he returned to Washington he wrote to Pilsbry of their findings and his work. "I am busy arranging our immense collection of Naiades, and it is a very interesting task."[25] Not only interesting, but "back-breaking" and "mind-boggling." "It sometimes happened when I got into a lot of such forms I either became brainfogged or lost all power to grasp or comprehend anything. These things look one way at 9 o'clock and another at noon and still another after lamplighting."[26]

To unwind from his confining work, Simpson would walk in Washington's Rock Creek Park, which he described as

> a large tract of broken land in the immediate suburbs of the city. . . . The surface was so broken that it had defied the efforts of the real estate men to level it up and make lots out of it. It was largely covered with primeval forest and thru it a considerable stream, Rock Creek, tumbled and roared down over granite rocks to the Potomac river. . . . [T]hose who had charge of it had the rare good sense and taste to preserve the forest and all the natural features with very little change. . . . Here and there . . . resting places were provided. . . . The result is that Rock Creek Park is one of the great attractions of Washington. . . . Trolley lines, jitneys and sight-seeing cars run to it, and the poorest people in the city can go there.[27]

One day in the future he would remember Rock Creek Park and apply its naturalistic design to a wilderness park in the Everglades.

Gradually, the rustic Simpson was learning to cope with office routine. Dall was in Tacoma, Washington, when Simpson wrote, "I found the routine and red tape a little difficult at first, but I think I am getting the run of it now and am trying to be very careful and not miss anything. Everyone, especially in Mr. Brown's office, is very kind. There has been a racket about copying ink lately. Mrs. V. and Mr. Y. came over to investigate."[28]

Simpson was moving ahead with his studies of the naiads, but he was unsure of his position at the museum. With no academic credentials to back his theories, he was cautious in expressing his ideas. Writing to Pilsbry in March 1895, addressed him in his usual custom as "My dear Pilsbry" and thanked him for his "very kindly criticism on my paper" on the distribution of West Indian land and freshwater mollusks.[29] He confessed: "I thought I took great risks in saying what I did. Dall grudgingly let the paper go into the *Proc.*, not that he could assail its positions, but he thought them too bold with too little foundation."[30]

This eight-page, handwritten letter, dashed off with great excitement and with little regard for punctuation, proved to be historic, for in it he elucidated the skeleton of his plan for the new classification of the freshwater mussels, or naiads, which was based on studies of the Brazilian malacologist Hermann von Ihering.[31]

> Iherings' head is level I think on the clams. I shall base my classifications largely on the shell & this is the gist of it. In Unionidae *all* genera have cardinals, laterals, or both—some unios almost obliterated, but always to be found in certain species. In Mutelidae *all genera have taxodont*[32] teeth or occasional vestiges of them never an arrangement of cardinals and laterals. The unionids are heterodont[33] the mutelids taxodont. There are other good conchological characters but these show the families to be widely separated. All genera known to have a lasidium[34] (Ihering's Mutelidae) have the vestigial taxodont teeth all known to have a glochidium have theirs heterodont.[35]

This, then, was the framework on which Simpson would build his classification. Though hotly contested from some quarters, it proved to be a workable system and stood the test of time.[36]

The additional pay promised in Dall's initial job proposal had not been forthcoming, and in May 1896 Simpson asked for a raise.

> I know that I am not a rapid workman and that I lack education, but I think I have done my duty reasonably well and have earned a reputation for faithfulness that is deserved. . . . In the first two years here I spent my leisure hours identifying materials sent by correspondents. Since then, I have devoted my time out of the office to the study of West Indian snails, etc. and now am putting in an average of three or four hours daily in preparing a synopsis. All this work will be turned to the benefit of the Museum and I only hope to receive the honor

of publishing it in my own name. . . . It does seem to me that my services ought to entitle me to a little recognition.[37]

His grievance met with no success. Though Dall approached G. B. Goode, the Smithsonian's administrator, on Simpson's behalf, funds were low and other persons with greater seniority held prior claims.[38] The faithful uniologist remained at his post for nearly six more years without a promotion or pay raise.

A MIDLIFE CRISIS

The winter of 1898 was bitterly cold. As Simpson bent over his tray of specimens, he complained of drunken janitors who forgot to turn on the heat. One night the temperature fell to seventeen degrees below zero, killing the "woman's tongue" tree (*Albizia lebbeck*) that had grown near his home and filled the summer nights with the pungent fragrance of its blossoms. Simpson would long remember the rustle of the papery pods on the dying tree, for since September he had known that his wife, too, was dying.[39] On Christmas Eve, Cornelia was admitted to Providence Hospital, where she died two days later of stomach cancer.

The day of Cornelia's funeral Simpson scrawled a brief note to Dall on a scrap of paper torn from a tablet: "I must ask your indulgence for being away Saturday and again today on account of the death of Mrs. Simpson who will be buried today. The funeral will be at 2 P.M. from my home, and I would be glad to have you and Mrs. Dall come if you could. Excuse this. I am all broken up. Yours, C. T. Simpson."[40] Cornelia was forty-seven. She was buried in the Congressional Cemetery in Washington.

Cornelia Couch Simpson transmits but a faint image. No letters, diaries, or other primary material referring to her have been found save a few remarks in Simpson's letters and in those of Pliny Reasoner to his mother. What is known is that, in frail health, she followed her husband to frontier towns in Florida and Nebraska, and to the nation's capital, yet remained closely bound to her childhood home in Illinois. She sometimes joined her husband on excursions, and when nearly seven months pregnant she embarked with him on a month-long cruise aboard a working sailboat with few personal comforts. She suffered nausea and numerous indignities with apparent good humor, winning the admiration of Hugh Culbert, a self-proclaimed misogynist. While in Bradenton she bore the loss of an infant daughter and stood staunch when her marriage and home were threatened. Until research reveals more, Cornelia's character rests on these premises.

In August 1899 Simpson completed the first draft of his paper "Synopsis of the Naiades, or Pearly Fresh-Water Mussels." Unsure of how his work would be received by the scientific staff at the museum, he tried it out on Pilsbry. "Will you give any suggestions or corrections on the enclosed blank paper? . . . I have never asked any advise [*sic*] here—I didnt dare to do it."[41]

A year later the "Synopsis" was published in the *Proceedings* of the U.S. National Museum. With over 550 pages and a distribution map of world populations of naiads, it was the first definitive reclassification of these mollusks since Lea's *Synopsis of the Family Unionidae* in 1870.

In the "Introduction" Simpson reviewed the history of the classification of the Unionidae and credited the work of his contemporaries Sterki, Taylor, and Kelly, though he reserved his highest praise for von Ihering. Simpson had drawn from the species-level work of many of his fellow uniologists, but it was von Ihering's findings that led to the new system of higher classification. Referring to von Ihering's 1893 paper, which recognized the Unionidae and the Mutelidae as families on the basis of different methods of reproduction and shell characteristics, he wrote, "I consider this the most important discovery that has yet been made in the study of the Naiades."[42]

The reaction to his "Synopsis" was slow in coming, but when it did the thin-skinned uniologist was sharply stung by his critics. Simpson found the objections of Arnold Ortmann particularly offensive: "[Ortmann] seems to me to stand with a club ready to jump on any of my mistakes,"[43] he blurted out in a letter to Bryant Walker some years later. Ortmann (1863–1927), who earned a Ph.D. in 1885 from the University of Jena in Germany, came to America from Germany in 1894 and was at this time curator of invertebrate paleontology at Princeton University. In 1903 Andrew Carnegie asked him to set up the Museum of Invertebrate Zoology at the Carnegie Institute, and he became its first curator. Highly respected among his colleagues and noted for his fair-mindedness, he became recognized as the chief American authority on the morphology and classification of the Unionidae. In later years he continued and augmented Simpson's system with his careful work in anatomy, especially gill structure.[44]

A review of Ortmann's published papers turned up only differences of opinion on points of nomenclature until 1910, when he criticized Simpson's new system as based on "insufficient material" and lacking "microscopic detail." Some called the "Synopsis" "careless," and in later years Simpson admitted that it "drew the criticism of those in authority."[45] Even von Ihering, whose work had inspired Simpson, was not unqualified in his praise. In the lead article in *Nautilus,* August 1901, he wrote, "It is for me the greatest satisfaction to felicitate Mr. Simpson upon having produced a work which will mark a new period in the study of fresh-water mussels."[46] However, he then continued to take issue with some of Simpson's conclusions. Simpson defended his arrangement, confident that when further histological studies were made they would confirm his findings.[47]

The unsigned review of the "Synopsis" in *Nautilus* can be safely attributed to Pilsbry, who was well aware of the uproar Simpson's "arrangement" would cause. "The classification of the family *Unionidae* is almost completely original with Mr. Simpson, and . . . must appear strange to those acquainted with the old arrangement of the group," he stated. After highlighting some of specific changes in the system, the reviewer invited the readers to give Simpson's system a try.

> We hazard little in saying that once this is done, the naturalness of his generic groups will win general acceptance for the new classification. . . .
>
> Regarding the synonymy, Mr. Simpson seems to have exercised fair and temperate judgment. He is no species-splitter, but on the other hand, he has steered clear of an equally dangerous reef, which has wrecked several promising investigators. In other words, he has never allowed the reaction toward extreme "lumping" of species which followed the era of Lea, to warp his judgment. As it is, the list of synonyms under some species . . . is appalling.

In conclusion the reviewer declared, "Mr. Simpson's synopsis is destined to work a revolution in the study of fresh-water mussels, though there will naturally be opposition to the new ideas and methods among some reactionists."[48]

Another student of the naiad mussels, Victor Sterki, while voicing criticism on some points, praised it as "a new era in our knowledge of these animals." And, in time, Ortmann would also accept and use the premises of Simpson's "Synopsis" as a foundation for future studies. Further recognition at this time came from conchologist James Ferris, who named a new bivalve *Lampsilis simpsoni* in Simpson's honor, with the tribute "to one who has given nearly a life work towards perfecting the history of the humble clam."[49]

The "Synopsis" was just one-third of the entire work. A year later, Simpson expanded it into his *Descriptive Catalogue of the Naiades, or Pearly Fresh-Water Mussels,* a monumental study of 1,540 manuscript pages with 7,600 entries. For months the catalog was reviewed and discussed, but the museum made no commitment to publish it. Finally it became apparent that it had been rejected. Privately, Simpson was angry and profoundly disappointed. He saw his life work as a failure. He had labored many long hours, much of it his leisure time, for minimum wages or none at all. His only reward would have been "the honor of having it published under my name. . . . I went out as a pioneer and blazed my way, there being no classification, worthy of the name, of the Naiades, and it was an immense task. . . . It was to be expected that I would make a great many mistakes. . . . But I blazed the way."[50]

Though often revised and still controversial, Simpson's work has not been equaled in the nearly one hundred years that have passed since its completion. Only Fritz Haas in his *Superfamilia Unionacea* published in German in 1969 has approached it. The reasons for the catalog's rejection are not clear. Apparently, Dall withheld his approval. The "Synopsis" had received a cool reception from some influential quarters, and the Smithsonian was a public institution, sensitive to criticism. Dall may have feared that Simpson's work was ahead of its time. Professional jealousy and Simpson's lack of credentials may have played a part. Ortmann had a classical German education and had studied under the noted Ernst Haeckel. As curator of a major museum, he held a position of authority. Simpson, on the other hand, though widely respected by his peers, was self-educated and occupied a position on the lower echelon of the museum staff. Money may have been another consideration. Mrs. Chamberlain had died since the project had been begun, and perhaps the family was unable or unwilling to continue their support of the work.

Frustrated and depressed at the rejection of his work, Simpson tied up the manuscript in three packages and "laid it aside." Seeing no future for himself at the museum, he looked beyond his disappointment to the fulfillment of a lifelong dream, a home in the subtropical region of Florida. He submitted his resignation to the museum and announced his plans. Whatever his feelings, apparently his departure took place with good humor, for Dall and other staff members corresponded with him and visited him in Florida.

Before embarking for Florida, Simpson remarried. Mutual friends, realizing his limited resources and his need for a companion, found a bride for him in Flora Roper, the widow of Edward Roper, a fellow conchologist, whose ads and articles on shells had run side-by-side with Simpson's in *Nautilus.* Simpson met Flora for the first time on September 17, 1902, the day they were wed by a Unitarian minister in Revere, Massachusetts. Though a marriage of convenience, it proved successful. Flora, a pleasant, intelligent woman of forty-two, found a good home for herself and her six-year-old daughter, Marion. And Charles found a wife accustomed to the ways of a naturalist, who brought to the marriage some financial assets and also many natural history books, technical papers, shell collections, and a copper microscope. The two had much in common, for Flora was educated in natural history and had taught botany in the public schools.[51]

With little more than his government retirement, Simpson's dream of living once more in Florida might have turned out very different. His marriage to Flora shaped the direction of his new life in no small way. So confident was he of her judgment that, according to a feature on Flora that appeared in the *Miami Daily News,* he sent her ahead to choose their homesite: "In 1903 Mrs. Simpson, to whom he had recently been married, came to look over the land in the Miami area. She found a 15-acre plot that answered the description he had given her of what he wanted. They bought the tract she had found and her place still comprises 10 acres of it."[52]

CHAPTER SIX

The Sentinels, 1902–1909

Whatever special nest we make—leaves and moss like the marmots and birds, or tents or piled stone—we all dwell in a house of one room—the world with the firmament for its roof—and are sailing the celestial spaces without leaving any track.

John Muir

A SUCCESSFUL TRANSPLANT

Simpson was only fifty-six when he retired from the museum, but he thought of himself as old and expected to spend his last years quietly investigating nature's secrets. However, life took a different twist, and the studious and sometimes contentious uniologist C. T. Simpson was destined to become respectfully known as "Charles Torrey Simpson," South Florida's much-revered naturalist. Ahead of him lay thirty years during which his reputation as a specialist in mollusks would be rivaled by his fame as a horticulturalist. Boxed up and stored was his catalogue on the pearly freshwater mussels. Not for twelve years would a patron be found to publish it. In the meantime, Simpson turned his attention to an equally engrossing member of the mollusk family, the Florida tree snail, *Liguus fasciatus.*

As hungry for light as a houseplant in winter, Simpson eagerly turned his face to the sun. Florida's soft climate would be a boon to his health, and though he sometimes claimed to be "broken down," he seldom wrote of "chills and fever," the constant complaint of his younger years.

The Community

A social item in the *Miami Metropolis* for January 16, 1903, under "Lemon City Notes" reported that "Mr. and Mrs. Simpson, late of Washington, and their son and daughter, have arrived and are at the Green cottage on Bay Street until a new home can be built."[1] To call it Lemon "City" was somewhat of an exaggeration. The little community had only three hundred residents when the Simpsons set down their bags, but it supported several stores and churches, a school, a hotel, and a physician.

Five miles south, Miami, the "magic city," was on the brink of "boom times." Henry Flagler's Florida East Coast Railroad had rolled into town in April 1896, and three months later, with 480 registered voters, Miami was incorporated as a city. In the next six years its population increased tenfold. The city boasted electric lights, waterworks, telephones, free mail delivery, three newspapers, and a fine rock-walled county courthouse. Flagler's mammoth six-hundred-room Royal Palm Hotel sprawled along the Miami River, and many substantial boardinghouses and health resorts catered to tourists and invalids. The Fort Dallas National Bank, patterned after a Greek temple, had capital of $100,000, and the Palladian-styled First Presbyterian Church, endowed by Flagler, had opened its doors along with churches of many other denominations. Pine forests and hammocks were felled to make way for the infrastructure of the new city, for fields of pineapples, tomatoes, peppers, beans, and potatoes, and for groves of coconuts, citrus, avocado, and mangoes.

The Land

The Simpsons bought fifteen acres on Biscayne Bay for fifteen hundred dollars. Located on the edge of Lemon City, their property is now incorporated into the city of Miami and would be found at North East 69 Street from Biscayne Boulevard to the bayfront. Though legally a resident of Lemon City, Simpson preferred the post office of neighboring Little River and used it as his mailing address.

Brother Joseph, whose botanical survey had taken him to this area in 1891, was overjoyed when he heard about his brother's property, commenting, "If it is a piece of that high hammock on Biscayne Bay just north of Lemon City then I must congratulate you ten thousand times ten thousand on the beautiful paradise you have selected."[2]

Up to this time Charles Simpson had been a rolling stone, never settled long in one place, but now he anchored himself firmly, as though with a byssus, to this promising site. His land was well suited to a natural-

Charles and Flora (Roper) Simpson, 1902. Courtesy of the Historical Association of Southern Florida.

ist, providing diversified ecosystems: rocky pineland, hammock, and, along the waterfront, all the vegetation associated with tidal flats. Like other classical naturalists before him—White at Selbourne, Thoreau at Walden, and his contemporary, Burroughs, at Slabsides—Simpson would devote himself to the leisurely study of this microcosm of earth. Little escaped his notice: the strange growth habits of the white, red, and black mangroves that grew on the shoreline; the antics of the land crabs that skittered over the mudflats at low tide; the golden spiders and arboreal snails that jeweled the hammock; and the frogs, owls, and chuck-will's-widows, whose raucous calls filled the night with music only a naturalist could love. "The glory of the place was a couple of acres of fine young hammock that lay within a few rods of my door. . . . Year in and year out its greenery, its peace and quiet have appealed to me and from it I have learned some of the most valuable lessons of my life. Within this bit of forest and a short distance from it I found growing wild over ninety species of trees and large shrubs, most of them derived from the American tropics from seed carried along on the Gulf Stream and cast on the shore by the sea."[3]

The tropical hardwoods of his hammock grew nowhere else in North America. Among them were the gumbo limbo, with its distinctive coppery bark; the lofty mastic, rising some eighty feet from massive buttress roots; and the royal poinciana, or flame tree, with its outstretched, muscular limbs and scarlet blooms. Giant oaks were loaded to the breaking point with ferns, air plants, and Spanish moss. Wild coffee, tetrazygia, and other sun-loving shrubs crowded the forest edge, while a tangle of vines and creepers sprawled and clambered over all. Two venerable pines stood near his homesite. "I called them 'the Sentinels' and from them I named my home. I felt that they would stand watch and guard me and mine."[4]

It was "the Sentinels" to the naturalist, but more often than not folks called it "Simpson's hammock" or "the Simpson place." In a denim shirt and overalls belted with a rope, Simpson was often found flush-faced, sweaty, and grimy-handed as he began to cultivate his land. Like his pioneer father, he was breaking new ground—not the thickly matted sod of the plains, but a plant cover with roots deeply embedded in the Miami limestone, a soft rock that yielded only to a pickax or a stick of dynamite.

Simpson cleared the natural growth selectively, replacing scrub trees with flowering and fruiting tropical plants. Among the first were a pandanus, or "screw pine," from Australia and a "woman's tongue" tree, whose branches, in later years, had a spread of ninety feet.

"The Sentinels," named for the two pine trees that stood in front of the house. They were both killed in the great hurricane, thus dating this photo as pre-1926. Courtesy of the Historical Association of Southern Florida.

A Most Unusual House

Simpson began to build his self-designed house almost at once. From his observations in the Caribbean and the picture of an inn in Honolulu, he adopted the concept of a house built on pilings, with the ground floor enclosed with latticework and the upper story encircled with spacious verandas. It was quite unlike any other house in the area, but it was geared to South Florida's climate.

To choose his site, Simpson made a light, portable scaffold about twelve to fifteen feet high. Standing on this "prospect tower," he studied the lay of the land, plotted views for the verandas and windows, and determined the limits of the open space to be set aside for lawn.

As the construction progressed, he did not lack for sidewalk superintendents. Among them was Ada Merritt, one of Lemon City's first schoolteachers, whom Simpson wryly described as having been "on deck since the Fall of Man." As she watched the pilings go in and the two upper stories rise high off the ground, she warned the newcomer that the very first hurricane would scatter it over one, perhaps two counties.[5]

In April 1903, though the house was far from complete, the Simpsons moved in. He wrote to William Dall, "We are living in the upper part and using the lower for storeroom, books, etc. Filled one side below eight feet high and twenty-four feet long with shelves for books. . . . Have built a slat house for starting young plants and it works admirable."[6]

When the house was virtually finished, he described it as "sort of an irregular cross, 46 feet one way and 64 the other, the whole elevated eight feet above the ground on massive posts. This basement being mostly latticed in, it makes an excellent laboratory, bathroom, storeroom, carpenter shop, etc. There is a piazza entirely around the main part 120' running length, an admirable place to lounge and one can always find a sheltered spot."[7] Simpson's house contrasted sharply with the northern-style, two-story frame houses, the pine bungalows, and Spanish-style villas common in his neighborhood, and though it was set apart on fifteen acres it drew many comments. "An atrocity," said some. "Monstrous," said others, but it suited the climate and, more importantly, its owner.[8]

The Waterfront

Aside from an access path to the bayfront, a boathouse, and a dock, Simpson left the shore in its natural state. Three species of mangroves grew in this littoral: the red mangrove, with trunks four feet or more in diameter and one hundred feet high and with enormous, arched roots; the white mangrove, a lofty tree as well; and, just north of his line, an immense black mangrove with half an acre of quills, or pneumatophores, the tree's breathing apparatus. Farther back—half on the sandy shore and half verging into the water—were giant buttonwoods, "a few of which stood erect like respectable trees, but the majority of which had fallen and were sprawling aimlessly over the mud."[9]

Simpson recognized the ecological value of this malodorous shoreline for building up the land and as a nursery and feeding ground for a host of small invertebrates, as well as for saltwater fish such as mullet, grey snapper, tarpon, and sea trout. Too many waterfront owners would have viewed such a tangle of sprawling roots and branches, rotting seaweed, and ocean detritus as undesirable and replaced it with breakwalls. As Simpson put it in *Ornamental Gardening in Florida,* "No sooner does the average man possess a water front than he considers it necessary to build a sea wall along it. In nine cases out of ten there isn't the slightest need for it; he simply builds it because it is . . . the fashion to do it, just as he would wear a collar a foot high around his neck if the other fellows did. There are cases where the sea or a stream is encroaching on the land and a wall is needed, but as a general thing it is not."[10]

The Hammock

The hammock was the crown jewel of Simpson's property. His first challenge was to retain its natural growth while opening up paths to its interior. "I cut a narrow trail just wide enough to walk in Indian file, getting down on my knees in the thick growth, and working it out with a hatchet. Nothing of value was destroyed in making this walk, for where I came in contact with a tree or any choice small thing I worked around and left it." The path, leading to curiosities of the plant world, took a circular route so that at no point could the edge of the wood be seen. "The impression was created that this bit of wood was quite a considerable forest, and I have been asked if there were not twenty acres of it."[11]

He introduced shade-loving palms along the walk and loaded the branches of oaks and boots of the palms with bromeliads, peperomias, ferns, and orchids, creating a virtual air garden. Many of these he collected on his travels with John Brooks Henderson in the Caribbean, and some he purchased with his meager income.

A neighbor, watching his patient work, commented, "If this timber were mine I would take my ax and cut out all the underbrush, the crooked and small trees, and I would pull off and burn all that long moss and clean up all the rubbish you have lying around. Then it would look as though somebody had been here and done something." Simpson's divergent view was, "That's just what the average person wants to do, to clean up and improve. He is sure nature hasn't properly finished up her work."[12]

The neighborhood kids dropped in to watch his progress, and one of them was five-year-old Elsie Mettair. She remembers herself as "a little, bitty kid, following him around, talking his ears off and asking him a million questions. If he needed two more hands to hold something I was right there. I never knew if I was a bother to him or not, but when I left, he would always ask me, 'What time are you coming back tomorrow?' "[13]

Elsie held his tools when he attached the first staghorn fern to the trunk of a sprawling oak and watched as he planted strelitzia, the "bird of paradise." Plants such as these had seldom been seen outside the conservatories of major botanical gardens. Visitors to Simpson's hammock were astonished to find them growing in nature. Soon they would be found in many South Florida gardens, but even as late as 1922 newspaper articles touted Simpson's plantings as "found nowhere else in America," and to a degree this was so.[14]

The Fern Pool

A striking feature of Simpson's hammock was what he called a "fern pool," inspired by the thick growth that covered the walls of the lime sinks, or "solution holes," commonly found in the hammocks of Florida's coastal ridge. To recreate this natural feature, Simpson blasted out a hole a foot or so below water level.

> I left the sides as irregular as possible, filled earth into the crevices and pockets, planted a lot of shade and moisture loving stuff and in a short time had a fair imitation of a natural fern pool. . . . A rugged sort of trail half path, half steps, is worked out so that it is possible to get down to water level, yet it is so constructed that it does not appear to be artificial. On its sides I have about twenty-five species of ferns, . . . Peperomias, Begonias, Dieffenbachias, . . . and a variety of other things. *Ficus quercifolia* and other creepers are beginning to cover the walls and a Monstera starting from near the water is creeping up and will ascend one of the trees on its bank.
>
> I have put native fish in all my pools and they not only prevent the breeding of mosquitoes, but they add to the attractiveness of the place. . . . In a sort of rough seat which I have worked out in the side of it I can sit and . . . now and then catch sight of a shy bird peering out and half afraid of me.[15]

Though he had no power tools or hired labor, he did have helpers. His stepdaughter, Marion, recalled that when constructing landscape features "Mr. Simpson" was the master planner, she was the hod carrier, Mrs. Simpson was the mason, and Pliny was the water engineer. And when a fishpond and mirror pool were called for, all the children in the neighborhood pitched in.[16] "He had a very strong will," Marion said, "and would push through what he set out to do at any cost."[17]

To complete his estate, Simpson constructed several ornamental outbuildings: a slathouse for orchids and cuttings, a boathouse, and a dock with a rustic pavilion overlooking the bay. In 1908 he wrote to Dall, "We put in a cement walk and did a lot of work in beautifying some low hammocks with a pond, rustic seats, bridge, walk, etc. . . . I have the place at last licked into shape. In fact it is visited by tourists and leading botanists and horticulturalists when they come to Miami."[18]

Simpson's orchid house and potting shed on the edge of his hammock, ca. 1910. Firecracker plant (russelia) in the foreground. From Simpson, *Ornamental Gardening.*

EXPLORING PARADISE KEY

South of Miami, long, wet fingers of Everglades stretched out through the rocky pineland where scattered truck gardens and the farming communities of Larkin (South Miami), Cutler, Perrine, and Homestead had been established. At the edge of the pineland a large island, remarkable for the royal palms that crested above the forest canopy, could be sighted. To any but the most determined explorer the island was inaccessible. Barred on the east by Taylor Slough, in the rainy season it seemed to float just out of reach in the shallow sea of the Everglades, like a Shangri-la, alluring but unattainable. Plume hunters and trappers knew it and dubbed it "Paradise Key," but few found its rewards to compensate for the effort needed to reach it. The Seminoles visited it in their dugouts and used it as their hideaway during the Seminole Wars (1835–42). Perhaps the soldiers who tracked them were the first white men to invade its fastness. If so, they left no record. Other adventurers in the Glades had drawn near the Key, but until John and Marian Soar, Little River nurserymen, waded to its edge in 1893, Paradise Key had never known the foot of a naturalist.

This remote Everglades island was one of Simpson's first trips to explore for plants. When he learned of the island, he arranged to go there in December 1903 with the Soar brothers and Alvah Augustus Eaton, a fern specialist Simpson recalled as "most companionable and altogether one of the best woodsmen I ever knew."[19] Earlier that year, the Soars had guided botanist John Kunkel Small to the Key. As Small commented, "In our phytogeography it is not duplicated. . . . It is . . . like the hammock islands which are scattered in myriads over the southern portion of the Everglades. However, it differs from these in that it is larger and higher, and consequently more rocky and with a more extensive flora. Furthermore, it has been always surrounded by water or damp sloughs and thus protected from fires. . . . Thus its vegetation has had nearly uninterrupted growth for ages."[20]

The expedition was planned for December, during the dry season when the water would be low and the menace of mosquitoes somewhat diminished. Although the party would spend only one day on the Key, the round-trip from Little River, which today takes about two hours by car, required seven days.

They set out from Little River in a horse-drawn open wagon that carried their provisions, bedrolls, and collecting gear. After driving for some hours over "preposterous" roads, they finally arrived at Camp Jackson on the edge of the Everglades. This was a makeshift depot for the surveyors of the Florida East Coast Railroad—little more than a rough board shed—and its only creature comfort was a deep, natural water hole. From there they hiked, carrying their camp outfit, three or four miles to the island.

> The surface was irregular rock which, as we proceeded, became covered with water and so slippery that we were constantly sliding into pot holes. In fact, the walking consisted mostly of slipping down and getting up again. At length we reached the headwaters of Taylor River and Soar suggested that we keep close together when crossing. Eaton asked why and was told that there might be alligators or crocodiles. He contemptuously offered to eat the entire saurian supply that might be found in Dade County, and boldly waded in. In midstream, the water to his armpits, there suddenly began a tremendous commotion and for a minute the surface of the stream was

> all arms, legs, blankets, and camp equipage, along with the tail and body of a monster alligator. Eaton finally crawled out looking very pale and explained that he had stepped on what he thought was a log. . . . After that I frequently reminded him of his promise to eat the alligator crop.[21]

When they finally reached the edges of the hammock, the ordeal of the trip was forgotten. Paradise Key lived up to its name—a "paradise" of virgin growth comparable to the rain forests of Central America. Eaton was delirious at the sight of head-high sword ferns growing thickly at the edge of the forest, while in the humid interior were filmy fern and maidenhair. Resurrection fern, so called because it shrivels up in dry weather but springs to life in the rainy season, formed thick mats on prostrate logs and the horizontal branches of oaks. In open spots, the bronze-green selaginella, a club moss, scrambled vinelike over the underbrush, and shoestring and Boston fern lodged in the boots of cabbage palms. Immense, broad-limbed oaks, some with trunks five feet in diameter, harbored orchids, and air plants and were hung with Spanish moss while gumbo-limbo and mastic trees, entwined with thick lianas, formed a canopy overhead and densely shaded the hammock. To Simpson the royal palms were the most stunning feature of this "noble and wonderful forest. Their great smooth, white stems appeared everywhere, and one could look up, up, up, away into the intensely blue sky where their glorious crowns were tossing the sea breeze."[22]

The men laid their camping equipment under a large royal palm and wandered off to explore. Simpson was filling his sack with orchids when he heard a shot. Soon Eaton and Soar arrived carrying a large rattlesnake, which Soar immediately skinned. Close to sundown, the men consulted and decided to return to Camp Jackson for the night. The trip in reverse was much like their entry—wading through the Taylor River, stumbling over rocks, and negotiating the sharp saw grass—except it was exacerbated by the gathering darkness and their heavy loads. All carried camping equipment plus bags of plant specimens—Simpson claimed his load of orchids weighed forty pounds but seemed as heavy as a freight car. To make matters worse, Soar became dreadfully ill, perhaps from the odor of the snake he had skinned, so Eaton shouldered his pack and Simpson went on to a scrubby growth and built a fire.

> Soar finally arrived in dreadful condition and he vomited most of the night. We were camped on a small ragged rock which nowhere rose more than a foot above the water and was full of potholes. Here

> we turned in for the night on the most wretched bed I ever saw. Towards morning we all slept, but at dawn I got up to stretch my cold, aching limbs. Within twenty feet of us was a fine dry island a rod across, almost perfectly level, covered with nice soft grass,—an ideal place for a camp. Eaton suggested that we each take turns kicking the others, and he basely attempted to lay the responsibility of the camp selection on me. . . . Poor Eaton! He went north, married the woman of his choice, and wrote me how supremely happy he was,—and then I heard of his sudden death. Had he lived he would have become famous as a botanist.[23]

Simpson returned many times to Paradise Key, and his writings about its natural history stimulated interest in preserving its natural wonders. This wild garden in the Everglades later became Royal Palm State Park and, later still, the nucleus of Everglades National Park.

CHAPTER SEVEN

Tropical Plant Distribution, 1909–1914

It was an education in the botany of the tropics to wander with this great naturalist through his place and hear him tell about his plants.

Dr. David Fairchild

FLORIDA'S PIONEER PLANTSMEN

South Florida, with climatic conditions found nowhere else on the North American mainland, had drawn many plantsmen. Early in the nineteenth century, Henry Perrine experimented with sisal and other tropical economic plants on Indian Key. As railroads and highways opened South Florida to northern markets, fruit growers, such as William J. and Isabel Krome in Homestead, cultivated citrus and avocados from Mexico, mangoes from India, and oranges from the Meditarranean. Dooryard gardeners tried out exotics like papaya, kumquats, breadfruit, lychee nuts, and calamondins, with varying results.

Industrialist Charles Deering (1852–1927), not to be confused with his brother, James, whose Italian renaissance Villa Viscaya in Miami is now a Dade County museum of the European decorative arts, was a retired chairman of the board of International Harvester and a patron of the natural sciences. At his estate near Buena Vista—just south of Lemon City—he supported a research project of the New York Botanical Garden by reserving twenty-five acres for planting more than forty varieties of imported and native cacti.

John Gifford, the first American to hold a doctorate in forestry and an early resident of Coconut Grove, shuttled back and forth between Miami and the Caribbean islands, bringing back seeds he thought would grow in Florida's hospitable climate, including those of an orchid tree and the scarlet-flowered coral tree he introduced to Dade County. He carried in his coat pocket a seedling of the first *Ficus altissima,* whose trunks and branches later covered half an acre. Farther north, Dr. Henry Nehrling, a German emigrant, had established a remarkable collection of bamboos, palms, and other tropical plants in his Palm Cottage Garden of Gotha in Central Florida.

DAVID FAIRCHILD

Simpson soon connected with Dade County's plant enthusiasts and was a frequent visitor to the plant introduction station on Brickell Avenue. This was a modest affair that had come about when the youthful David Fairchild and his cohorts in the U.S. Department of Plant Pathology spearheaded the idea for the section of Foreign Seed and Plant Introduction of the U.S. Department of Agriculture, informally known as "SPI." Given the reins of the new section in 1898, Fairchild recognized the need for a place with a warm climate where seeds and plants sent from foreign ports by agricultural explorers could be planted. For this purpose the department leased six acres between Brickell Avenue and Biscayne Bay, and Florida developer Henry Flagler subscribed one thousand dollars to build a laboratory there for the study of plant disease. Fairchild visited the station in the winter of 1898 and later recalled, "I found the laboratory only half finished, and but a few plants in the garden—some guavas, a few citrus varieties, and a single Carob tree grown from seed which I had sent from the Mediterranean. To us young fellows, this six acres seemed quite marvelous. It was the first land available to us where we could plant anything we wanted."[1] Miami's 1904 directory pictures the "U.S. Sub-Tropical Laboratory," as it was originally called. Later it was more frequently referred to as the Plant Introduction Station or the "little" garden on Brickell Avenue.

After his initial visit to the station, Fairchild did not return for fourteen years, though he shipped many plants there during the interim. A quiet, studious fellow with heavy-rimmed glasses, a bushy head of hair, and a thick, boxy, casually barbered moustache, the youthful Fairchild found delight in such arcane studies as the nuclei of alga and the mushroom gardens of termite colonies. However, a chance shipboard meeting with Barbour Lathrop, a wealthy philanthropist and inveterate traveler, led to an invitation to accompany Lathrop on an odyssey to search the world for economic plants to benefit America. Fairchild took leave of

U.S. Department of Agriculture Plant Introduction Station, Miami, ca. 1904. Also called "U.S. Subtropical Laboratory." Courtesy of the P. K. Yonge Library of Florida History, University of Florida.

the Department of Agriculture and, from 1898 to 1904, traveled with his benefactor around the globe. They shipped back for testing plants that endured extreme heat, drought, high altitude, and other special growing conditions as well as promising new cultivars. From their travels came strains of barley, hops, and alfalfa; spineless cactus and seedless grapes; and water chestnuts, tung oil seeds, Egyptian cotton, and many bamboos. Exotic fruit trees especially intrigued Fairchild, and he introduced many new strains of avocados, mangoes, and the calamondin, as well as Miami's famous sausage tree, which has been the subject of countless tourists' photographs and postcards. A fruit of his travels in Japan were the flowering cherry trees that each spring create such a spectacle around Washington's Tidal Basin.

When he returned to Washington in 1904, he met and married Marian Bell, the daughter of inventor Alexander Graham Bell. Fairchild, perhaps more widely conversant with the agriculture of the world than any other American, again took the helm of the Foreign Seed and Plant section. His keen ability to judge character and his gift for leadership were impor-

tant assets in his department, which required the selection and nurturing of the intrepid, independent breed of botanists who chose to become plant explorers.

The Brickell Avenue station not only provided information to truck farmers, fruit and flower growers, and home gardeners on fertilizers, plant diseases, and horticulture in general, but it also distributed free seeds and cuttings. "It was a social center as well as an experiment station," recalled Gifford, "In fact, it was there that many people first learned to know many of these tropical things."[2]

THE SIMPSON PLANT COLLECTION

Simpson acquired many plants through the experimental station or directly from the SPI office in Washington. Others he purchased from local nurseries, collected in the wild, or grew from seed sent to him by foreign correspondents.

It is astonishing how quickly he established his plantings. "Simpson Botanical Garden a Veritable Eden" was the headline for a *Miami Metropolis* article in 1913, just ten years after Simpson acquired his "naturalist's paradise." While the newswriter may have inflated the figures, he described "three thousand varieties of plants, which include seventy-five species of orchids, fifteen of oleanders, 150 of palms, twenty of rubber plants, 100 of young fruits of all kinds."[3] Among the palms were an African oil palm, two species of California fan palms, the sugar palm from the Malay Archipelago, the gingerbread palm of Egypt, a chamerops from southern Europe, the wine palm of India, an immense sabal from South America, and the salt-tolerant nipa palm from the Philippines.

The Simpson place attracted a constant stream of visitors. Every kind of motor car, from Deering's Rolls Royce to Gifford's Model T, could be found parked in the drive. Charles Brookfield, who raised limes on Elliot Key and was for many years associated with the Tropical Audubon Society, recalled Simpson's cordial greeting, "Come in, come in," he would say. "I am so glad to see you."[4]

Simpson gave freely of his advice to those who asked. Deering, for example, who employed several landscape gardeners, consulted Simpson on developing a hammocklike arboretum on a section of his property. Simpson never charged for this kind of service. People were awed by his knowledge and addressed him respectfully as "Professor Simpson," but the modest plantsman tagged himself as "the old man with the hoe."

On weekends Simpson's hammock was a popular place for outings. Picnic lunches were shared on the piazza or taken to the Simpsons' bay-

"The old man with a hoe." Courtesy of Special Collections, Fairchild Tropical Garden Library.

front pavilion. While the grown-ups strolled around the grounds sampling new varieties of tropical fruits, discussing the weather or inquiring about this plant or that tree, the children played with the menagerie of dogs, cats, and chickens that overran the place or clambered in the mangroves, picking up sea wrack caught in the arching, matted roots. Sometimes the group would pile into Simpson's launch for a "plunge in the surf" on the ocean side of the adjacent key, soon to become Miami Beach. Simpson recalls one such occasion when a "cheeky" land crab dragged his socks, garters, and one sleeve of his shirt into a hole. "It might be supposed the crabs wanted these articles for nests, but as their bodies are very hard, they certainly could have no use for a bed. I have dug into a good many of these burrows . . . but have found no bedding so I am led to believe that our clothes were stolen out of 'pure cussedness.'"[5]

Simpson, a light sleeper, often dozed during the day and was too alert for sleep at bedtime. On these occasions, when the balmy, humid air equaled body temperature, he would give his household fair warning and stroll nude in his garden.[6] He relished the moonlight glimpsed through a vista to the bay or brushing with silver the feathery leaves of bamboos and palms.

> To walk in one's grounds at night is to discover a new world; the trees are larger, their forms have changed and their well-known branches are shapeless blots against the sky. Unexpected noises startle and almost terrify one. The day birds have gone to rest and a new and different set have taken their places, as if Nature were working her employees in shifts.

The night sounds, like the mating calls of the chuck-will's widow, held him spellbound.

> From early twilight until sunrise, rarely after, the males pour out their discordant song. I know no bird so earnest about securing a mate; hence their terrible clatter. . . .
>
> This bird almost entirely replaces here the much pleasanter-voiced whippoorwill of the north . . . but it does in fact inhabit our part of the country. Once or twice a season I catch its lonely, plaintive call.

The sounds of night hawks, owls, field crickets, and frogs claimed his attention as well.

> As soon as the early summer rains flood the low places, the nights resound with frog music, and the clacking, snoring, screaming, and gurgling are heard from dusk to dawn. . . .
>
> Now and then the deep voice of the bullfrog (*Rana catesbyana*) is heard, a voice of such power that it sometimes carries for miles. To me its note uttered at intervals sounds like "o-onk, o-onk," while to others it is variously interpreted as "br'wum," or "be drowned," or "more rum."
>
> Some of the music of this nocturnal serenade may be produced by the tree frogs. . . . In the brackish swamp I have occasionally heard at night a contralto frog note which sounds like "gul, gul, gul; guggle, gul" slowly repeated. . . . I know of no sweeter sound in all nature than the song of this frog and it must be a stony-hearted female that would be deaf to it. . . .
>
> I love the night with its silence, its strange sounds, its beauty and mystery. . . .It is then largely because of the stimulation of the imagi-

nation that the night is so wonderful. Under its spell we create a world of our own and revel in the make believe—like the children of a larger growth that we all are.[7]

For all appearances, Simpson was a rich man. He owned a large piece of waterfront, dabbled in expensive, exotic plants, was well traveled, and seemed to want for nothing. In fact, property assessments were rising, and the retired naturalist found it hard to pay his taxes.

His meager resources improved somewhat in 1908 when he reached retirement age—sixty-two. In a letter he informed Dall: "I was allotted a time-service pension [for military service] the other day. I never had the audacity to swear I was 'used up' and I think I will spend this for books, shells, and rare plants."[8]

Sometime in 1911 Simpson sold six acres toward the road, reserving an easement for access to his property. The nine remaining acres, intensively planted with fruit trees and exotic plants, were more than enough for a man in his mid-sixties to maintain single-handed.

Much of the credit for Simpson's rise to prominence as "the patriarch of Florida naturalists" belongs to David Fairchild, who recognized Simpson as an environmental spokesman for Florida and encouraged him to write and publish. He put him on his staff as an agricultural agent and nominated him for a prestigious medal for plant introduction. On many occasions he drew the reticent Simpson into the limelight and used his influence to assist in the publication of Simpson's books.

Though they did not meet until 1912, the two men both began their careers in Washington in the same year, 1889. While Simpson, a man of forty, was immersed in his shells in the tower of the Smithsonian, Fairchild, a lad of twenty, toiled as an apprentice plant pathologist in the "attic" of the mansard-roofed Agriculture Building. Their paths never crossed until Fairchild, returned from his travels and again at the helm of SPI, visited the USDA's outpost in Miami. Reminiscing about his first visit to his correspondent in Miami, Fairchild recalled that, "like John Muir and John Burroughs [Simpson] had gathered about him all kinds of trees and plants, which he loved to handle and classify and study. His charming personality and unfailing generosity towards every one who came for information or plants made his place a general rendezvous. Professor Simpson and I took a liking to each other from the start and a friendship developed which lasted to the end of his life."[9]

The two plantsmen were a good match. Like Simpson, Fairchild had a warm, friendly nature, and ready laughter as well as an inquiring mind.

Fairchild's son Graham recalled, "When the two got together the world became a sort of unexplored botanists' paradise. C.T.S.'s interest in plants coincided with Pa's—they wanted to grow and enjoy them. Neither was much interested in taxonomic botany, but both would go into ecstasies over some rare and exotic plant that they hoped would grow in Florida. The less likely it was to survive, the more they would cherish it. Gardeners to the core, both of them."[10]

A HANDBOOK FOR FLORIDA'S HOME GARDENERS

When they met, Fairchild and Simpson discussed the need for a handbook that would answer the questions of the home gardeners. Mabel Dorn, who came to South Miami from Chicago, was typical of these recent arrivals. She asked with a gasp of disappointment, "Where are the flowers?" She expected to see them everywhere, and the gaudy foliage plants, such as crotons, "irked me to the depths of my being." She recalled desolation of their homesite, scraped clean of vegetation. "There was not a spear of green anywhere. . . . The glare was terrific."

South Florida's weather patterns, too, were strange. "When it was wet enough to plant nasturtiums, . . . it was too hot and they wilted. When it was cool enough in the fall, the sand was too dry."[11] In the spring she dug out a little garden and planted sweet peas and asters. But summer brought the rainy season, and her garden of temperate-zone plants succumbed to the onslaught of bugs and fungus.

Then, suddenly, she awakened to the lush tropical growth—both wild and cultivated—that surrounded her and embraced a totally new kind of horticulture. Later, at a women's club meeting, Mabel teamed up with Marjory Stoneman Douglas to start a class in tropical horticulture. So began Mabel's long and fruitful career as a tropical gardener, teacher, and writer about South Florida's plant life.[12]

To encourage settlers like Mabel, Fairchild suggested that Simpson's paper "Native and Exotic Plants of Dade County," which had been recently published in the *Proceedings of the Florida Horticultural Society,* be issued as a pamphlet for free distribution. Charles Deering donated the money, and it was circulated by the experimental station. This much-needed publication heightened Simpson's visibility. Somewhat to his dismay, strangers stopped him on the street and asked his advice on plantings. Garden clubs and civic groups invited him to speak, and various publications solicited his articles. Even the noted Liberty H. Bailey called on him to write for his encyclopedia of American horticulture.

When Fairchild returned to Washington he kept in touch with Simpson, and in May 1914 he appointed him a collaborator of the SPI office and gave him an annual salary of three hundred dollars. In his new post Simpson would not only act as a collector, propagator, and cultivator of new varieties and mentor to budding botanists; he would also be a record keeper of such things as the blooming dates of fruit trees and the effect on plants of weather extremes such as frost and drought.

CHAPTER EIGHT

Revival of the *Catalogue*, 1910–1914

The Descriptive Catalogue . . . contains the full exposition of the principles of Simpson's classification which has revolutionized the study of the Naiads. It should certainly be in the hands of all interested in fresh-water mussels.

Review in Nautilus, *September 1914*

AFIELD AND ABROAD WITH THE CONCHS

Those who knew Simpson questioned whether shells or plants came first in his life. Certainly it was the latter as he was gaining a foothold in south Florida. Bitter thoughts of his failed work on the bivalves were here pushed aside. His shells remained boxed up in his laboratory, and, except when one of the "conchs" visited, he seldom spoke of the matters that had once been so close to his heart. What he had learned during his twelve years at the Smithsonian, however, could now be applied to a new member of the molluscan race, the Florida tree snails.

His old friend, Henry Pilsbury, was equally intrigued by the tree snails. Simpson referred to Pilsbry as "the greatest malacologist who ever lived. He could look at a thing and tell all about it, whereas I'd have to study like a demon to get the first principles."[1] Pilsbry was gathering material for his "Variation and Zoogeography of *Liguus* in Florida," a study of the races and distribution of the tree snails, and in April 1909 Simpson joined him with a party from the Philadelphia Academy on a trip to the Keys. It proved to be a "dry cycle" for *Liguus.* Though they scoured the hammocks from Key West to Bahia Honda, they found not one living specimen and very little of anything else.[2]

Foul weather also hampered the expedition. While the party was stormbound for six hours in a narrow passage east of Boca Chica Key, Simpson's observations of the fury of the wind driving the water across the Keys and through the channel supported his theory that the lower Keys, from Little Pine Key to Key West, were originally one large island that had been divided by wind and wave action over the centuries.

Henderson, now in his late thirties, was another winter visitor. After receiving his law degree from George Washington University, he succeeded his father as a regent of the Smithsonian and entered the diplomatic service. Though a popular figure in Washington's social circles, he was serious about his molluscan studies and was making some inroads on a catalog of Cuba's large and puzzling groups of land snails. During the winters Simpson often accompanied him when he cruised in the Caribbean, stopping at the islands to collect land snail fauna and dredging at sea for marine specimens. After Simpson's retirement, he accompanied Henderson on six cruises to the Florida Keys, Jamaica, Haiti, or Cuba that were documented in published accounts. No doubt there were more.

Embarking from Miami aboard Henderson's sailing yacht, the *Eolis,* they would sometimes be gone for two months at a time. The *Eolis* was equipped with sounding and hoisting machinery as well as deep-water dredges. Simpson recalls a curious sea animal found in a haul off the Pourtales Plateau.

> Perhaps the most astonishing thing we took was an *Ophiuran* or "brittle star," one of the *Echinoderms,* and related to the starfishes. . . . The species are mostly small, but some of the specimens we dredged had the amazing length from tip to tip of opposite arms of two and a half feet! . . .
>
> We were all delighted over these wonderful things, and Mr. Henderson declared this Ophiuran was new to science. He said, "Won't Professor Clark" (the echinoderm expert at the Smithsonian) "be astonished over this? He'll surely have a fit when he sees them!" In Washington H. hastened at once to Clark and proudly exhibited the trophies,—undoubtedly new and the largest in the world. Clark had no fit at all; he didn't even fall off his chair; in fact, he seemed but mildly interested.
>
> Finally Clark observed quietly: "Your specimens are quite inter-

Henderson's dredging yacht, the *Eolis,* ca. 1910. Courtesy of the Division of Mollusks, National Museum of Natural History, Smithsonian Institution.

Simpson and George H. Clapp, Carnegie Institute of Pittsburgh, returning to the ship in the tender with gunnysacks of land shells after collecting trip ashore in the Caribbean islands. ca. 1914. Courtesy of the Division of Mollusks, National Museum of Natural History, Smithsonian Institution.

esting, but we have others from the Pacific which measure about ten feet across!" It is related that H. required restoratives.[3]

Sometimes Henderson brought aboard a diving helmet, which the men used by turns when the *Eolis* drifted over Florida's coral reefs.

> This device consists of a brass hood which encloses the head while resting on the shoulders, so weighted and adjusted that the wearer can walk with ease on the bottom or study and collect his specimens while air is being pumped down as into an ordinary diving suit. Through a glass plate one can get an excellent view about. With this aid one comes into the closest contact with the reef and its marvelous life; it was like entering into a new world—like visiting another planet.[4]

When Henderson visited, they talked about Simpson's still unpublished *Descriptive Catalogue of the Naiades, or Pearly Fresh-Water Mussels.* Simpson despaired that it would ever see print, but Henderson never lost hope. Early on he had solicited the support of philanthropist Andrew Carnegie, asserting, "Those faults of method and carelessness which were evident in the *Synopsis* have been remedied. . . . The critical species of the Naiades in nearly all the collections of the country have been determined by Simpson and his word on the subject has been generally accepted by everyone . . . a monument to his life work and labors."[5]

Henderson's appeal to Carnegie met without success. The Carnegie Museum was of such recent origin that all funds may have been earmarked for its development. Also, Arnold Ortmann, its curator of invertebrates, had been one of Simpson's critics. Simpson kept abreast of the ongoing controversy his "Synopsis" aroused over the classification of the naiads, but after leaving the museum he took no public stand on the issue.

Sometime in the winter of 1909, Henderson arrived with the good news that Bryant Walker, a Detroit lawyer and amateur conchologist, had agreed to publish Simpson's *Catalogue.* Heartened by this development, Simpson turned once more to his shell collection, which, when he had joined the museum, numbered several thousand freshwater, marine, and land specimens gathered over many years of field work, purchases, and exchanges with foreign and domestic correspondents. In one of his first letters to Walker he noted, "Most of this stuff has been packt up for over 20 years and untoucht, some for considerably longer than that. I can't describe the feeling of unpacking at last."[6] This letter confirms that although generally museum personnel were expected to either sell or give away their preexisting collections, an agreement had been reached between Dall and Simpson allowing him to store his shells, provided he add nothing to them while employed by the museum.

From now until the old naturalist held his hardbound, linen-covered, volume in his suntanned, work-worn hands, his plant collecting and investigative field trips into Florida's wilds would be interleaved with periods of sorting his shells, editing copy, and reading proofs. It would not keep him, however, from continuing his pursuit of the tree snails and developing what was, in essence, the first public tropical garden in North America.

BRYANT WALKER

Bryant Walker, the publisher of Simpson's *Descriptive Catalogue of the Naiades, or Pearly Fresh-Water Mussels,* was a widower of fifty-four and a graduate of the University of Michigan Law School. Along with his father, he represented the auto industry in negotiations with the labor unions. A civic leader in Detroit, Walker sat on the boards of the Museum of Art, the Zoological Society, and other community organizations. As a boy he had collected butterflies and birds' eggs, but when he was eleven years old his father sent him an article on "The Land Snails of New England," and he was drawn to a study of mollusks that was to endure for seventy years. When he began work on Simpson's *Catalogue* in 1910 he was honorary curator of mollusca at the University of Michigan, and two years later he received an honorary doctorate of science from that university.

It is hard to reconcile Walker's busy law practice with his scientific achievements. He published 155 papers on freshwater and land mollusks and proposed 133 new taxa.[7] His shell collection—acquired mainly through purchasing collections and exchanges—was so large that he added a two-story wing to his house to store it. Calvin Goodrich, in his eulogy in *Nautilus,* explains that Walker was able to accomplish much in his free time because he had a "singularly retentive memory" and wrote his papers quickly and without revisions. "Facts, references, footnotes and everything needed marshalled themselves for him like proud, regimented soldiery and the end of the paper actually meant the end and not irksome reincubation."[8] Friend of Henderson and Pilsbry and mentor to Harvard University's future malacologist, William J. Clench, Walker was, simply, one of the "conchs"—that brotherhood of men who shared a devotion to the mollusks.

Walker had some reservations about the *Catalogue.* Since Simpson had completed it ten years previously, it would need to be made current, but, since coming to Florida, Simpson had embraced a whole new biota, leaving the study of naiad mussels far behind. He felt too out of touch with current literature and advancements in the science to take on the task. It would be up to Walker to make hard decisions and add new material. Differences of opinion among fellow students of the naiads were legion, and Walker had no wish to exacerbate these controversies. On the other hand, his legal training led him to dislike untidy ends, and he wanted their classification on a solid scientific foundation. He found this in the system proposed in Simpson's "Synopsis" of 1900. With this in mind, Walker agreed to publish the *Catalogue,* well aware that it would upset the established order. In so doing he found himself in the role of peacemaker, walking the narrow line between calming the excitable Simpson and placating other unio specialists.

OPENING OLD WOUNDS

Walker's letters to Simpson have been lost, but Simpson's letters are preserved with Walker's papers in the archives at the University of Michigan. Writing with an open scrawl, Simpson addressed his benefactor respectfully as "My Dear Mr. Walker." In one of the first letters he wrote to Walker in 1910, he refers to a letter from Dall: "He said he hoped I could get time to work with my shells now and then for old association's sake and somehow it all softened me greatly. Perhaps Dall like good whisky gets mellow with age. . . .

Regarding classification of the naiads, he notes that "Ortmann seems to be making quite a good many discoveries in the Unionidae. I think he is a little inclined to place undue stress on the anatomical [soft parts] characters for classification and to ignore the shell. . . . There is *very* much to learn yet about the anatomy of the Naiades and in very many cases I stumbled along with scarcely anything to guide me for in classifying one must put everything *somewhere.*"[9]

Twine-tied boxes of shells and unwieldy papers on the unios bulged out of Simpson's pigeonhole at the Little River post office during these years. A letter to Walker in December 1910 discusses the shell characteristics of certain unios and reveals that the naturalist was pinched for cash. "I came to a halt unpacking and cleaning my shells sometime months ago on account of running out of shell trays and couldn't send for more at the time. A short time ago I was able to raise the wind and have ordered more but they havent come yet."

He also speaks freely in this letter of his critics, one of whom was Ortmann. While Ortmann was a hero to many fellow scientists—untiring in his quest for specimens and an enthusiastic researcher and teacher—to the thin-skinned Simpson he was a threat: "[Ortmann] seems to me to stand with a club ready to jump on any of my mistakes as he would on to a rat. He has made some mistakes in correcting what he supposed were mine." In a postscript Simpson asks Walker to let him know when Ortmann's paper on Unionidae anatomy will be published: "I want to get it. He has never sent me any of his papers."[10]

More than a year passed, and little progress was made on the *Catalogue.* From the gist of Simpson's letter of February 9, 1912, it appears that Walker was engrossed in updating the *Catalogue* and mediating the arguments of other conchologists. Simpson writes,

> Your letter regarding the monograph is here and as Uncle Remus says "It done hope me up mightily." I have felt *very blue* over the whole affair since Ortmann and Sterki have been whacking at me so and to get words of commendation from you is certainly comforting. I still believe that my classification and arrangement of the Naiades of the U.S. as proposed in the Synopsis is a fairly good one. Of course there will have to be some changes made in it when we have more knowledge of the anatomy of all the forms. . . .
>
> I think I understood the predicament you were in when Ortmann and others attackt it as they did. Still I will be very glad to see it published in some form. I fully agree with you that under the circumstances the sooner it is out the better. . . .
>
> There will be lots of things to be learnt about the Naiades when you and Sterki, Ortmann, Haas and I are gone and the monographer of the group 50 years hence will no doubt call us all a lot of numbskulls and wonder how we ever could be so ignorant."[11]

In March, having finally "licked the rest of the ms of the catalogue into shape," Simpson mentioned to Walker that several sheets were missing. "This part of the ms remained at the National Museum till shortly before I left for my home here. I would dislike to think that anyone took these sheets out in order to prevent the work being published. . . . I couldn't possibly tell the museum [catalog] number of any of the new species. It would be a good idea to have them in, but I am doubtful whether Dall or Bartsch would give them to you."[12]

In a subsequent letter Simpson again voices doubts about the reception his work would receive at the museum: "Still I don't feel any certainty that [Dall] would approve of having the work published and he might attempt to block it. Most of the types of my mss are in the Nat'l Museum, no doubt."[13] His fears proved foundless, however; some months later, when he visited the museum, his colleagues assisted him in verifying details for the catalogue, and their support eased Simpson's mind.

Simpson was most incensed with the criticism of Lorraine Frierson, a Louisiana cotton planter and amateur conchologist, who championed the cause of Rafinesque. Frierson's "racket" over some point of classification touched a sore spot. He complained to Walker,

> He is a d—d skunk and I never had any use for him. He has hung on my flanks ever since he knew that a clam was a bivalve. . . . Whenever he has been able to pick out some little mistake . . . he has thrown up his arms and shouted as though he had discovered a break in a Mississippi River levee. He systematically used me for years at the Museum to identify his material and hunt up information and then publisht what I told him as his own discoveries. . . . He also sent material to me time and again for opinions, . . . and he insisted that I return it, & usually didnt send postage, but he never would spare a shell either to the Museum or me. . . . He lives in a sawmill . . . has his own collections and some literature he has pickt up. I dont believe he has ever studied any of the great collections or libraries and how in h—l can he know so much I don't know. I am tempted to write to him and give him my opinion of him.[14]

After a "delightful" visit in March 1912 from Henderson with the promise of a trip to the Bahamas in April or May, and a mollifying letter from Walker, Simpson softened somewhat. "No, I shall not write to Frierson. My second sense dictates that it is wise to keep still. I have kept out of print so far in defending my work and expect to [continue to do so]. . . .

O yes, Frierson *is* bright and he must have done a lot of hard studying. He ought to go where he could have access to libraries and collections. I cant see how he can work fixed as he is."[15]

What triggered Simpson's outburst against Frierson or his defensive attitude toward Ortmann and Sterki is unclear. Their papers on naiad classification from the period offer no explanation. Their opinions may have been voiced in private meetings or letters and passed on to Simpson. However it reached his ears, it would appear he overreacted. Ortmann's monograph of the naiads of Pennsylvania, published in 1911, acknowledged that "the family of the *Unionidae* in Simpson's sense is accepted."

Sterki had already given the "Synopsis" his stamp of approval. Simpson's premise was generally applauded, though some individual species, synonymies, and matters of nomenclature were disputed.

On these matters, even Walker and Ortmann found Frierson unreasonable. After the *Catalogue* was published, Walker, Ortmann, and Frierson formed a committee to arbitrate disputed nomenclature in a judicial manner. Pilsbry was rung in as final arbiter if the three could not agree.[16] The group soon ran aground. Ortmann wrote to Walker in April 1920:

> Pilsbry has sent to me, last week, a bundle of Frierson's Objections etc., telling me that he has sent the same to you. . . . I do not think it worth while to go again into detail. . . . Frierson's arguments are not new to us. Indeed *we have considered them,* and it is of no use for Frierson to repeat his arguments again and again. . . .
>
> But we have concluded to leave the decision with Pilsbry and if I can do so, and you can do so, I do not see why Frierson can *not*! Nothing could be fairer than that. . . .
>
> Frierson seems to be offended that we do not accept *all* his dicta as gospel-truth. He entirely forgets that we have accepted quite a few of his suggestions. . . . We want to be fair to all parties concerned, not only to Rafinesque, and we have no bias against anybody, none against Lea, and none against Frierson.[17]

In the draft of his introduction to the *Catalogue,* Simpson credited no other researchers in the naiads, but he wanted to acknowledge his debt to Bryant Walker. "I hope you will leave my reference to you stand in it. I realize that besides large expense . . . you are taking on a lot of hand drudgery."[18] Walker, however, demurred despite Simpson's continued urging.

When Simpson addressed Walker in March 1913, the strain of putting his shell collection into order and satisfying the demands created by his remarkable botanical collection was evident. "The older I get the more . . . is forced on to me and the more I *must* do. I do not have a moment of leisure, hardly one that I can steal. . . . I haven't been in my shell room for weeks. This has become a show place . . . as high as 40 to 50 visitors here in a single day this winter to see and admire the plants and place, newspapers have sent reporters to write it up and I am in the limelight."[19]

The months flew by as the catalogue went into final production, and, in August 1914, the first copies came off the press. To "My Dear Mr. Walker," he wrote,

> I can hardly describe my feelings this morning when I was handed the bulky package from you and realized that at last the thing I had hoped for, then buried, then again hoped for was at last a reality.
>
> It is, as far as the make-up, printing, and paper go, a clean, respectable piece of work and I am not ashamed of it. I feel like most heartily congratulating you now that your long and most arduous labor is at an end. The only thing I feel badly about is that there is no recognition of yourself in it. . . . not that I want to saddle my many mistakes and errors on you. I am ready to bear them all myself.
>
> I can't thank you in words for what you have done. But for you my life work would have never seen the light.[20]

The publication of the *Catalogue,* to Simpson the crowning achievement of his life, was somewhat of an anticlimax in terms of content. Simpson's system had already been elucidated in the "Synopsis," and the *Catalogue* was merely an extension of the earlier work. The shouting and loud protests had been vented on the first publication. The review in *Nautilus* commented, "Mr. Simpson's *Synopsis of the Naiades,* 1900, next after the *Observations* of Lea, has done more than any other work to stimulate and direct the study of fresh-water mussels. . . .

After the *Synopsis* was launched, Mr. Simpson began the more comprehensive work now before us. . . . The synonymy has been given in full, and keys have been made to the species of many genera. The index contains about 7600 entries."

The reviewer went on to praise Bryant Walker for undertaking the publication of the "monumental monograph" and completing the descriptions for the period from 1902 to 1913. "Mr. Walker has earned the gratitude of conchologists for his part in it."[21]

CHAPTER NINE

The Naturalists' Cruise to Cuba, 1914

No one uninoculated with the virus of nature study can quite understand the feelings of a naturalist who first stands upon the threshold of his promised land.

John Brooks Henderson

UNCHARTED TERRITORY

Henderson considered Cuba "the richest island in the world for land mollusks,"[1] and his enthusiasm for exploring this region was irrepressible. He had long contemplated leading a joint expedition with the Smithsonian and the government of Cuba to the Organ Mountains in the northwest and the Colorado Reefs off the northwest shores. In early spring 1914 the prospects for the expedition looked promising, and he began plans for a two-month trip beginning in May, the onset of the rainy season, when the land snails would be emerging from estivation. The primary mission of the voyage was to make a full collection of these gastropods. Another goal was to expand the National Museum's collection of Antillean marine shells, which was considered deficient. The types—the actual shells described—were in Europe, and Henderson found their figures and descriptions "inadequate and faulty."

CARLOS DE LA TORRE

Henderson relied on Carlos de la Torre, a Cuban malacologist who had accompanied Henderson and Simpson on previous expeditions, to plan their itinerary. Torre, termed by Pilsbry as "that overflowing dictionary of Cuban shell-lore," was then professor of zoology at the University of Havana. In Cuba he was regarded as a national hero, combining his prowess as a scientist with a flair for politics. He had been mayor of Havana, rector of the University of Havana, and, briefly, acting president of the Republic. As a malacologist he was unsurpassed in the Caribbean.

Thomas Barbour, former director of Harvard University's Museum of Comparative Zoology, recalled Torre as "a captivating character, a naturalist from his early days . . . and unpredictable. When he would go to bed or when he would arise, when it would occur to him to eat, no one knew . . . he was a law unto himself. . . . I could never make out whether he rose very early in the morning or whether he simply never went to bed at all. At any rate, he was always on hand, sorting his shells, doing them up in little packets with the most minute information regarding locality tied up in each one."[2]

Torre suggested that the Colorado Reefs would be the ideal field for their quest. This region was then uncharted and little known to naturalists. Henderson explained, "We were delighted with the thought of untouched coral reefs, unvisited islands, and many hundred square miles of crystalline tropic waters. Besides all this, exceptional opportunities for shore work and collecting upon the northern slopes of the 'Sierra de los Organos' would be presented."[3]

In addition to Henderson, Torre, and Simpson, the scientific personnel on the voyage included Victor J. Rodriguez, an assistant from the University of Havana's biology department; Manuel Lesmes of the Cuban fisheries; George Clapp of the Carnegie Museum in Pittsburgh; Paul Bartsch, then the National Museum's curator of marine invertebrates; and George W. Gill, a specialist in the treatment and preservation of specimens. Simpson, at sixty-eight, was the senior member of the group, and identified by Henderson as an "expert in two specialties, conversant with the land shells of the Antilles and an authority on the Antillean flora."[4]

Torre, whose persuasive powers were legion, knew the owners of a charter fleet of two-masted fishing schooners, and when he explained to them the mission of the expedition they placed their best and newest ship at his disposal, declining to accept any fee. "Thus materialized our dreams of a naturalists' cruise in Cuban waters. It was like seeing burst into full flower a cherished plant one had long and tenderly nurtured," wrote Henderson.[5]

The *Tomás Barrera,* berthed in Havana, was a sixty-five foot schooner known in Cuba as a "vivero" because she was equipped amidships with a large tank designed to hold live fish. This proved very helpful to the

Carlos de la Torre. From John B. Henderson, Jr., *The Cruise of the Tomás Barrera.*

The *Tomás Barrera*. From John B. Henderson, Jr., *The Cruise of the Tomás Barrera.*

party in keeping live specimens until they could be preserved. The vessel, captained by its part-owner, Gaspar Pellicer, had no auxiliary engine but was outfitted with a rowboat, a gasoline tender, and a twenty-five foot gasoline launch with Capt. Sidney W. Greenlaw, skipper of Henderson's yacht, at the helm. A crew of six Majorcan islanders completed the crew.

The party assembled in Havana during the first week in May. Simpson described the scene: "The schooner . . . was something like a floating bee hive. Besides the scientists and crew, we had two very loud-voiced dogs, and numerous coops of chickens, ducks, turkeys, and geese. There were provisions, liquid refreshments, tents, folding chairs, dredging apparatus, [preserving] alcohol in tanks, piles of bedding and cots, water pails, basins, pans, scoops, nets and a hundred other things; in fact there was scarcely any room to stand, sit or sleep in."[6]

On May 8 the *Tomás Barrera,* with Greenlaw and Gill aboard, departed from Havana with orders to proceed to La Esperanza, the gateway to Viñales and the region the naturalists wished to explore. The remainder of the party traveled overland on the Western Railway to avoid the less productive sea voyage and to allow a day or two in the field around Viñales.

THE ORGAN MOUNTAINS

At Pinar del Río, "our last outpost of civilization," they hired a ramshackle taxi. "With a clanging of bells, . . . scattering of children and domestic animals, our chauffeur fairly shot out of Pinar, taking the Vinales road with a rush that made us beg for mercy," wrote Henderson.[7] Along the way they stopped to explore a mogote. This distinctive geological feature of the Cuban landscape is an isolated remnant of a limestone sierra, worn down into a steep elevation and covered with rich vegetation. Henderson described the great mountain ridges of the "Sierra de los Organos," or "Organ-Pipe" mountains, found in the northern half of Pinar del Río province:

> They are always very steep, often displaying vertical walls of quite one thousand feet elevation . . . densely overgrown wherever vegetation can find lodgment . . . and harbor a rich and varied fauna both altogether different from that of the *lomas* or of the lower plains. It is upon the sierras that Cuba's astonishing wealth of molluscan life exists. As these land mollusks cannot maintain themselves away from the limestone of the sierras, their restricted little world may be said to consist of the "continental area" of the sierras and the "islands" repre-

> sented by the *mogotes.* . . . The constant mutations slowly going on in all living species are most strikingly shown by a comparative study of the life, especially of the mollusks, that have suffered isolation upon the lesser sierras and the *mogotes;* indeed the answer to most of the puzzles concerning the origin and the development of the Cuban fauna must be sought in the modified faunas of the *mogotes.*[8]

Continuing on, they spent the night at an inn in Viñales, and in the morning were on the brink of their great adventure. "No one uninoculated with the virus of nature study can quite understand the feelings of a naturalist who first stands upon the threshold of his promised land," Henderson wrote.[9]

After a strenuous day of collecting, the party took a motor bus to La Esperanza. It was after dark when they reached the port and boarded the launch for the *Tomás Barrera.* Once on deck they groped for their beds, which were set up on deck, because the cabins below were overcrowded with all those necessities for preserving, cataloging, and describing their specimens. Their bags were upended on the floor, and, as Henderson put it,

> To open any one of them necessitated doing violence to another's outfit. . . . Everyone exchanged his land costume of khaki and leggins for the nautical white duck. It is a phase of human vanity to wish to appear sartorially all right at sea, especially at the start. There were none to admire our fine clothes, yet we bedecked ourselves as if to appear at a yacht club regatta. In a very few days, however, we were a sorry looking lot of half dressed vagabonds, and had it not been for the painful effects of a vertical sun, we would likely have reduced costumes almost to the "altogether" and thereby scandalized our crew. The modesty of a Spaniard or a Cuban and his objections to nudity while in the water was to us a matter of some surprise. We always stripped for the morning plunge and our crew never recovered from shock at sight of such outrageous immodesty.[10]

Henderson's log, unlike the published account of the cruise, revealed that harmony did not always prevail aboard ship. Personality clashes arose, aggravated by cultural differences. Henderson observed that Manuel Lesmes, the "fish expert," disagreed with almost anything that was said, which he found "amusing if one is well, but if one is not, it is irritating."[11] The great "shark debate" was a case in point. Manuel insisted that all man-eating sharks were dangerous, while the naturalists contended that sharks attack only under special circumstances. When the Americans stripped and plunged into the sea for their morning swim, Manuel hovered at the rail, direly warning of killer sharks.[12] The patron, however, was more concerned about shark attacks in the murky water of Bahia Honda harbor.

As the cruise progressed, great piles of brine-soaked clothing and bags of specimens accumulated above and below deck, creating a stench that even sea air could not overcome. Whenever the shore launch left or arrived, all was pandemonium. Dogs barked, the chickens cackled, and everyone shouted, but once the skiff departed for a day of collecting, Henderson found the resulting peace like "running into some delightful port after a week of storms."[13]

Shore parties were often interrupted by Torre's different lifestyle. Henderson noted in his log that

> Simpson wanders about impatient of the delays that postpone collection . . . his disappointment as great as his pleasure. . . . Torre's idea of the expedition is to have plenty to eat served in three formal meals and no collecting arrangements can be completed without some serious conflict with plans for foraging expeditions ashore to get ice or some eatables of a luxurious kind. We are very hopeful, however, of having some time so we can do a little collecting—not much, but just a little.[14]

As the expedition continued, however, crew and naturalists forgot their differences and warmed to each other, swapping stories in the evening. A crew member declared that he once saw a man so frightened that he ran on the surface of the sea. "We were all stunned to silence," wrote Henderson. "From the total of our combined experience and reading we could recall no such defiance of the laws of gravity save possibly the one of biblical reference which delicacy forbade mentioning. Then Dr. Torre forged to the front and saved us from a humiliating route. With great solemnity Torre recounted a tale of a man who ran so fast that he could not stop until he seized himself around the waist!"[15]

Despite his years, Simpson survived the trip well, except for the time he nearly fell fifty feet over a cliff and, "hanging on by all fours," found himself face to face with a ten-foot Cuban boa. Fortunately, the snake was as surprised as Simpson and soon slithered out of sight.

The original mission of the expedition—to collect marine and land mollusks—had expanded to include "good specimens of every living thing, animal or vegetable, that inhabited the reef," as well as insects, birds, reptiles, small animals, and rock specimens. It took two full days to pack for shipping the material the naturalists had collected for their institutions. Henderson noted, "Of the thousand or more jars of alcoholics, but one was broken when the crates and barrels were unpacked at the National Museum. The immense amount of material was soon separated into its phyla and consigned to the various specialists who will in due time report upon it."[16]

CHAPTER TEN

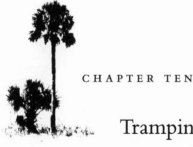

Tramping in the Keys, 1915–1920

We cannot win this battle to save species and environments without forging an emotional bond between ourselves and nature as well—we will not fight to save what we do not love.

Stephen Jay Gould

FLORIDA TREE SNAILS

Pilsbry indicates that Simpson began his serious study of *Liguus fasciatus,* the Florida tree snails, in 1915.[1] Actually, he had been devoted to them since 1885, when he discovered his first—the form *crassus*—on Big Pine Key. Since his permanent settlement in Florida, his explorations had greatly expanded his knowledge of the origins of these colorful land snails. Puzzling over their history was a natural extension of questions that had plagued Simpson since childhood—where things came from, and how the land was formed—matters that were integral as well to his work on the naiads at the National Museum.

The ranks of the tree snails have been diminishing for many years, as is apparent in this passage, written in 1923:

> Unfortunately no thorough collecting was done within our borders before the beginning of the destruction of the hammocks, in which alone they live, and now we find them exterminated throughout a large part of their former territory. In many places only dead shells or mere fragments are found, often so bleached that they cannot be

> identified. . . . Yet I believe it is possible from what evidence we can get from these snails alone to learn something of their migration and development, to fairly well reconstruct the past history of the land and sea in Lower Florida. The effort to work this out is a good deal like attempting to read from the pages of an old, faded and half destroyed book.[2]

Simpson found that the Florida tree snails inhabited a narrow range that includes certain of the Keys, the Ten Thousand Islands and Chokoloskee Island on Florida's west coast, the hammock islands of the Everglades, the Pinecrest area south of the Tamiami Trail (now U.S. 41), and the Atlantic ridge as far as Pompano Beach on the east coast.

These air-breathing mollusks are hermaphrodites: each animal has both male and female reproductive organs. Individuals mate with a mutual exchange of sperm, and both may produce eggs. Unlike bivalves, which produce many thousands of offspring, these gastropods lay only eight or ten eggs, which are buried in forest debris at the base of trees. In cold and/or dry weather they estivate in knotholes, under loose bark, or in some other protected place, attaching themselves firmly by exuding a gluey mucus. With the coming of the rainy season this mucus dissolves and they become active, feeding on lichen and mold. They do not eat chlorophyll-bearing leaves and so live cooperatively with their tree hosts. Until the coming of humankind, their enemies were few: tree-climbing mammals such as raccoons, opossums, and certain rats, and large birds such as crows.

In the many thousands of years since their colonization of South Florida, they flourished undisturbed, gradually evolving into subspecies. Although modern taxonomists recognize only one species, *Liguus fasciatus,* with many colorforms, Simpson recognized three: *L. solidus,* a large, light, slender porcelaneous shell sometimes more than two inches in length that, with few exceptions, is found only on the Lower Keys; *L. crenatus,* distinguished by a white apex or "jewel" on its spire and a white columella; and *L. fasciatus,* distinguished from the other two by its rich color markings, often with a pink jewel and columella, and found mainly on the mainland and Everglades Keys.

Simpson's investigations suggested that the *Liguus* had emigrated from Cuba, which was thought to have a much older geological history than the Florida Keys and mainland. This, however, raised problems. How did they make the journey? Why are they found on some keys and not on others? Big Pine Key, for instance, had several varieties of *solidus,* but nearby Bahia Honda had none. Skipping up the island chain to Lower Matecumbe, Simpson found varieties of *solidus* thriving. What caused this gap in distribution? The shell structure and coloring also varied in different locations. The *Liguus* of the Lower Keys bore thin, glossy, elongated shells with pastel markings, while the housing of those found in the Miami hammock land and upper Key Largo was heavier, more oblate, and often deeply colored with bands of chestnut brown on ivory and rosy tips and columella.

Related questions concerned the geology and flora of the region. Why are the Upper Keys long and narrow and the lower ones oblate and massed against the axis of the chain in a north-south direction? What caused the difference in the flora found on the mainland from that on the Keys? These questions and variations of them were what the old naturalist meant when he described the purpose of his tramps as finding solutions to "a number of interesting problems that remain to be studied and worked out."[3]

THE HAZARDS OF COLLECTING

To this end the determined Simpson, grizzled and approaching seventy, waded, crawled, and hacked his way into over three hundred hammocks throughout the region. No roads went where he wanted to go, and until the coming of the Florida East Coast Railroad the only passage to the Keys was by water. He described the hazards of making a landing in *In Lower Florida Wilds.*

> The beach consists of terribly ragged rock, often extending beyond the low tide mark. One is liable to get aground and injure his boat and once on land walking is well nigh impossible. Usually near the shore the sea is very shallow and the bottom of soft, sticky mud. The explorer at times cannot get within many rods of such a beach, even with a light skiff, and he must get overboard and wade. Too often the shore is fringed with an almost impenetrable barrier of mangroves which may be a quarter of a mile wide. One must work in somehow to the edge of these, dragging his boat and making it fast to the arching roots, then climb like an awkward monkey over and through the dreadful tangle to dry land. If a naturalist he likely has to carry bags for specimens, grub hoe, spade, ax, and camera besides various other collecting gear, some in his hands and more slung about him. The least slip means a fall into the water or among the sharp oysters attached to the roots. Often the growth is so dense and tall that the

harassed explorer can only see a short distance in any direction and he can rarely find the sun owing to the dense foliage. . . . If he does reach terra firma and complete his collections he can only guess on the way back where his skiff may be. He will likely crawl a long distance out to find the water,—but not the boat. It is better to blaze the trees going in and hope to be able to see the marks going out. At last too he finds the tide fallen and he must wade again and drag the unwilling skiff,—seemingly miles.[4]

Thorns, prickles, and mosquitoes were major obstacles in a day of collecting.

On the Upper Keys there are acres of stunted century plants, often growing so densely that it is impossible to get through; with them are several kinds of prickly pears and the terrible *Cereus pentagonus* [cactus] which sprawls over all. In lower ground a Bumelia . . . usually a dense shrub, has narrow leaves and vicious thorns. . . . One could no more force his way through a haystack than through a patch of this shrub. And everywhere the whole is literally bound together by the pull-and-haul-back (Pisonia), the vilest thorny shrub in Florida.[5]

We encountered swarms . . . of immense black mosquitoes which shone as if freshly varnished. They came with a slow, steady motion, as if they were sure of their victims and had no need to hurry. The front part of the insect was bent down in a remarkable manner, probably to let the proboscis get into action before the rest of it arrived. The Doctor [Mercer] at once called them "Dirigibles" which we soon shortened into "Blimps." . . . When loaded with blood and calmly sailing away this insect was certainly suggestive of a small edition of a zeppelin.[6]

Mosquito-control programs were unknown in Simpson's day, and these voracious insects were a serious hazard to the naturalist. Once, on Big Pine Key, they were life-threatening.

I have had a good deal of experience with mosquitoes, in the Green River swamps of Illinois, among the Ten Thousand Islands on the southwest coast of Florida, along the south shore of the mainland, at Cape Sable and on the Keys, but I believe I can honestly say that for numbers and fierceness . . . what I saw and endured that day exceeded anything I have ever known before or since. . . . [T]hey covered the exposed parts of my body until they were gray, and whenever I wiped

> them from my face, neck or hands the blood dripped on the ground.
>
> The effect of the stings of such a swarm soon became something like that of morphine, producing a stupid, drowsy sensation, and in addition to this my cheeks and eyelids swelled until it was difficult to see. . . . Twice I went to the side of the track where I dropped down and gave up, but had I remained there I would have been dead in ten minutes. . . . Finally I reached the main part of the island and realized that my tormenters were becoming less numerous. I passed through the village and on to where I was stopping, but I could not eat or sleep and was sick all night. The old postmaster . . . told me the next day that I was the worst used up man when I passed him that evening than he had seen in a thirty years' residence on the Keys.[7]

Summing up the perils he had faced, the determined explorer wrote, "I have had a good deal of experience as a naturalist collector in temperate, subtropical and tropical regions and I am ready to go on record with the statement that the wilds of Lower Florida can furnish as much laceration and as many annoyances to the square inch as any place I have ever seen."[8]

A RACE AGAINST TIME

The period when the historic colonies of tree snails could be studied by trained investigators was very brief. Loss of habitat, changing weather patterns, and human intrusions were severely impacting the *Liguus* population. Simpson was aware of this, and the knowledge intensified his quest.

The forest homes of South Florida's tree snails had been diminishing for some time. Charles Vignoles, in his "Observations upon the Floridas 1823," wrote: "Key Largo formerly abounded in mastic, lignumvitae and mahogany, but the most valuable has been long cut down, and there is none now but very young timber."[9] Early in the nineteenth century, farmer-settlers from the Bahamas had cleared hammocks on the Keys for plantations of pineapples or lime trees. When the thin soil of the rocky islands failed, the fields were abandoned and the process was repeated in a new site.

With the conclusion of Indian wars in 1858 and the coming of the Florida East Coast Railroad in the first decade of the twentieth century, people moved into Florida by the thousands. With them came the need to clear land for homes and crops. Throughout the Keys and on the mainland, the great hammocks were falling, their tropical hardwoods uprooted and burned and the ashes used as fertilizer. Along the bay the new city of Miami was rising, and the great Brickell hammock, where Simpson had identified thirteen color forms of *Liguus,* was being grubbed out for streets and homes, hotels and shops. Tree snail colonies were additionally pressured by collectors as railroad and automobile routes made remote hammocks more accessible. Commercial snailers prized the glossy, brightly painted shells and gleaned them from hammocks by the bucketful to sell as souvenirs to tourists. Women wore them as earrings and dangled them on bracelets and necklaces. Pilsbry notes that a store at Goodland Point around 1909 sold baskets trimmed with as many as thirty or forty tree snail shells.

Other collectors removed the live snails from their historic habitat and transplanted them to other localities. Even Simpson did this, colonizing a few on his property. Specimens found in isolated locations became suspect. Pilsbry speculated that *Liguus* found on Chokoloskee Island may have been transported and established by Indians. Varieties were being hopelessly mixed up, and population records would soon become worthless.

Another factor compelling Simpson to intensify his search was the knowledge of his own mortality. Though just shy of seventy, he repeatedly referred to himself as the "old man." "My health is not good," he complained to Dall. "I have broken myself down by hard work so I can accomplish but little any more."[10] In reality, many years of accomplishment lay ahead.

A RAILROAD TO THE KEYS

The completion of the Key West extension of the Florida East Coast Railroad in 1912 eased Simpson's passage to the Keys, though he deplored the cost: the wreckage of the hammocks. On Key Largo, he noted,

> a few years ago a hammock that was perhaps the finest and most extensive in the lower part of the State covered the latter [Key Largo] island for several miles in the vicinity of Cross Key. The Florida East Coast Railway cut a right of way through this for the Key West extension of its line and piled felled timber along the edges of the clearing. When it was fairly dried out it was set on fire by sparks from the locomotives (so claimed) and this unfortunately communicated to the forest. For months the fire slowly ate its way through the peatlike soil and as it crept along its ruinous way the grand old giants of the hammock toppled and fell, a tragedy in every fall. Every vestige of the soil

> was consumed and today the charred ruin glares in the sun as a silent and pathetic protest against useless waste and folly. A few young trees are springing up here and there and thorny vines are beginning to scramble over the melancholy wreck. Nature will in time conceal her wound beneath a green mantle—but the fine forest is forever gone.[11]

He admitted that progress had its advantages: "In days gone by the only way a naturalist could visit the Florida Keys was by boat, but since the completion of the Florida East Coast Railroad he can get off the train at Jewfish on Cross Key, tramp to Largo, to Long and Windleys islands, Upper and Lower Matecumbe, Long, Grassy, Crawl, and Vaca keys, Bahia Honda, Big Pine, . . . and a number of islands of lesser importance until at last he reaches Key West."[12] It became his custom to take the train to Big Pine Key, make his headquarters in Watson's Hammock there,[13] and then wend his way north or south along the railroad tracks, collecting in hammocks along the way and returning by boat or train.

Travel on the overseas railroad was uncertain at best. "The stupendous arches carry a single track line and are too narrow for a train and pedestrian to pass, but the company has hung out wooden cages over the side at regular intervals and the tramp, if he watches, can always reach one of them in time to avoid danger."[14] The trip from Little River to Big Pine Key took from six to eight hours, depending on the weather and the number of stops. If the wind velocity exceeded fifteen miles an hour on the bridges, the trains did not run at all, because the bridges—one was seven miles long—tended to sway.

Most naturalists who came to Miami to observe South Florida's flora and fauna or to write travelogues for northern publications shopped around for a camp outfit and hired a guide and someone to carry their equipment. Simpson, however, traveled light and shouldered his own pack: "For several years I went alone, trusting like an army to live on the invaded country, but I have been so often taken for a tramp and driven away that several times I came near starving. Of late I have carried a small tent, blankets, food, and even drinking water, and by so doing I could camp wherever night overtook me."[15]

Other items stowed in his gunny sack included a knife, a compass, a toothbrush, and a water glass for observing marine life. Despite the outlaws and tough characters that could be encountered in the Keys, Simpson did not list firearms in his inventory, perhaps because they were taken for granted in pioneer days. He had a gun at the Sentinels—a precaution against roving panthers, rattlesnakes, and the raccoons that robbed his

Simpson's "headquarters" on Big Pine Key. From Simpson, *Out of Doors in Florida.*

hen house—but when on the move he may have found firearms excess baggage. Though outspoken and easily aroused, he was a peaceable sort. It is tempting to believe he chose to depend on the protective coloring of a foolish tramp to disarm any dangerous characters he might meet.

Simpson's modest demeanor and independent nature made him a living legend to some of the younger shell collectors. William Clench, Harvard malacologist, encountered the old naturalist in the Keys about 1930, as did Nick Winkleman, Glades naturalist and sheller, who described a hard-of-hearing, disheveled Simpson, seated on a log by the Florida East Coast Railroad station, his face flushed from exertion and swollen with insect venom. As he doggedly shaved the cactus thorns from his legs, he was explaining his home remedy for mosquito bites.[16]

One evening Simpson requested hospitality at a farmer's house, and even though he explained himself as a wandering naturalist the lady of the household turned him away as nothing but a tramp.

> Then I went out to the railroad and looked myself over. I wore a tolerably whole suit of khaki, not too clean, however, for I had lately gone through a freshly burnt district and I was covered with black marks. My coat and wool hat were torn by "pull-and-haul-back" vines and my strong leather shoes were literally cut to pieces on the sharp rocks, so that I had been compelled to tie them on to my lacerated feet with old pieces of cloth. If anything else was lacking in my makeup to prove that I was a genuine knight of the road, the two-

quart water can which I carried completed the evidence. So I "'unted up a hempty 'ouse" as the woman had suggested, put up my bar, made a bed of grass, and as the weather had moderated, I slept royally. The next afternoon I flagged the train and arrived home after dark, having been thirty-eight hours without food.[17]

Simpson toyed with the question of how the *Liguus* had made the ninety-mile voyage from Cuba. Darwin's *Origin of Species* speculated on the role of drift timber in transporting organisms from islands to distant shores. Thinking along this line, Simpson wrote, "It is easy to believe that decaying logs in tropical forests might be a means of dispersing mollusks. Some of the ground snails live on such logs, and arboreal species lay their eggs in their crumbling surfaces. These logs are washed out in times of violent rains and carried out to sea."[18]

To test his theory he tried one of Darwin's experiments: "On one occasion I immersed a lot of Liguus in fresh water and after they had been kept beneath the surface for thirty hours I found nearly all were alive and able to crawl away. . . . Suppose that decaying logs . . . or living trees bearing snails or their eggs were thus carried out to sea from Cuba; that after a voyage of some weeks or even months the whole were cast high and dry on the Florida Keys. There would be absolutely nothing to prevent them from crawling off the packet on which they took passage and establishing themselves as immigrants into the United States."[19]

Simpson carefully observed the activities of *Liguus* on his own property in an effort to understand how they migrated from one hammock to another. One day during a heavy rain, he discovered an individual crawling on the ground among the pine trees, away from its natural habitat. He marked the spot and watched the snail from day to day, sometimes finding it fully twenty-five feet away. He repeated this experiment often, and it led him to believe that during the rainy season a tree snail could travel from one hammock to another, assuming it was not devoured by an enemy. Finding a parallel between his pioneer ancestors and the snails, Simpson observed that "there is something very courageous about these little fellows who leave their sheltered homes, their food, and companions and set forth to wander in the hostile pine woods to find a new hammock. They forsake all and risk all in answering the call of one of the strangest animal instincts—the founding of new colonies, the extension of their race."[20]

Against all obstacles—mosquitoes, fire ants, alligators, and snakes; vicious cacti and thorny vines; numbing cold, hunger, thirst, wind, rain, heat, and humidity—Simpson sought out the *Liguus* in their forest homes. Although he was past seventy he cut his own trails, stumbled, crawled, and even climbed trees to collect and interpret the history of these tropical, arboreal snails.

PRESERVING PARADISE KEY

Mired as he was in the stuff of Florida's wilderness areas, Simpson joined wholeheartedly in efforts to preserve them. Paradise Key was a case in point. That pristine tree island he had first visited in 1903 was no longer isolated. A highway had been completed to its vicinity, and the trip that once took nearly a week could now be made by car in a few hours. Truck gardeners coveted its fertile soil, and rumors circulated that it would be sold and cleared. The Key's unique biota, formed during centuries of isolation, was threatened with extinction.

Florida's water-control measures also threatened the wildlife of this once isolated island. Although the drainage canals that extended from Lake Okeechobee to Florida Bay were not yet completed, they already affected the water table in the Everglades. Taylor Slough and the wet glades that surrounded Paradise Key had protected it for centuries from the wildfires that swept over the Glades. Now the broad expanse of water was diminished, and during the dry season the Key was defenseless against fire.[21]

Simpson saw the danger, as did botanist John Kunkel Small, David Fairchild, and other natural history specialists who knew the ground. But it was a group of women, many of them veterans of the "feather fight"—the successful campaign to pass legislation to protect Florida's plume birds from commercial exploitation—who led the way.

> Mrs. Kirk Munroe began to agitate in favor of saving the magnificent forest from destruction, entering into correspondence with people of influence and talking in favor of the project with friends. Finally the women of the Florida Federation of Woman's Clubs took up the matter and attempted to get the Legislature of the State to cede it to them for a public park, and led by Mrs. William S. Jennings, a strong fight for it was made which finally proved successful.
>
> The late Mrs. Henry Flagler generously donated nine hundred and sixty acres of land, an amount equal to what the Legislature had given, and this was exchanged for State land adjoining the park, thus giving them 1920 acres in a solid block that included the entire key and the whole was called "The Royal Palm State Park."

. . . There ought to be a monument, a great block of native oolitic limestone left in a natural state . . . with a bronze tablet containing the names of all the women who worked to save the park.[22]

Once the land was secured, the work of developing Paradise Key into a public park began. Simpson advocated retaining the traditional name "Paradise Key" but was outvoted in favor of "Royal Palm," a name that he noted could be just as easily applied to half a dozen other South Florida hammocks. Some members of the park committee proposed tearing down the untidy lianas that hung out of the trees, clearing open spaces for picnic grounds, and planting flowering shrubs. A wide, straight road had already been cut through the hammock at the expense of several venerable oaks, and contractors were preparing to blast rock from the hammock edges for road building.

Simpson was alarmed at the turn things were taking and pleaded that the hammock be left in its natural state:

> No matter how beautiful any work of nature is our people are possessed with a desire to "improve it." They must "clean it up a little," they must add to or take away, or change or absolutely destroy the finest piece of landscape it has taken nature ages to produce. The desire to . . . chop down or mutilate trees seems to be second nature to all mankind. We destroy the lovely hammock to plant rows of Australian pines and Chinese Hibiscus. . . .
>
> The proper thing to do may be summed up in just three words; LET IT ALONE.[23]

To illustrate, Simpson cited the laissez-faire management of Washington's Rock Creek Park, whose rough terrain had been so restorative to him during his years at the National Museum. In his recommendations for the tropical park, the naturalist conceded the need for a caretaker's lodge to accommodate visiting botanists and other natural scientists, a pavilion with picnic tables, and narrow trails leading into the hammock.

Royal Palm State Park was officially dedicated on November 22, 1916, before a crowd of 750 friends and supporters. The 150 autos that brought them there demonstrated the need for the park's first parking lot.

Everglades National Park would not take shape for nearly thirty years, but Royal Palm State Park was its genesis. The voice of Charles Simpson in lectures, radio broadcasts, and books and articles on Florida's natural history would be instrumental in preserving this unique natural region for future generations.

CHAPTER ELEVEN

Field Trips with John Kunkel Small, 1916–1918

Why should an old man, past the age when most persons seek adventure, leave a comfortable home and plunge into the wilderness to endure such hardships? What rewards can he receive for it?

Charles Torrey Simpson

A COLLABORATION

Simpson's fellow defender of Florida's wild areas was botanist John Kunkel Small (1869–1938), whose book *From Eden to Sahara: Florida's Tragedy* is a classic protest against the environmental cost of progress. While head curator for the New York Botanical Garden, Small had explored extensively in the southeastern states, making his first forays into Florida about 1901. He called it "the land of the ferns" for the more than one hundred varieties he had identified in the state, over half of them found exclusively in South Florida. Small, who had received a Ph.D. in science from Columbia University and wrote more than ninety papers, is widely recognized as Florida's most important historical name in botany. His *Flora of the Southeastern States,* first published in 1903, describes more than 5,500 species. He was a devoted student of plant evolution and distribution, and his explorations contributed much to the demarcation of the climatic regions where temperate and tropical plants intermingle, as well as the influence of plant migration from the West Indies. H. Harold Hume, in a tribute to Small, commented, "As a result of his labors, the foundations for botanical knowledge of the southeastern plants have

Botanist John Kunkel Small. Courtesy of Kathryn S. Blankley.

been placed upon a basis that possibly would not have been established otherwise except after the lapse of many years."[1]

An energetic, stocky, short-statured Pennsylvania Dutchman, Small was tireless when he was on the move in Florida's keys and hinterlands. As long as light remained in the sky, he thrashed through the thick, prickly undergrowth in quest of botanical specimens. John Soar, who often accompanied him on expeditions, recalls that the botanist was a keen marksman and could cut down with one shot a cluster of palm seeds swinging ninety feet in the air. Small balanced his devotion to the plant world with a close family life and sometimes brought his wife and four children along on his Florida field trips. An accomplished flutist, he occasionally performed with the Metropolitan Opera Company, where he was famous for his solo flute rendition in the *William Tell Overture*. Each of his children played an instrument and the family enjoyed performing together. Brilliant, witty, and urbane, Small was friend to Thomas Edison and industrialists George Eastman, Henry Firestone, and Henry

Charles Deering, industrialist and patron of the natural sciences. Courtesy of the Historical Association of Southern Florida.

Ford, who sought him out both for his knowledge of the economic value of plants and for the cheerful conviviality of his home in Queens.

Small and Simpson had common interests, compared notes on botanical matters, and often went plant hunting together. As was often the case when Simpson encountered scientists, however, he was wary of Small. The warmth and affection, the confident give-and-take that was characteristic in Simpson's friendships with Henderson, Pilsbry, and Fairchild was less spontaneous between Simpson and Small, and the teasing and bantering was more likely to offend. The two men quibbled about taxonomical questions, and Simpson freely criticized Small's botanical prose. If any friction existed, however, it was of little consequence, for they had a mutual respect for each other and joined forces in urging the preservation of South Florida's wild places.

It is said that when Charles Deering and Small learned of each other they were so eager to collaborate that their letters passed in the mail. Small sought a place to plant and observe the specimens he collected in Florida before they were uprooted by the region's development. Deering was a willing ally, deeply interested in native and exotic plants. On his estate at Buena Vista, just north of the Sentinels, he was testing the climatic tolerance and commercial possibilities of cactus and tropical fruits.

Deering nurtured on his estate not only tropical plants, but animals as well. Over two miles of artificial canals wound through the property, and mangroves and swamp plants were added to provide suitable habitat for a variety of animals. Alligators and crocodiles basked in large, substantial pens while their smaller relatives, the ubiquitous green anoles, iguanas, and purple skinks, scampered among the rocks. Monkeys and exotic birds were imported from Asia, Australia, and the Orient. The monkeys were isolated on a small island, but eventually they overcame their fear of water and escaped, becoming a nuisance in the neighborhood. Flight cages—some said to be as large as four city blocks—were built for the birds, but at nesting time some were released into the wild to breed, only to be shot for their plumage or captured and caged as curiosities. Others fell prey to bobcats and alligators. The scheme was finally abandoned as impractical.[2]

EXPEDITION TO CAPE SABLE

At the end of March 1916, Simpson and Small embarked on a two-week exploration, sponsored by the New York Botanical Garden and Charles Deering, to the Cape Sable region of the Bay of Florida. The party also included nurseryman John Soar and his brother, Victor, who was then grounds supervisor of Flagler's Royal Palm Hotel. Deering loaned the expedition his boat, the *Barbee,* along with its captain, Paul Matthaus, and a cook, Laban Bethel. The *Barbee* was a light-draught motor launch about thirty-two feet long and twelve feet abeam. She was admirably suited to navigating the shallow bay waters, which sometimes diminished to little more than "heavy dew."

The purpose of the expedition was to study the distribution of plants in the region, photograph the outland areas, and bring back for Deering a cargo of native palms, cacti, and orchids—especially the cluster palm, *Acoelorraphe wrightii,* commonly known as the "paroutis" palm. Grubbing out and hauling cactus and palms is tough, sweaty work, but it is doubtful that Simpson was paid. He accompanied Small as a fellow scientist. His reward was a free junket to Florida's nearly inaccessible wild places.

As was often the case, the adventure got off to a bad start as a cold front swept in with high winds and heavy seas, keeping the party hopping to secure supplies, cameras, and collecting gear from the water. It was four days before they reached Flamingo. Along the way they collected and botanized at Lignum Vitae Key and Upper and Lower Matecumbe. Small was elated to find an undescribed species of cactus.

Anchoring off Flamingo, they went ashore and, after exploring in the hammocks and prairies in the vicinity, engaged John Douthett to guide them into the interior. At daybreak, Simpson and Small disembarked from the *Barbee* into Douthett's motorboat, trailing two boats for transporting plants, and headed into a wall of mangroves for a point of uncertain location called Cuthbert Lake.

As the boats vanished through the towering mangroves into an almost-concealed creek, they entered a dimly lit world where orchids, bromeliads, and vinelike cacti grew in profusion. Simpson observed that cacti—usually associated with an arid habitat—flourished in this damp, muddy environment where, at high tide, their roots might be underwater. "In fact it seems that these desert-loving plants are attempting to become aquatics. Along our strange course where the ground becomes too swampy, they grow as epiphytes, attaching their roots well up on the trunks of living or dead trees."[3]

They proceeded slowly through channels so clogged with sunken logs, branches, and mangrove roots that they were obliged to get out and lift the boat over obstructions or lie down to pass under overhanging vegetation. The propeller on Douthett's boat had only one blade, and that threatened to shatter as it struck against the rocky bottom. They navigated through six small lakes before reaching Cuthbert Lake, which Simpson described as a "large, nearly circular body of brackish water a mile across."[4] Here they found a large stand of the paroutis palm and went to work digging them up and loading them onto the boats. Simpson noted,

> This locality is one of the last resorts of some of our most beautiful and interesting wading birds. Here in days gone by resorted vast numbers of gorgeous flamingos, scarlet ibises, roseate spoonbills, and roseate terns. This was one of the chief breeding places of the ethereally beautiful egret (*Herodias egretta*) and the even more perfect snowy heron (*Egretta candidissima*). Owing to woman's vanity and man's greed they are now well-nigh exterminated. The men who raid these heronries are toughs and outlaws, and there is not one of them today who does not gloat with satisfaction over the foul murder of the faithful game warden, Warren [Guy] Bradley, who was shot down by their gang while trying to preserve these birds. This entire region should be set apart by the federal government as a great bird reservation.[5]

The return trip, with two boats loaded to the gunwales with plants, was even more difficult than the first. It was after dark when they reached the bay. And then the engine quit. Douthett cranked it and coaxed it without success, so the party settled down to a miserable night in the open. Simpson recalls, "A cold wind arose from the northwest and the sky was overcast with ominous clouds. We were exhausted, wet and hungry, as we had had no food since morning. No doubt . . . [as] I was much the oldest of the party I suffered greatly with the cold.[6]

At last, to warm his chilled body, Simpson began to pole. Later Douthett joined in, and when they spotted a launch around midnight all hands sent up a cheer. After a long, cold ride in saltwater-drenched clothes, everyone was eager to get aboard; they clambered over the rails, only to discover it was the wrong boat! As Small told it, "The occupants of the boat were perhaps as much surprised as we were, for no resistance was offered and no attempt at arrest for our apparent act of piracy was made."[7] On discovering their mistake they quickly disembarked and began the search again; at last—"joyful sight!"—they found their own boat.

At sunrise the next morning the party went ashore at Flamingo, secured a horse and wagon, and set out for Snake Hammock—near Coot Bay, about four miles distant. Snake Hammock proved to be the highlight of the trip, "Unless some richer orchid locality is to be discovered in Florida . . . this hammock is the most marvelous natural orchid garden in the United States. All but one or two species of our epiphytic orchids grow there . . . in greater profusion and to greater size than I have ever seen them elsewhere," wrote Small.[8]

Cyrtopodium punctatum, the cow-horn or cigar orchid (named for its cylindrical pseudo-bulbs), grew in great masses on fallen tree trunks. One plant that Small photographed had thirty-one four-foot flower stalks, each bearing hundreds of blossoms. The party reaped two wagonloads of orchids. So copious were their numbers that their harvest could scarcely be noticed.

As the party proceeded they observed billowing clouds of smoke arising the pinelands and crossed through some areas that had been burned over. South Florida was experiencing a prolonged drought; little or no rain had fallen for several months. Tropical trees that normally shed their leaves only gradually were completely bare, and the forest floor was a tinderbox of dry debris. Now, parts of the prairie and woodland were aflame. The phenomenon of these natural fires and their influence on the growth habits of plants intrigued Simpson.

> Undoubtedly lightning fired the forest long before human beings inhabited the region. Then came prehistoric man, later the Indian, and at last the Caucasian. At all events it is almost certain that from the very beginning of the forest, fires have swept through it at inter-

Hauling out cacti (*Cereus deeringi*) from Lower Matecumbe Key in 1916. *Left to right,* Paul Matthaus, Francis Soar, Laban Bethel, and Simpson. Photo by John Kunkel Small. From Simpson, *In Lower Florida Wilds.*

Collecting paroutis palms at Madeira Bay, Florida, 1916. *Left to right,* Simpson, John Soar, and Paul Matthaus. Photo by John Kunkel Small. From Simpson, *In Lower Florida Wilds.*

Charles Deering's shallow draft launch, the *Barbee,* offshore in the Keys with a load of cacti in 1916. *Left to right,* Paul Matthaus, Simpson, Francis Soar, and Laban Bethel. Photo by John Kunkel Small. From Simpson, *In Lower Florida Wilds.*

vals of a few years. I have seen such fires during a drought period rush through the pines before a furious wind with the speed of a horse. The fire leaps to the tops of the tallest trees and with a hissing burst of red flame consumes their leaves. Young pines, fully eight inches in diameter may be killed outright. All herbaceous and shrubby vegetation is instantly devoured, including the oily leaves of the palmettos; only their charred stems are left.

He notes, however,

But visit the forest a fortnight later and young tender growth is springing up everywhere. . . . Look carefully at the bases of small oaks and other shrubs and see the young shoots beginning to grow just at the ground or a little below the surface. Now the *vital part* of all these plants is safely hidden *below* the surface of the earth. This is the lesson that has been forced upon the dwellers of the inflammable pine belt. . . . The plants of the pine woods *must bury all that is essential to their existence down where the heat cannot injure it, or if it is above ground it must be fireproof!*[9]

The comptie, with its flowers and fruits armored by the thick plates of its reddish brown cone; the saw palmetto (*Serenoa repens*), which creeps on the forest floor, burying its stem in the ground; and the bright yellow star grass, which stores its nourishment deeply underground in a corm—Simpson noted all as examples of "lessons" these plants "learned" to protect themselves from fire. The growth habits plants develop to adapt to their environment led the naturalist to toy with the idea of plant intelligence. "I may be told that . . . trees are simply obeying the fixed laws of nature yet somehow I like to believe that in all this there is a purpose, soul, intelligence, almost thought, that these things reach results in somewhat the same fashion I do."[10]

The men explored the entire length of Cape Sable and the next day continued on to Chokoloskee Island. There Charles posted a card to Deering, noting, "We got in here a short time ago under stress of weather. Have done well so far, got a lot of the *Acoelorraphe* [*Paroutis wrightii*] and have orchids for you."

From sunup to sundown the party botanized and collected, stopping at Lostman's Key, Sawfish Hole, Sandy Key, Bamboo Key, Umbrella or Windley's Key, and Jewfish Creek. It was April 9 before they finally tied up at Deering's dock on Biscayne Bay, with a cargo of plants that nearly swamped the launch.

ORNAMENTAL GARDENING

Miami's *Tropic Magazine* published several articles by Simpson about his explorations, but the naturalist had a gripe with the editor, LeBaron Perrine. In a 1915 letter to Roland Harper, a botanist-writer who collected in Florida for Professor Charles Sargent of Harvard University's Arnold Arboretum, Simpson wrote, "Do you know that this snipe of a Perrine (related to the GREAT Perrine) has teazed me in and out to write for his paper without pay and then when he got out a number he . . . put it on sale for weeks before he would send even a copy? And these with my own articles in them. I would have to write again and again to get extras."

Simpson also complained to Harper about authors of plant guides. "I don't think Dr. Britton or any of the N.Y. Botanical Garden ducks can write a botany that anyone can work with. They all put a few dry facts and measurements into the hopper, turn the crank, and grind out the driest, dreariest and briefest mess of stuff on earth."

Simpson's appraisal of Small's writing was tempered by his admiration of the noted botanist's wealth of plant lore.

> I fear I may have offended him by my very plain talk . . . about his work. He askt me to frankly criticize & I thot the descriptions should be full enough for the average amateur to be able to identify plants with certainty and that there should be comparison of one plant with another.
>
> . . . Small is really a fine botanist in the field, a hard worker, and he has a wonderful knowledge of the plants of this region . . . but he ought to stop there and turn his work over to someone competent to describe. I went for him again about his awful descriptions, but all I got out of him was a grin. I could beat him describing.[11]

These critical comments reflected Simpson's old complaint against "closet naturalists," his pet peeve as a conchologist—professional scientists who discouraged amateurs by changing classifications and presenting few facts. It was a subject he gabbed about to Fairchild, who agreed with him, but Fairchild was more diplomatic, acknowledging the need for systematic botanists but wistfully pleading for sympathy for men like himself who dealt with live plants outdoors under all kinds of weather. "The world of the Kew Index with its thousands of Latin names is a very different one from that of the horticultural world where nothing is fixed and where tags are blown away by storms or become illegible when one's back is turned."[12]

Simpson had acquired a typewriter and taught himself how to use it, much to the relief of his correspondents and editors, who had pondered long over his open-handed scrawl, truncated words, and informal syllable divisions. Now, with the encouragement of Fairchild, he was working on a new plant manual for South Florida.

The resulting publication was *Ornamental Gardening in Florida: A Treatise on the Native and Exotic Decorative Plants Adapted to Florida and Their Cultivation, with Suggestions for the Ornamentation of Our Homes and Gardens.* Self-published in Little River in 1916 and printed in New York by J. J. Little and Ives, *Ornamental Gardening* was a hardbound, 198-page book with 42 black-and-white photographs. Simpson dedicated the book "to Charles Deering who instead of destroying the hammock is creating it."

With chapters on the "Natural Style of Gardening," "Wild Gardens," and "Fern Pools," Simpson introduced to South Florida a new form of tropical landscape design: a departure from formal, geometric plantings. Influenced by the American rustic trend seen in other parts of the country, Simpson had demonstrated his concept on his own grounds at the

Sentinels. Now his innovative ideas would change the way many Floridians viewed their property.

> Nature is the great landscape gardener; she plants single trees, clumps or masses of them; she makes open grassy spaces from which we get the idea of lawns. Here and there . . . she may leave a recess even deep enough to allow a vista into it. She puts banks of shrubs against masses of trees . . . she provides stretches of water, and charming views at a distance. In fact about all we do in the matter of making a landscape is done by this great master designer and planter.[13]

Conceding the need for an open space or lawn around a house in Florida's humid climate, he discussed the planting of the lawn border.

> Its outlines should be careless and irregular, though no effort ought to be made to render them so. If the expanse is large, a point of the planting may project into it in one or more places and this ought to be finished up with striking things, one or more palms, a clump of bamboos or bananas, or perhaps a mixed lot of bold vegetation which may contain yuccas, Furcraeas [large, flowering succulents], . . . or century plants. . . . When one looks into the space at the back, it is almost twilight below while higher up the foliage may be bathed in brilliant sunlight.[14]

A signature of Simpson's landscape design was an island of deep-shaded foliage—palms and bamboos of varying heights—pointing into an expanse of sunlit lawn. This may have been inspired by memories of his boyhood landscape, where belts of shady, green forest verged out from riverbeds into broad, sunlit prairies.

Simpson deplored the developers' practice of scouring building sites of all vegetation. It pained him to see noble trees, some eighty feet tall and more than one hundred years old, toppled over and grubbed out. While writing *Ornamental Gardening,* the old naturalist, whose love and respect for the mangrove was of long standing, could see these ancient giants being uprooted and dragged away by mules on the sandy key across the bay where "Miami Beach" was taking shape. Dredges plied back and forth in the bay, pumping sand over the glaring white surface of the scarified island. Long lines of barges brought in soil from the Everglades, and grass was planted sprig by sprig. Hibiscus, bougainvillea, and allamanda replaced the jungly tangle of mangroves, palmetto palms, and tropical vegetation that Simpson so loved.

More destruction of the native landscape was taking place near Simpson's home, where a swampy tract, rich in wildflowers, was being filled and parceled into building lots. Hot words like "atrocious" and "hideous" flared up in his writing as he criticized the destruction of what he called "the patient work of nature."[15] The problem was not that Simpson was a native plant purist or that he objected to flowering plants.

> Here in Florida we do not have half enough flowers in our gardens. We are satisfied with trees with fine form or handsome foliage, with palms, bamboos, and other things. . . . There is no reason why we may not . . . plant abundantly things that furnish handsome blossoms . . . such trees as . . . the coral trees, the splendid royal poinciana, the silk cotton . . . and Jacaranda, . . . and the great queen crepe myrtle are glorious while moon flowers, Allamandas, Antigonons, Bougainvillea, the Bauhinias [orchid trees], the oleanders and hibiscus furnish a mantle of lighter decorative beauty.[16]

More than half of *Ornamental Gardening* was devoted to a listing of the native palms, ornamental trees, shrubs, vines, and herbaceous plants—as well as exotics—that thrive in Florida's climate. In addition to detailed descriptions of each plant, Simpson's catalog contained practical advice on its habits and cultivation. He dealt with Florida's climate and soil, fertilizers, propagation, and pest control and offered advice on modes of architecture suitable for the subtropics. He decried the use of artificial ornaments on lawns, including a structure then in vogue called a "rockery."

> This may consist of a rather regular pile of stones, often smooth and rounded; sometimes broken pieces of plaster images or crockery ware are introduced and mingled with the pile to add to the effect. In some places the mound is of earth into which the stones are imbedded and the whole looks like an enormous pudding covered with raisins.[17]

The preservation of Florida's wildflowers was of great concern to Simpson. In his chapter on wild gardens he stressed

> bringing them in from the woods, the swamps and prairies to save and care for them. . . . The state is being rapidly settled and large areas of our territory are being devastated as a consequence. Already a few things found nowhere else in the United States have been wiped out and others are on the verge of extinction.
>
> If one has a piece of untouched high pine forest I would suggest that it be left for a wildwood garden.[18]

Simpson's practical guide to Florida gardening was welcomed by plant lovers. It was the first book of its kind, preceded only by botanies compiled in the northeast containing limited coverage of subtropical flora. The *Miami Metropolis* reviewer called it "a most notable achievement not only for the state but for the distinguished author . . . a delightful medium between a technical thoroughness . . . and a lively readableness . . . a book to fascinate the most amateur gardener and the student at the same time."[19] Many discerning property owners adopted Simpson's innovative guidelines for naturalistic planting, and their influence can still be seen in Dade County's older sections, such as Coconut Grove, Lemon City, Little River, and Buena Vista. Not until recent times, however, would the high value Simpson placed on native plants be recognized and the practice of clearing mature trees from construction sites prohibited by law.

In February 1916 the Fairchilds purchased a large strip of property in Coconut Grove that extended from Old Main Highway to Biscayne Bay for a winter home. Perhaps it was Simpson who steered them to the place, because Fairchild records that his old friend "spread the news that we were looking for a place." For the Fairchilds it was love at first sight: the tumble-down stone barn, the shack that had been the former owner's jelly factory, the modest, low-roofed frame bungalow with its native rock fireplace, the wildflower meadow sloping to the beach, and the twelve royal palms growing along the property line all filled the new owners with "a cosmic feeling of happiness."[20] Because the many small buildings on the property suggested a Javanese village, they named their place "the Kampong."

The Fairchilds could not move in until the following year, but before returning to Washington, Fairchild invited the Simpsons to look over the new property. Flora, whose specialty was wildflowers, identified the plants found along the rocky slope leading down to the shore, and Simpson, ecstatic with his friends' great prize, offered suggestions for landscaping. In a letter addressed to "My Dear Mr. and Mrs. Fairchild" in Washington, Simpson expressed his delight at the prospect of having the Fairchilds for "sometime neighbors," writing, "I am so full of your new place . . . that I must open the faucet and write you or suffer the consequences. I lay awake for hours the night after visiting it thinking of the wonderful possibilities for beauty which you have there and looking out again over Biscayne Bay, trying to imagine how it will look when you have been on it ten years."[21]

The Fairchilds moved in just a month before the freeze of February 2, 1917. Simpson called it "a terrible freeze which wrought the greatest damage I have seen in twenty-seven years. Every tender thing was cut down if not killed. No contrivance that I know of could have saved most of the stuff on that dreadful night."[22]

Some farmers kept their overhead sprinklers going all night and in the morning found the trees weighted down with icicles. The temperature dropped to twenty-seven degrees at daybreak and hovered around thirty-five throughout the day. Fairchild dropped in and the two commiserated in funereal tones, mourning the loss of so many beloved plants. Much as they grieved over the effects of the freeze, from a practical viewpoint it was an opportunity to assess plants' hardiness and experiment with methods of protecting them from frost as well as restoring cold-damaged stock.

War was declared against Germany on April 6, 1917. A submarine and naval training station was established in Key West, and patrol vessels, biplanes, and dirigibles kept watch for enemy activity along Florida's coastline. Fear of espionage and rumors of sabotage made Floridians jittery. Simpson heard that "two loud-mouthed Bolsheviks" on Big Pine Key had been caught shipping in gasoline to establish a German submarine base. He declared, "I wish to God they had shot the pair of Anarchists!"[23]

In South Florida, property values soared and taxes skyrocketed, causing retirees like Simpson to dip deep into their pockets. He wrote to Fairchild in Washington about the possibility of selling the Sentinels. He regarded his property as "in a sense an experimental station of the Department of Agriculture. . . . It would be to me like a mother selling her child to part with it."[24]

During the war Thomas Edison and the auto industrialists talked to Small about a domestic source for natural rubber. Their search centered in Florida, where a hybrid of goldenrod seemed a good candidate. Then DuPont introduced artificial rubber, and the problem was solved.

In May 1917 Simpson accompanied Small on another expedition financed by Charles Deering, this time to Lake Okeechobee. Both Simpson and Small had visited the lake region several times in the past and were quick to observe changes brought on by growth. At the mouth of the Disston Canal, which they remembered as an unbroken wilderness, stood the flourishing town of Moore Haven, with a bank, theater, hotel, stores, electric lights, and "all the belongings of modern civilization." On the southern rim of the lake only remnants of the pond apple hammocks and other plant communities remained. Some areas had been cleared to plant vegetables destined for northern markets. In many parts of the country-side the peatlike "soil," deprived of its seasonal water by the canals, was smoldering under the surface. Wisps of smoke rose from these subterranean fires through minute craters. Simpson wrote, "All the glamour and mystery which once surrounded the great lake, all the wildness and loneliness, . . . its peace and holiness are fast disappearing before the advance of the white man's civilization and soon it will be only a sheet of dirty water surrounded by truck gardens and having winter homes on its eastern shore. . . . It should have been preserved as a state or government reservation where its rare flora and rich wild fauna, its mystery and beauty could have been kept forever."[25]

A recent drought had so lowered the lake level that it took many hands to keep the *Barbee* afloat. Time and again she mired down and the men doffed their trousers and jumped into the murky waters of the lake—in defiance of alligators and giant catfish—to perform an operation referred to as "shirtailing the boat." As Simpson wryly observed, "It made me realize the necessity of water for navigation."[26]

The party was drenched by storms, lost in the dark, and plagued by horseflies and scourges of giant grasshoppers, but these minor annoyances only spurred them on. When the party reached Fort Lauderdale, however, they joyfully embraced the amenities of civilization and phoned Buena Vista for an automobile to complete their journey.

Shortly after returning from this trip, Small named a tropical tree he had recently discovered *Anamomis simpsonii* (*Myrcianthes fragrans*). In thanking Small, Simpson wrote, "I think I can stand it to have that fine Anamomis named after me, at least I'll brace up and try hard. . . . I only hope that some son-of-a-gun didn't name it away back in the time of Aristotle. . . . I have had two genera of freshwater mollusks named after me and a number of species, but I believe this is the first time that any plant has been . . . called for me."[27]

In 1918, when funding for Royal Palm State Park was threatened, Simpson asked for Small's intervention.

> Dear Dr. . . . Mrs. Jennings has just written that the Dade Co. Commissioners have cut out the entire appropriation for the Royal Palm Park, thus leaving it to the mercy of vandals who will steal right and

Simpson (center) at Moore Haven in 1917 on botanical exploration to Lake Okeechobee with John Kunkel Small, Victor Soar, and Paul Matthaus, captain of the *Barbee,* which can be seen moored under the bridge. Photo by John Kunkel Small.

"Shirt-tailing the boat." All hands overboard when the *Barbee* ran aground in Lake Okeechobee in 1917. Left to right, Simpson, Victor Soar, Paul Matthaus, and Laban Bethel. Photo by John Kunkel Small. From Simpson, *Out of Doors in Florida.*

> left and very probably burn up the lodge. Please write an appeal to Hon. E. D. V. Burr, Arch Creek, Florida asking him to present it to the Board at its next meeting, and if you can get Dr. Britton to write or any other person of influence, so much the better. It will be a calamity to leave the park unprotected. Please don't say you were asked to write. Sincerely, Simpson.[28]

Simpson can hardly be regarded a "shy" man in the usual sense of the word. In articles, books, and correspondence he gives full vent to his feelings, yet here he preferred that his influence be anonymous.

BROTHER JOSEPH'S DEATH

Charles kept in touch with his brother Joseph by mail and visited him in Bradenton from time to time on return trips from the north. Though still active, Joseph's years of accomplishment were long past. Subject to a host of unspecified illnesses and severely handicapped with acute arthritis, he moved about only with great difficulty. Like Charles, however, a fierce desire to possess the things of nature pursued him all his life. He wrote to E. N. Rose of the Botanical Department of the U.S. National Museum, offering to exchange plants or samples of wood and bark for minerals or fossils. "While I am so badly crippled that it is difficult to walk any distance from home, yet if it is botanical specimens you want I am willing to endure considerable pain or inconvenience if I can only get minerals."[29]

In September 1918 Charles received a telegram informing him that Joseph, at the age of seventy-seven, had died. The news was unexpected because that very morning Charles had received a letter from him. His brother, despite his poor health, had been confined to bed for only two days.

The National Herbarium holds some 5,000 specimens attributed to Joseph, who was listed in the world directory of botanists. He mounted a display of photographs and specimens of the flora indigenous to South Florida that was displayed at the World's Columbian Exposition of 1893 in Chicago.[30] Many plant species were named *simpsonii,* which caused Charles some embarrassment. "People think these plants are named for me. They are not. They are named for my brother, Joseph. . . . Brother Jo became a most excellent botanist; discovered many new Floridian plants . . . he could have done original work, but he had less ability to get in and work his way among people than I have."[31]

A bit of a malcontent, Joseph grumbled that botanists named plants for him but never published them, the honor then going to others. His brother commented, "Poor old Jo Simpson dug up a large number of new things in Florida, far more I think than he ever was credited with. I had urged him repeatedly to publish his own new things, but he has felt timid about it and feared he would publish something not really new."[32]

Joseph's interest in plant lore extended to their medicinal properties, and he claimed to have arrested his mother's respiratory illness with pulverized root and bark powders and to have cured himself of "elephant foot" and yellow fever with natural remedies. Disillusioned in his youth with the orthodox church, Joseph had become a Spiritualist, and, in deference to his wishes, no funeral services were held. Interment was in the Palma Sola Cemetery in Manatee County. Describing Joseph to a relative, Simpson wrote, "He was . . . a chip of his grandfather, David Conger Simpson, no business ability whatever. He bought a lot of land in B. [Bradenton] and finally deeded it all to a man who was to take care of him for the rest of his life, but who really misused him. At the time he died the land was worth at least $50,000. He was all brain, but no world wisdom."[33]

The Brickell Avenue experimental station, which Fairchild had established in 1898, was under siege periodically as appropriations for its funding were threatened, but each time committees were formed and petitions written to keep this popular facility in business. Now managed by Ed Simmonds, its function as a proving ground for new tropical plants and its important experimental work in support of Florida's flourishing fruit industry had long outgrown its six acres. When the war was concluded and attention focused once more on domestic affairs, Fairchild began looking for another site. Deering, already host to the experimental plantings of the New York Botanical Gardens, offered a tract of land near his Buena Vista estate. The Department of Agriculture accepted Deering's offer, with the stipulation that if it no longer used the property as a plant introduction garden the land would revert back to Deering. The little garden on Brickell Avenue was later abandoned—to the regret of the many plant lovers, who would always associate it with a handful of seeds, a seedling, a flowering vine, or a new variety of palm they had received for free and planted. Mabel Dorn acquired one of her first tropical plants, *Spathodea campanulata,* from the Brickell Avenue garden.

"A tall ornamental tree from West Africa, bearing huge trusses of flame-colored tulips. . . . I have always felt greatly indebted to that beautiful plant immigrant from Africa, . . . while developing its own roots, [it] carried mine also deep into South Florida's rocky soil."[34]

CHAPTER TWELVE

A Passion for Knowing, 1919–1921

There speaks the naturalist as we have all learned to love him, a man who does not know where to stop in his great passion for knowing.

Donald Culross Peattie

RECORDING FLORIDA'S NATURAL HISTORY

Simpson was an inveterate reader and an obsessive book collector. He claimed he would sacrifice a meal for a book, and if this were true he must have gone hungry often, for one wall of his study was lined to the ceiling with books, and more were piled on the floor and strewn over the work table. Among them were volumes on the study of plants, birds, insects, shells, earth science, and the history of humans while others dealt with language and reference. Highly prized were his nineteenth-century editions of classics such as the seventeen-volume *Prodromus, Systematis Naturalis, Regni Vegetabilis* of De Candolle, for which he paid forty-five dollars. Nature travelogues—including Ernest Wilson's *A Naturalist in Western China,* Isabella Bishop's *Among the Tibetans,* and Arthur Adams's *Travels of a Naturalist in Japan and Manchuria*—accounted for many of his books. Others concerned field exploration in the Caribbean and South America. These accounts were popular in Simpson's day, and he found in them inspiration for a book about his own explorations in what still was, to most Americans, terra incognita.

By April 1919 the book was finished. Henderson put Simpson in touch with G. P. Putnam's Sons, who published it in 1920 at the price of $3.50. Titled *In Lower Florida Wilds: A Naturalist's Observations on the Life, Physical Geography, and Geology of the More Tropical Part of the State,* it included chapters on "The Building of the Land," "The Florida Keys," "Cape Sable," "The Everglades," "The Planting of Our Flora," "The Origin of the Hammocks," and "The Secrets of the Sea." It explained to the curious-minded the dynamic forces that formed the Floridian land masses and the origin of its animals and plant cover. One chapter, "The Story of the Land Snails," traced the life history of these "jewels" of the Keys and Glades. *In Lower Florida Wilds*'s 404 pages were lavishly illustrated with sixty-four black-and-white photographs and a color plate of sixteen varieties of tree snails. Tourists and residents alike, many of whom never strayed far from city streets, were fascinated to see Simpson's "vagaries of vegetation" (strangler figs), "the most villainous cactus," profusely blooming orchids, the dense growth of tropical hammocks, reef fishes, corals, and sea fans (photographed with an underwater camera), and oddities like mollusk egg cases and giant land crabs. Cameras were standard equipment on board Henderson's *Eolis* and in Small's pack, so photographs were taken not only of nature, but also of the adventurers themselves.

Two fold-out maps were tipped into the back cover. One showed South Florida from Fort Lauderdale south to the Keys and Dry Tortugas and marked and named the rivers and ninety-one of its islands or keys, as well as the capes, passes, and reefs. It also delineated that slim crescent of land at the tip of Florida that supported tropical life forms. The second map, by E. H. Sellards, depicted the extent of Florida's submersion between glacial periods based on the distribution of marine shell marls and limestones.

GEOLOGICAL QUESTIONS

In Lower Florida Wilds introduced Simpson's hard-won theories on geology and distribution. His ideas were not original. Their premise had been postulated by Darwin in his writings on geological distribution and in the works of other scientists whose books were in Simpson's library. However, it is unlikely they had ever before been applied to southern Florida.

A Single Large Island

In *In Lower Florida Wilds* Simpson theorized that the Lower Keys, extending from Big Pine Key to Key West, had once been a single island,

and that, along with the "Miami mainland" (Atlantic coastal ridge), they were "elevated above the sea" when the Upper Keys were still a "living coral reef."

> I feel sure that the lower group of keys is a remnant of what was once a single large island which lay along the northern part of this great ocean river and which had been raised above the sea by the first Pleistocene elevation. . . . While this large island was entire, . . . various animals and the seeds of tropical plants were brought to it, largely by the Gulf Stream; these became colonized and finally generally distributed over it. At the time of the second depression (during later Pleistocene) the island subsided slightly, but not sufficiently to drown out completely its dry-land life.[1]

Simpson speculated that over long periods of time, ocean surges divided the island into the group of existing keys. His concepts were based on his informal plant and animal inventories, fossil findings, and his personal observations. "The mainland of the Miami region, including the rocky ridge just mentioned, has a mixed flora, a majority of its species being migrants from the American tropics. These are, to a very considerable extent, identical with plants found on the Lower Keys."[2]

Simpson's botanical studies indicated that more than 140 species of tropical plants common to the Atlantic ridge and the Lower Keys do not occur in the Upper Keys at all. "I can conceive of no better evidence that the Miami coast and the Lower Keys . . . were above the sea and were receiving life drifted from the American tropics a long time before the Upper Keys had become dry land. If I am correct the Lower Keys should be far richer in tropical life than the upper ones. This is in fact the case."[3]

The Land Bridge

Simpson also believed that plant and animal life migrated from the Upper Keys to the mainland over a land bridge that once existed from Lower Matecumbe Key to the mainland east of Flamingo. He noted, "Before the Florida East Coast Railway dredged a channel across the mud flat back of Matecumbe it would have been possible by following the tortuous shoals actually to wade from it to the mainland near Joe Kemp's key, a distance of fully thirty miles, in water nowhere more than two feet deep."[4]

He cited the difference in plants and animals found on the Lower Keys, Upper Keys, and mainland, such as *Liguus solidus,* "a large beautiful arboreal snail" that almost exclusively occupied the Lower Keys; a native cotton rat; and a cotton mouse that occurred abundantly on the upper chain of islands but never on the lower. Not the raccoon, the opossum, the Florida panther, or the wild cat—in fact, no wild mammal, so far as was known—was found in Simpson's day on the Lower Keys.

Simpson readily conceded that his geology was that of an amateur, but —except for one major flaw—his theories have largely held up. Although he was aware of the glacial periods, he did not recognize their effect on the rising and falling of the ocean level.

Thomas Barbour, a seasonal visitor to Florida since his youth, knew Simpson well and wrote,

> The best account of the Keys with which I am acquainted is in Charles Torrey Simpson's *In Lower Florida Wilds*. . . . I can strongly recommend the reading of his book, but I think this reservation is worth making: In connection with the formation and dissection of these islands, Simpson frequently postulates an "uplifting" of the land. I believe that it is much more likely that what happened was a lowering of the surface of the sea. . . . Nevertheless as I see it, each time the earth passed through one of the several epochs of extensive glaciation there was such an enormous amount of water tied up in the gigantic polar icecap that the surface of the sea was lowered.[5]

In Lower Florida Wilds was addressed to the amateur naturalist, and throughout the book Simpson aimed to entertain his reader. With metaphors drawn from Shakespeare, the Bible, mythology, and the military, he pictured a world in a state of flux, one where plants and animals found ingenious solutions to problems of survival. He slipped in lessons in geology, plant adaptation, and forest succession among tales of his misadventures in the "wilds of lower Florida" and aboard the *Eolis* on the Caribbean.

Reviewers greeted Simpson's new book with the flowery enthusiasm typical of the day. One columnist dubbed him "one of the princes among naturalists" and went on to say, "But once you have seen Florida through his eyes, you have seen it emerge from the ocean bed . . . you have watched the palmetto invent its cunning defense against fire, and seen the villain of the jungle, the strangling fig, carry out its slow, stealthy, murderous campaign."[6] *Booklist* reviewed it for the trade as "a curious though pleasant, blending of the scientist's delight in naming, describing or explaining and the artist's sensitiveness to vivid coloring, ethereal lights or deeps of forest."[7] Botanist Roland Harper, writing in *Geographi-*

cal Review, said, "Mr. Simpson's work stands out in refreshing contrast to the mass of irresponsible or sensational gush about Florida. . . . His book is . . . packed with accurate first-hand information about . . . this most tropical part of the United States."[8] The *New York Times* cautioned, "He has written well and has presented his material in as popular a form as was possible, but the reviewer would be failing in his duty if he did not warn the casual book-buyer of the scientific nature of this volume with so attractive a title."[9]

In Lower Florida Wilds sold out its first printing and went into a second impression. Simpson sent a copy to the public library in Tiskilwa, sparking a review and commentary by the editor of the local paper. Simpson was unimpressed. To his cousin, Helen Simpson, he wrote, "[The editor] said I was the 'most wonderful man' living and 'the greatest naturalist on earth';. . . they had a hurrah meeting in the library and passed similar resolutions, all of which were just as far out of the way as the esteem I was held in as a boy."[10]

Shortly after the publication of his new book Simpson had another cause for celebration—the publication of "New Floridian Subspecies of the Genus *Liguus*" by the *Proceedings of the Biological Society of Washington* (December 1920). In it he described eighteen new color forms.

PILGRIMAGE TO DEEP LAKE

Ever curious about oddities of nature and always looking for something new to write up for regional journals or his next book, in February 1921 Simpson set forth on a "pilgrimage" to Deep Lake, a peculiar but little known body of water in Collier County's Big Cypress country. His companion was Dr. Edward Mercer, a retired Philadelphia physician, whom Simpson described as "a man I go roughing with."[11]

Mystery surrounded the origin and nature of the lake. Simpson wrote, "I had been told that its depth was very great, in fact unfathomable, and again that it was rather shallow, that it was a small body of water and also that it covered a considerable area; in fact, it had even been asserted that no such lake existed. . . . I determined to pay it a visit and, if possible find out something of its origin and natural features."[12]

Indians once had a camp in the Deep Lake hammock land, and during the second phase of the Wars of Indian Removal (1855–58), a reconnaissance patrol ripped up Billy Bowlegs's banana patch and trampled on his crops to see "how old Billy would cut up," thus setting off what was called "Bowlegs' War." Two-thirds of the fertile, three-hundred-acre hammock

Aerial view of Deep Lake, ca. 1974. Photo by Douglas Schneider.

had been cleared for grapefruit, and rails were put in to carry the fruit to Allen's River for shipping.[13]

Deep Lake is about thirty miles north of Everglades City (ninety miles northwest of Miami). It is an easy two-hour trip from Miami today, but in 1921 the only trans-state route was from West Palm Beach to Fort Myers. To reach their destination, Mercer and Simpson had go almost full circle on a course that covered nearly four hundred miles and used almost every form of transportation except horse carriage. This did not dismay Simpson, for he had a big agenda. He was hankering to check over the Lake Okeechobee area, which he had explored five years earlier with John Small; he wanted to reinforce his theories about the flora of the west coast; and he was irresistibly drawn back to Marco Island for its tree snail population. Above all, he loved the out-of-doors and longed to go camping.

At seventy-five, with cataracts blurring his vision, Simpson could hardly have embarked on this trip alone, but he claimed he only asked Mercer along for the value of his tie.

> He is one of the kind who looks dressy in any old clothes; he carried a linen collar and a red imitation four-in-hand tie of about the vintage 1900 which fastened to the collar button with some kind of bent wire. Whenever we needed accommodations at a house, he buttoned on his collar, hooked up the tie, and with a smiling face and the most absolute assurance he knocked and asked for any favors. If I kept out of sight, and the tie, which was a little unreliable, didn't come loose, he always got whatever he wanted."

They traveled light, camping out in Simpson's pup tent and lunching on dry bread and beef jerky supplemented with fresh fruit and whatever hospitality might be offered along the way. Blankets, collecting gear, notebook and pencil, compass, and matches completed their outfit. Both men wore leather leggings as protection against the prickly brush, and Simpson dressed in army surplus khaki pants and jacket, with a stiff-brimmed hat set at a jaunty angle.

Departing from Little River, they traveled north via train and bus to Loxahatchee, where a launch conveyed them through canals and west across Lake Okeechobee to Moore Haven.

> While the other passengers went to the hotel, my companion and I hunted for a camping place. It was getting dark, and we searched in vain for something for tent poles and stakes. Finally we saw on the bank of the canal an old upturned canoe resting on a couple of saw horses. We spread the tent over the boat so that it shut off some of the keen northwest wind and pulled a little dead grass for a bed. . . . We passed a miserable night and when we got up in the morning, stiff with cold, we found the ground covered with frost.

From Moore Haven they took a steamer through Lake Hicpochee to Citrus Center, where they traveled by bus on a dirt road to Fort Myers. There they joined three other travelers on the mail bus headed down Dixie Highway (U.S. 41) for Marco Island. The road was "improved" as far as Naples, but from Naples to Marco it was another story.

> A track had been cut out barely wide enough for the passage of a car and our machine constantly dodged from side to side to avoid the larger trees and stumps. . . . The driver ran his car at the rate of twenty miles an hour. . . . There were five of us and all except the driver held on to the car and each other while he clung to the wheel, the result being that we were thrown violently in every direction a dozen times a minute. . . . One of our party, a Florida cracker, dryly remarked after an unusually difficult performance, "I reckon thish hyer road is thist nacherly drunk."

Camping at Marco Island

The mail bus discharged its passengers at the Marco Island landing, where they crossed the channel on a ferry boat. Their destination on Marco Island was Caxambas, where, in 1885, Simpson had discovered his first tree snails.[14] It was sundown when they arrived, and a cold wind was blowing. The shell mound where Simpson had camped in the past was smothered in cacti, prickly pears, and sharp-spined century plants, but Mercer cleared off a place for their tent while Simpson looked around for tent poles. "Everything I got hold of proved to be erect cactus stems. Finally I found in the darkness a little tree which I thought would do and when I drew it towards me something came off in my hand which to my joy and astonishment proved to be a large, fine, tree snail. . . . Then I said, 'When I find a place where I can gather Liguus in the dark, a few cacti or century plants isn't going to ruffle my feelings in the least.' "

When Simpson crawled out the next morning he discovered that without moving from the door of the tent he could spot over fifty *Liguus* feeding on the lichen-encrusted bark of deciduous coral trees. "There were two forms," he recalled, "the sub species roseatus having a white shell with broad yellow or orange bands, and lineolatus with the same ground color and a narrow reddish band on the last whorl. In both the axial region is pink or purplish."

Simpson and Mercer lingered a day around Caxambas, visiting and collecting in other hammocks and examining the great sand dunes and shell mounds of the area. When evening came, "the Doctor" happened on a tin pail and suggested they treat themselves to coffee for supper.

> Then as the stars came out we sat by our fire and ate grapefruit, hard bread, dried beef, guava jelly and drank hot coffee. And as we feasted in perfect content we exclaimed, "This is the life, this is the real thing!" We were tramps, as happy and free as children. With our little tent and everything carried on our backs we could stop anywhere when night overtook us or even earlier and stay as long as we liked. The nights since starting had been chilly, hence we had slept with all our clothes on, even to hats, shoes and leggins. Tramps hate to bathe, hence we found abundant excuses for not doing so—the chilliness of the morning air, the difficulty of getting water, and I am afraid, sometimes the want of any real desire to do so. It was so easy to say, "Oh, let's not wash, let's put it off till its warmer or we have a better chance." Anyhow it all fitted in well with the kind of vagabond life we were leading.

By Handcar to Deep Lake Groves

Embarking once more, they took a mail boat down the coast to Everglades, where they hunted up a boatman. He piloted them up Allen's River to the terminus of the railroad, which Simpson described as of standard width but with very small, crooked rails. "We climbed aboard a gasolene handcar while the driver stowed our bags among the machinery. The Doctor and I bade each other a long farewell and the machine sprang into motion. . . . It required all our strength to hang on as it swung, lurched, shook, wabbled and jumped, often entirely clear of the track, the rate being over fifteen miles an hour." Though much bounced about, the men were safely deposited in front of a house surrounded by citrus groves.

The Wonderful Lake

> We were guided by the kindly man who lived there, first through more grapefruit groves and then very heavy timber to a bit of a glade, and the wonderful lake lay before us. It apparently covers an area of about four acres and is somewhat quadrate in outline. Three sides are swampy, only that on which we approached was high and dry. It is a wonderful mirror of water set in a frame of dense, lofty, evergreen forest. . . . At the time of our visit a dozen or more alligators were

Deep Lake, ca. 1920. From Simpson, *Florida Wild Life.*

in sight and they seemed to be without fear as they swam and caught fish close to where we stood. One was a monster and was believed by the man in charge of the place to be sixteen feet long.

As to the origin of Deep Lake, Simpson believed it to have been an enormous spring that has long been dead.

Away back in Pleistocene time the water which extended in a sheet from the Appalachian region to Lower Florida under impervious rock found some crevice opening to the surface at the present site of this lake through which it was forced with great power. . . . It eroded and dissolved the soft limestone until a big basin was formed. . . . Silver Spring was formed in the same way, but it is still active; something has choked up the underground channel of Deep Lake and it is dead. A sounding line let down into it might touch on a shelf and register not more than ninety feet, but if it went down the mouth, the water might well be unfathomable.

Geologists today regard Deep Lake as a sinkhole lake, one of several in southern Florida. Limnologists make annual studies of its temperature and chemical properties. Their soundings indicate that its sides drop off sharply in a cone shape to a depth of ninety-five feet. Another peculiarity of the lake is that most years its waters do not completely overturn with seasonal temperature changes.

As evening drew on, the two travelers rigged up their tent and, despite their aversion to water and their apprehension about dangers posed by the reptilian residents of the lake, took a swim before retiring.

> Slowly the darkness fell on the great forest and the holy beauty, the peace and stillness of the night brooded over the landscape. There was something almost weird and overpowering in the thought of the immense depth of the water that lay at our feet. We sat close to the shore and out on the lake an alligator rose and made a rush after a fish which splashed as it fell back. Insects churred in the trees around us; we heard the mournful notes of a whip-poor-will and in the distance an owl hooted. Finally we crawled into the little tent beneath our blankets and were lulled to sleep by the witchery of the night and the voices of the forest.

The next morning, as they were packing, Mercer discovered that his money belt, containing more than a hundred dollars, was missing. A diligent search was made to no avail. Mercer remembered removing it when they went swimming, but he could not recall where he put it. Later, he had cleaned up the campsite and burned up the trash. Searching for the missing belt, Simpson found a folded piece of cloth with charred paper in it and concluded that the belt had been raked into the fire.

> It cast a decided gloom over the expedition for we hadn't money enough left to take us home. That evening we camped in our old place at Caxambas and after supper as we sat in gloomy silence the Doctor remarked that he had a thorn in his foot and took off his leggin in order to get it out. As he did so something dropped out and on picking it up it proved to be the missing belt with the money undisturbed. . . . Joy reigned supreme in our camp and to properly celebrate we made up a big can of coffee, got out provisions, and went in for a regular tramp spree.[15]

CHAPTER THIRTEEN

An Icon for Nature, 1922–1925

In the glorious luxuriance of
the hundred plants he takes delight.

Inscription on the Meyer Medal taken from a poem by Chi K'ang, poet of the Tang Dynasty, A.D. *618*

THE GREENING OF MIAMI

South Florida was enjoying economic growth, and signs of progress and prosperity were everywhere. Simpson said that hotels were so full that the "guests arms and legs are sticking out the windows," and he claimed that he dared not venture out at night for fear he might "stumble and fall over a new fifteen story building."[1] The population of Miami had tripled since Simpson's arrival. By 1922 it was over 30,000, and though Little River boasted only 317 residents, it, too, was growing fast. Near Simpson's home, lots were cleared in the piney woods once home to fields of wildflowers and a fine stand of native royal palms.

A state motor route sixty feet wide was being built from Miami to Jacksonville, and Simpson told Fairchild that "a solid mile at least should be planted with two rows of royal poincianas."[2] The poinciana, known in its native Madagascar as "flame of the forest," has an inflorescence of scarlet blossoms twelve to eighteen inches across emerging in a blaze of glory on leafless branches.

Simpson and Fairchild both served on Miami's "Scientists Committee," formed to recommend landscaping for streets and highways. When Dade County commissioners appropriated $27,000 toward the planting of "Paradise Boulevard" from Biscayne Bay west to Hialeah, Simpson in a newspaper story proposed a large collection of palms, both native and rare. "The Royals which grow so tall, placed in the center, with lower forms graduating down to the stemless ones bordering the entire mass . . . fan and feather palms mixed would impart a dome effect. . . . In the Everglades section should be planted bamboo masses with great beddings of oleanders—the white, the pink, and the red."[3] To Fairchild he wrote, "Such a highway would be worth millions to Miami and would pay for itself many times over." Simpson asked nothing but the pleasure of seeing his landscape plan realized, and toward that end he contributed two hundred dollars to the Miami Parks Department to buy trees.[4]

ROADKILLS

The downside of Florida's new highways was the toll the automobile took on human and animal life. When one of his friends was killed in an auto accident, Simpson wrote a scathing letter to the editor of the *Miami Daily News* condemning "criminal drivers. . . . An unprincipled person sitting at the wheel of a car can strike a pedestrian, bowl him over and make a clean getaway at the rate of fifty miles an hour with almost no risk of detection whatever."[5]

He cursed this "new enemy," not only for its toll in human life but also for animals killed on the road. "Somehow, the smooth, oiled roads have a fascination for many forms of life," he explained, and he recalled that once after a summer rain he found the road so littered with dead crabs pulverized by the wheels of autos that he could not step without treading on their shelly remains.[6] Simpson's list of roadkills included whole armies of "lubbers," the large Florida grasshopper; sparrows, blackbirds, ground doves, and blue jays; rats, rabbits, mice, opossum, racoon, and mink; and a dozen species of snakes, including the diamond rattler, water moccasin, black snake, scarlet king snake, corn snake, and hog-nosed snake.

Horse-drawn buggies had caused little injury to animals, he observed, because these vehicles moved slowly and the rattle of the wheels and the vibration of the horses' hooves telegraphed the approaching danger. "But the automobile . . . comes so swiftly and silently that they neither see nor hear it until it is too late."[7]

An abandoned limestone rock pit near his home spoke of South Florida's new affluence and foretold the coming problem of waste disposal. "Now it is used as a dumping ground for the offal of a rapidly growing town, the wreckage of civilization. Among the heaps of rubbish are old trunks, broken stoves, tubs, smashed crockery and window glass, barrels and kegs, bedsteads, packing boxes, iron pipes, papers, rags, cast off shoes, window screens, tin cans, bottles, many of which are flat and have doubtless fitted into coat or hip pockets and the ruins of automobiles."[8] Despite this "wreck of civilization," Simpson often visited this old quarry, monitoring its plant growth and counting seventy-six species of flowering plants and three ferns thriving there amid the junk.

MENTOR TO THE GARDEN CLUBS

The flowers in the rock pit, the toll on wildlife taken by automobiles, plants for landscaping public places—all no doubt were subjects Simpson reiterated when the garden clubs met at the Sentinels. Groups had been formed in Miami, Jacksonville, Ormond Beach, and Winter Park, and in 1924, at the Jacksonville Spring Flower Show, the Florida Federation of Garden Clubs was formed, a part of the growing national garden club movement. As "watchdogs of beautification," their mission was to promote the wise use of natural resources and to foster civic pride in the natural surroundings. They fought for billboard regulation, parks, and street plantings. Through flower shows they set horticultural standards and encouraged home landscaping. To serve Florida's growing population, they planted trees in the yards of new schools and hospitals and landscaped other public places. "Professor" Simpson became a mentor to these public-spirited plant lovers, sharing cuttings and seeds, speaking at their meetings, and leading them on plant-collecting trips.

Simpson was drawn more and more into the public eye as illustrated articles introducing "Lemon City's most distinguished early resident" appeared in both the *Miami Herald* and the *Daily News.* One such story, headlined "World-Famous Naturalist Lives at Little River," described Simpson as one who started life "as a poor boy, and is still a poor man, rich only in the priceless treasures with which he has surrounded himself."[9]

The publicity brought to the Sentinels a mixed bag of visitors. Along with the botanists and other professionals came home gardeners, schoolchildren, and "visiting firemen" escorted by city officials, as well as curiosity seekers and young people looking for an afternoon outing. Often they surprised the old naturalist pushing a wheelbarrow full of mulch, caring for his plant friends, or, hammer in hand, repairing his roof, but Simpson always made time for visitors. He piloted them around, keeping up a lively banter as he pointed out his gigantic staghorn fern; the pandanus, which at thirty feet was the tallest of its kind in the United States; "a tree that walks" (the mahoe); and the bromeliads, which he claimed broke the prohibition law every day by using their cups as minia-

Simpson yoked to his wheelbarrow, 1924. In the background, a glimpse of his veranda and the latticework that enclosed his laboratory. Courtesy of Special Collections, Fairchild Tropical Garden Library.

John Brooks Henderson, ca. 1916. Courtesy of Research Library, Rosensteil School of Marine and Atmospheric Science, University of Miami.

ture "stills" to ferment water with fallen debris and drowned insects. His impromptu stories were lessons in plant adaptation, reproduction, and survival, meant to draw his visitors into natural world.

Though outwardly genial, in private the old gentleman sometimes lost patience with his visitors. "I am perfectly willing to give time to those interested in plants, who want honestly to learn, but a class comes that has no brains, . . . has not an atom of interest in plants, horticulture or nature and simply wants to brag to their friends that they stand in with the old man," he confessed to Fairchild.[10]

The second printing of *In Lower Florida Wilds* was nearly sold out, but the publisher balked at bringing out another. With more than sixty photographs, the book was expensive to publish, particularly because the wages of pressmen and bindery hands had peaked during the postwar period. Henderson came to the fore and sent $500 as the down payment on 1,000 copies and endorsed Simpson's $1,000 note for the remainder, explaining to the publisher, "Mr. Simpson is a man of limited means and the payment of the costs of manufacturing is only accomplished by considerable sacrifice on his part. It is regarded here as a sort of guide to the wilds that all should have who intend to get off the hotel piazza."[11]

Henderson's gesture was one of many favors he had tendered to Simpson over the years. His generosity enabled some of Simpson's trips to Ohio for reunions with veterans of the Civil War and to Philadelphia and Washington to hobnob with the "conchs." It was a symbiotic relationship, for the capable Simpson was a hard worker on expedition and assisted Henderson with his research.

In January 1923, Henderson was hospitalized for a routine operation and died suddenly from complications. He was only fifty-two. His passing was a heavy blow for Simpson. Like Pliny Reasoner, Henderson had been just a youth when he and Simpson shared their first collecting trips. He had supported Simpson in difficult, even hopeless, times, always firmly determined to find a publisher for Simpson's *Catalogue.* The aging naturalist admitted to "completely breaking down" in the winter of 1923, and the untimely death of yet another valued companion may have been a contributing factor. Henderson's colleagues at the Smithsonian held a memorial meeting and recorded "profound sorrow at the loss of a fellow worker and friend, whose personal charm and unassuming helpfulness endeared him to every one." After summarizing Henderson's scientific achievements, the resolution stated: "By his sudden death a career of great promise was cut short."[12] A question that plagued Simpson was what would become of Henderson's twenty-five years of research on the evolution and distribution of the West Indian land and marine mollusks.

A MEDAL FOR PLANT INTRODUCTION

In February, as Simpson was packing his gear to go camping with Flora on Big Pine Key, he received a letter from the American Genetic Association. He had been elected to receive the Frank N. Meyer Medal for Foreign Plant Introduction "for your twenty odd years of study of the whole subject of plant introduction carried on at great personal financial sacrifice; for your publications on the subject, and for the countless conferences and hospitalities which you have granted to all who have visited your arboretum."[13]

The letter was signed by the twelve members of the association's council, including David Fairchild, O. F. Cook, and Gilbert Grosvenor. Attached to the letter was a list of fifty plants Simpson was credited with having introduced to the United States, among them varieties of feather and fan palms, an orchid, bromeliads, hibiscus, philodendron, flowering vines, trees, lilies, ferns, and cacti. Most of them he had collected on his trips to Cuba. Others he had grown from seeds sent from his correspondents in Italy and Germany. Simpson hastened to reply to Fairchild, president of the association. "I cannot possibly see what I have done to deserve a medal, but if any scientific society sees fit to present me with one I shall receive it gratefully and cherish it greatly. One thing let me ask of you, if you have anything to do with it and that is that there be no spread or ceremony about it. You know I shrink from anything of this kind and it would make me very uncomfortable."[14]

The Meyer Medal was struck in honor of Frank Meyer, one of Fairchild's plant explorers. Meyer, a Dutchman, had been a gardener at the Amsterdam botanical garden. Coming to America in 1900, he was employed by Fairchild for SPI and served from 1905 to 1918 in China, Turkestan, and other parts of Asia. Fairchild reminisced, "The first thing that attracted my attention to Frank Meyer was the story that he wept because his superior refused to allow him to protect the tender roots of some imported bamboos. . . . [T]his was characteristic of Meyer. . . . [I]t was his love for the plants themselves that kept up his spirits and enabled him to stand the awful solitudes of life where every personality around him was strange and every word spoken unintelligible."[15] A brilliant conversationalist and good company when he chose, Meyer also had an unpredictable temper and suffered from acute fits of depression. In 1916, while in China tracking down reports of a wild pear reported to grow in almost pure sand, he disappeared from a river boat. Though his body was recovered, it was never known whether he had fallen in the river, been murdered, or committed suicide. His will disclosed a legacy of one thousand dollars to the staff of the Office of Foreign Plant Introduction, to be used to defray expenses for an outing or divided equally among the staff. Instead, Meyer's friends chose to use the money for a tribute to his memory: a medal to be awarded for distinctive service in the field of plant introduction.[16]

Simpson was the fourth to receive the medal, and only the second American, the first having been Barbour Lathrop.[17] The Fairchilds invited Charles and Flora to a "smoker" a week in advance of the festivities, but Simpson begged off, writing, "You know I am deaf and when I am in a room where a lot of people are talking the strain to understand is nerve wracking so I think I had better stay home and brace up against the events which are to follow."[18]

On the day of the presentation, Fairchild and Barbour Lathrop arrived at the Sentinels with representatives from the American Genetic Association and other notables, including the medal's designer, Theodore Spicer-Simson, and William Jennings Bryan, the famed orator, who was neigh-

Simpson and David Fairchild in the bamboo grove at the Sentinels. Courtesy of the Historical Association of Southern Florida.

bor to the Fairchilds in Coconut Grove. Perhaps they had arrived early, for Simpson was still in his work clothes. Marjory Stoneman Douglas reported the event for the *Miami Herald*. She wrote,

> An old man with bared grey head stood beneath an enormous pine tree in the late afternoon sun. The wide, green clearing about him brimmed with a golden and windy silence clear to the great crests of jungle wall which foamed in leafy spray against the blue brilliance of the Florida sky. The dull brown of his plain shirt and suspendered trousers seemed the same stuff of the grass stems and the huge pine trunk, harmonious, related. . . . And so also the high serenity of his face was very substance with the strong and unconquerable green of his trees about him, the look of one who has served for a lifetime, alone and silent, the tremendous holiness of earth.[19]

Frank N. Meyer Medal for Foreign Plant Introduction, inscribed "C. T. Simpson" and with the initials of the medalist, Theodore Spicer-Simson. Courtesy of the Otto G. Richter Library, University of Miami.

David Fairchild presented Spicer-Simson's bronze medal, which honored Frank Meyer on one side with an engraved inscription in Chinese characters of a Tang Dynasty poem. Freely translated it said, "In the glorious luxuriance of the hundred plants he takes delight." Flanking the inscription was a fruiting branch of the jujube and the white-barked pine, both plants brought to America by Frank Meyer. On the reverse was a relief of the recipient.[20] Describing the moment of presentation, Douglas wrote, "Mr. Simpson received the medal in his hand and his splendid, weathered, beautiful face twisted with emotion. The people looking on at a significant moment in the life of a remarkable man swallowed a little hard. Mr. Simpson only bowed and said slowly, 'I cannot say anything. I thank you very much.' But beneath the quick spatter of hand-clasping [hand-clapping], his eyes flooded." Lathrop broke the solemn moment, grabbing Simpson's hand and saying, "Well, I'm damned glad you got it!" Bryan stepped up and touched him on the shoulder, "It's better to feel, as you do, Professor Simpson, than to talk as I do!"[21]

TALES OF A NATURALIST

Simpson was becoming a celebrity, and this caused him some anxiety. When Spicer-Simson suggested that he use a photo of the medal in *Out of Doors in Florida,* the new book Simpson was writing, he declined, writing, "I shrink from any publicity and many times wish I knew no one but my immediate neighbors and a few dear friends. . . . I hope you and the Doctor will not feel offended because I do not want to have any picture of myself published in the book. Certainly it is not for want of appreciation of the picture or your great kindness, but just because I shrink from the limelight."[22]

Left to himself, Simpson was content to spend his days nurturing his plants, working in his laboratory, and tramping in the Keys. He wrote to Fairchild about a trip he was planning.

> There is the ruins of a great hammock on Big Pine where we will camp and I hope to haunt it. I may possibly find a few of the wonderful tree snails, and anyhow there are or should be two tropical trees there found by Dr. Blodgett seventy-five years ago and lost ever since. He found three on that island never reported elsewhere in the U.S. and Professor Sargent believes he faked them. I have found one of them [*coupania*] in considerable numbers . . . and hope for the other two. If I could get one of them it would be another "tut" haul.[23]

Despite Simpson's retiring nature, Fairchild encouraged him to continue writing. "Daddy always urged him on," recalls Fairchild's daughter, Barbara Muller. " 'You must do it,' he would say."[24] With this encouragement, Simpson had began compiling another book.

Out of Doors in Florida: The Adventures of a Naturalist Together with Essays on the Wild Life and the Geology of the State came out in the fall of 1923. Published by the E. B. Douglas Company of Miami, it was packed with black-and-white photos, but no formal portrait of the author appeared. It did, however, include several undignified snapshots of "an old tramp" making notes in front of his tent, hitching a ride on a section car, and shinning a tree to capture a tree snail. In the volume's preface Simpson again urged that the hammocks and other natural features of Florida be preserved. "It is high time that an organized effort should be made to save some of the useful and beautiful things for those who are to come after us." Over and over he would bark out this urgent theme of the preservation of wild Florida.

Out of Doors in Florida was more autobiographical than his previous books, reaching back nearly forty years to describe his cruise "Down the West Coast" of Florida in 1885 with Cornelia, Pliny Reasoner, and Capt. Hugh Culbert. Other chapters recounted incidents in his childhood, his trip to Honduras, and his adventures in the Florida Keys hunting the elusive tree snails. He extended his range to include Merritt's Island, the Caloosahatchee River, and Lake Okeechobee.

This new book dealt with many topics: plant reproduction and adaptation, native flowering plants and shrubs, hurricanes and geology. In answer to visitors to the state who asked "Where are the wildflowers?" Simpson pointed out that in locations where a vivid display of native flowers is seen, they bloom only during part of the year. In contrast he noted, "I have never seen a time in south Florida when I could not gather at least fifty species of wild plants in bloom."[25]

Out of Doors in Florida won many fans for the "sage of Biscayne Bay," as one reviewer called him. Margaret Bailey, in her "Summer Reading" column, described his new book as "written in such a clear-cut, entertaining and popular way, that the layman can understand it, and catch the contagion of Dr. Simpson's eager enthusiasm."[26] The *Miami Herald*'s Eleanor Bisbee, on the other hand, criticized the book for its "technical language" and "scientific explanations" but also noted "the charm of the 'old man' as the writer calls himself has always been his deep enjoyment of odd incidents and one follows him with the utmost delight in his conversational detours to recall some humorous happening."[27] Both reviewers noted the strong appeal that Simpson's book made for the preservation of Florida's wild things. Simpson's books were being stocked in bookstores throughout the state, and a columnist from the *Jacksonville Sunday Times* reviewed both *Out of Doors in Florida* and *In Lower Florida Wilds,* stating, "Nothing I ever have seen in the book line on Florida has appealed to me so powerfully and in such an absorbing way as Simpson's two nature books."[28]

LETTERS TO FAIRCHILD

As Simpson became increasingly deaf and cataracts blurred his vision, Flora was never far from his side. She entertained his callers with pitchers of lemonade served on the Sentinels' high veranda, cleared the paths in the hammock of fallen limbs, "towed" him to luncheons and various social engagements, and pulled on her boots when he wanted to go plant hunting in the swamp. Marion Roper referred to her mother as a "swell sport . . . on a camping trip" and said she would go "deeper into the woods than anyone."[29] On one such excursion to the Keys, in January 1924, the Simpsons ran into a "norther" with heavy rain and winds of thirty miles an hour. Their tent blew down, leaving them to sit the night out on the beach. "It was a fine chance to meditate," Simpson wrote to Fairchild. "Camping out is fun in dry weather, but it is what Sherman called war when it is wet!"[30]

Simpson's letters to Fairchild, preserved with Fairchild's papers at the Fairchild Tropical Garden in Miami, disclose Simpson's declining years. The two men wrote even when Fairchild was in Coconut Grove, sending bits of leaves, flowers, and seeds back and forth for identification. It was a trip of some distance between the two villages, and although the Simpsons had a telephone, the old gentleman found the mail service more suited to his needs. Though Simpson wrote of the state of his health and pocketbook, his letters never discussed family matters.

In March 1924 he wrote Fairchild, "I have just returned from a four day trip to Paradise Key [Royal Palm State Park] because I utterly broke down under the high pressure and had to get out."[31] The phrases "utterly broke down" and "breaking down" had become an oft-repeated complaint. Simpson himself explained it: "I am breaking down, partly because I am naturally growing old—partly from too much hurrah caused by the gang that streams in here now thruout the whole year."[32]

By "breaking down" Simpson may have been referring to nervous exhaustion, caused partly by physiological changes associated with aging and partly by the frustration of constant interruptions by visitors, the pressure to accomplish his scientific goals, and financial worries. Another contributing factor may have been domestic friction. His household included Flora's sister, known as "Aunt Annie," and his stepdaughter, Marion Roper. Pliny, now working in the building trades, no longer lived at home. Marion, in her mid-twenties, may have tried his patience, for she was a strange young woman with physical as well as personality defects. She was about the age of the Simpsons' neighbor, Elsie Picot, and when Charles and Flora went on collecting trips Elsie stayed with Marion, helping to get her meals. Elsie said, "She was not very bright . . . did not talk very good. . . . One part of her mind was brilliant, but she just didn't know how to go about ordinary things." Graham Fairchild remembers that she was "unobtrusive" save for her "occasional non-sequiturs which would bring the conversation to a startled halt."[33] She completed a home nursing course, however, tended the neighborhood children, wrote sensible essays and stories, and used a Brownie camera. One of her pictures appeared in *Ornamental Gardening.* She also mastered the typewriter and sometimes typed Simpson's manuscripts, but her special personality may have grated on Simpson's nerves.

Although the cause of his breakdown was not clear, the cure was always getting back to nature, and his visit to Royal Palm State Park (formerly Paradise Key) restored his spirits. He occupied himself escorting visitors about, identifying plants, and discussing plans for the park with Elizabeth Skinner, chair of the Park Committee. "She wants to artificialize somewhat and I countered all I could. . . . The first great thing is a scenic highway with a wide moat all around the island as a fire guard, and I am trying hard to keep this from being made a mere fortification. It can be a beautiful as well as a useful thing. An exotic garden is planned and I

e former lodge in Royal Palm State Park, ca. 1924. Simpson talking to Charles Mosier t), first custodian of the park. From Simpson, *Out of Doors in Florida.*

hope I can prevent this from being made a blot and eyesore."[34] In closing, he thanked Fairchild for "the small package from Coconut Grove containing a dried plant" and speculated on whether it would grow at the Sentinels.

Property values skyrocketed during the twenties, escalating the value of the Simpsons' bayfront property. Paying their taxes was a hardship, however, and they considered selling. Then the Rotary Club launched a plan to buy the property for a public park. Simpson liked the idea and was willing to sell for a nominal sum with the provision that he be permitted to occupy it during his lifetime as its custodian. The *Miami Herald* called it "A Wonderful Park Opportunity" and urged public support for the project, but eventually it fell through for lack of interest.[35]

Simpson wrote to Fairchild to discuss the matter.

> It is quite probable that we will sell our home, the Sentinels. . . . It is enough to break my heart, the thought of giving this up, of turning away from all these dear plants and seeing them no more forever but . . . as the man who acts as agent says, ". . . Isn't it better to sell now and have a little good of your money than to struggle in poverty till the end and let someone else have it?"

. . . As yet I am able to give the place some kind of superficial care, but in a short time I cannot do that. The stream of idiots increases from year to year and matters grow worse. I have given fully half my working time to the public for the last 15 years without any recompense and I feel as if I owe it nothing. I would like to have a few years at the end of my life I could call my own. I have some scientific work I want to do but never will get to do it as things are going. Once I broke down a year ago last winter and three times last winter I had to quit and go into the woods to rest.[36]

Fairchild had asked Simpson to write an article for the *Journal of Heredity* about the life history of the *Gongora* orchid that grew in his hammock. For months Simpson watched the flower, though his eyesight was so blurred that close work was almost impossible. Finally, he was able to write Fairchild. "I held the mss, ashamed to own that I could do nothing with it and yesterday when there was a crowd surging around me in the laboratory bothering the life out of me the solution of my problem flashed on me and I yelled and pawed the ground to the consternation of the dear public. So I have rewritten the sketch and am sending it to your editor."[37]

Simpson was never content when plants held their secrets from him, and nothing gave him more delight than solving these puzzles. In this case, by patient and close observation he had followed the journey of a pollen-laden bee into the interior of a flower and discovered how the orchid manipulated the insect to operate the ingenious mechanism of reproduction in its ovary.

Though speaking before large groups was an act of courage on Simpson's part, he continued to accept invitations. As he told Fairchild, "I have taken up talking in public once more—of course about gardening etc. I was called to Jacksonville to talk to the Women's Garden Clubs there and at the [Florida Federation of Garden Clubs] flower show."[38] His speaking engagements helped sell his books, though the income did little to lighten the burden of taxes. His finances improved, however, when he signed a contract with a real estate syndicate that agreed to buy the Sentinels, giving the Simpsons a reverse mortgage with the right to live there—a satisfactory solution to their dilemma.

The Fairchilds were stranded in Europe en route to a plant-hunting expedition in the summer of 1925 when Simpson learned that continued funding for the Plant Introduction Station at Chapman Field looked uncertain.[39] This was the former eight-hundred-acre World War I airfield at Cutler Ridge that through Fairchild's efforts was granted to the USDA after the war as an experimental plant station. Simpson wrote to offer his support:

> From time to time I have been hearing bad news of your expedition and later that the War Department is to take away the Chapman Field, also that the garden at Miami is to go back and that Mr. Deering is to have the 25 acres he gave for a Plant Introduction Garden. All this has filled me with genuine sorrow. . . .
>
> Since the death of my beloved Henderson you have been to me the one great friend left. The relation between him and me was a very dear one but he was born to the purple and somehow I never could feel the sense of closeness and familiarity with him that I have done with you. I want to say now that if in any way possible I can be of service to you just call on me and I will gladly do all I can.[40]

The Simpsons' income from their pooled resources was about ten thousand dollars a year, of which Charles had half. He used some of it to assist several needy "comrades of the Civil War," but most went to benefit the horticultural projects of the Miami Parks Department, which he called "local patriotism," and other "little things I want to boost."[41] In August 1925 he typed a letter to Paul Bartsch, curator of mollusks at the U.S. National Museum, to inquire about the status of Henderson's work on the West Indian land snails. Explaining his concern that the research would be laid aside, he wrote,

> I am under the deepest obligation to John B. Henderson who was my devoted friend for more than 30 years and who constantly showered favors on me. No doubt at one time and another he has spent $10,000 on me and nothing would make me happier than in some way pay back a little of this great debt of love.
>
> I am wondering if it will be possible to have this work published in case money necessary for various expenses could be furnished. I have, of course, no idea of what it would take. . . it might be beyond my means . . . but if it is not, I would be only too glad to furnish funds for its publication. . . . I would almost be willing to live on bread and water to put this thing through. . . . Please overlook mistakes as I cannot see what I am writing.[42]

Bartsch soon replied,

> I can't tell you how deeply I have been affected by your letter. I think it is one of the most touching tributes that I have ever known come to any man. Having loved J. B., as anyone who came intimately in contact with him was compelled to do, I understand so fully the motives which actuated your letter. . . . Also I hope you will have no objections to my showing it to Mrs. Henderson, for I have been working with her ever since John's death to have her set aside a little something of the Henderson fortune to enable the carrying on of that work which John had projected. So far I have not succeeded, but I am not sure that this failure on my part has been largely due to the fact that the Henderson fortunes were very much tied up about the time of John's death. However, from conversations with Mrs. Henderson, I have been led to believe that the clouds have lifted, and that fair weather and good sailing is ahead.[43]

Simpson offered to send the museum fifteen hundred dollars, despite anticipating the expense of cataract operations on both of his eyes. As to Bartsch's suggestion that he help compile the monograph, he replied, "I feel flattered that you should think I could do anything helpful at my age and because I have been so long out of the harness. But I fear I cannot attempt to help in this way. My eyes have been bad for a long time. . . . When I lived in Washington I was obliged to sit in a darkened room at night for several years and dared not use them by artificial light."[44]

Simpson continued to make contributions to the museum for publication of Henderson's work, even after the twin disasters of the 1926 hurricane and the Depression further depleted his income. Though Mrs. Henderson did give a small donation to the museum to aid in the completion of the catalog, Henderson's work was never finished.[45]

Henderson had had another project in the works at the time of his death—an index to *Nautilus,* the journal of malacology published by the Philadelphia Academy of Natural Sciences. Now Henderson's friends collaborated to complete this index as a memorial to their fellow "conch." William Dall edited the some eighty thousand citations, and George Clapp and Bryant Walker published it. The *Index* was "affectionately" dedicated to "John Brooks Henderson, ardent lover of nature and investigator of tropical American faunas, steadfast friend; comrade of many excursions afield, and nights around the campfire."

CHAPTER FOURTEEN

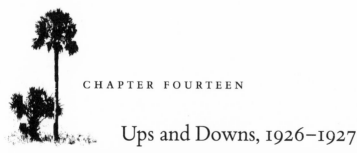

Ups and Downs, 1926–1927

He exerted an extraordinarily beneficent influence on the lower Florida community and has left a treasured memory behind him.

Thomas Barbour, former director,
Harvard University Museum of Comparative Zoology

TIDES OF CHANGE

One night in January 1926, robbers sacked Simpson's hammock, making off with many of his finest specimens. Elsie Picot was there that morning and recalled the old naturalist's fury, "He stomped up and down and swore. Oh! He swore like a sailor! The air turned blue."[1] Simpson wrote to Fairchild, "Thieves broke in and stole a thousand dollars worth of my beloved orchids and air plants. . . . There are not 25 orchids left in the hammock. This is the pay for denying myself all these years in order that I might make a garden and throw it open to the public. Christian and civilized hogs do such things; the natives of Borrioboola Gha would not be so infernally mean."[2]

Later that month, Simpson was hospitalized for a cataract operation on his left eye, the one he used with the microscope. While recuperating, he told Fairchild that "a flood of such brilliant and beautiful light pours into that eye that it seems I never saw." His vision was not well defined, but he agreed, "It is about a million times better than being blind!"[3]

His surgeon was Dr. M. P. Deboe, a noted Miami ophthalmologist. Both Deboe and his wife were outdoor people, and they occasionally took field trips with Simpson. Dr. Deboe treated Simpson for the remainder of Charles's life, but he never sent a bill.

Changes were taking place too quickly for the nearly eighty-year-old Simpson. "Everyone agrees that the boom in Florida is busted . . . but the papers do not say that—They call it 'readjustment' but it means that the 'binder boys'[4] are starved out and have gone. . . . It means that the land that sold at any price its owner asked for it isn't worth one half today," he told Fairchild.[5] Charles Deering had sold his estate at Buena Vista to a land developer, reportedly for $30,600 an acre, and had built a new villa on the bay at Cutler Ridge, twenty miles to the south. His exotic birds and animals were shipped off to zoos, and, although some of the finest palms and rare plants were reestablished on his new estate, many of his tropical fruit trees were destroyed. Bemoaning the loss, Simpson wrote Fairchild, "The company that bought it is murdering it in a dreadful fashion. They . . . literally slaughtered most of his magnificent mango and avocado grove, chopping it down and burning it as if it was a wild scrub. I never saw such devastation. . . . And C.D. has taken back the 245 acres he so nobly gave to the U.S. Dept. of Agriculture and sold it in with the rest to be destroyed. Bah! Rats!"[6]

Fairchild, too, agonized to see the Deering groves and choice plant specimens destroyed.

> Mr. Charles Deering's Buena Vista Estate, where beautiful canals wound through the mangrove forest and beneath overarching coconut palms, contained a collection of succulents planted by Dr. John K. Small and an arboretum of rare trees, many of them supplied by our Office . . . yet it all disappeared overnight in the boom of 1925 and 1926. Even the magnificent *Ficus nitida,* the wonder of the Miami region, was torn to pieces and dragged out by tractors as the entire place was turned into a ghastly waste of suburban lots. This wrecked land is a tragic memorial to those crazy mad days in which the trees of the "hammocks" went down, destroyed by an army of road builders, carpenters and cement mixers.[7]

Simpson sought solace from his changing world in the hammock, his "holy of holies," where he could "retire alone from the strife, the cares and worries of the world."[8] He had formed a rustic bench of native limestone and cement.

> In this seat I sit sometimes and visit with my plants, the fish and tadpoles which inhabit the pool and the woodsy people that come to

npson, ca. 1925, in his hammock, where he could "retire alone from the strife, the cares
l worries of the world." Courtesy of the Historical Association of Southern Florida.

it. Mud wasps hang about the water and make up balls of limy mud which they bear off to build their nests with—without even asking permission.

The pool is a great resort for butterflies. . . . Conspicuous among them is the Heliconious charitonious, a lovely, slender-winged species of a deep black color with diagonal yellow stripes. Sometimes fifty or more of them may be seen on the wing about the pool, moving with a peculiar trembling flight. When at rest they hang themselves up by the feet, allowing the folded wings to hang down as though they were dead. I have frequently seen twenty of them hanging thus together on the long moss or a dead twig, and I have no doubt that this is adopted as a means of protection.[9]

The once tireless field explorer was slowing down, but he was determined to complete some projects before he "turned up his toes." One of these was a paper on *Liguus.* In May 1926 he approached Paul Bartsch. "I believe you said you thought the National Museum might publish my paper on the genus *Liguus* in Florida provided I would furnish the figures. I have had . . . a glass made for [my left eye] and am now able to read and write so I want to finish this paper which I have been getting data for forty years."[10]

Another project that consumed his attention at this time was a new edition of *Ornamental Gardening.* The first printing had sold out, and as soon as his eyesight improved he began to revise it, including information about the freeze of February 1917, expanding the section on native plants, and adding plant lists and suggestions for gardeners in North and Central Florida. Describing it to Fairchild, he wrote, "I have a magnificent lot of photos for it—about 80 full plates . . . it will be a stunner and you should read it with smoked glasses."[11]

HURRICANE

All in all, 1926 was not a very good year. On September 17 the weather services reported a tropical storm headed in from the West Indies. Overcast skies and wind gusts throughout the day hinted of the coming storm, and the old-timers boarded up their homes and stocked essential provisions. New residents, however, having no prior experience with tropical hurricanes, were unprepared when the big blow struck just after midnight. Simpson had no doubt that it was the most severe storm Miami had experienced in a hundred years or more.[12] Its core was some thirty miles across, extending from Lemon City to Homestead. The Miami weather station's wind speed instrument recorded 125 miles per hour before it blew away, but Simpson felt sure that occasional puffs of wind reached a velocity of 150 miles per hour.

Some compared the storm's strength to a severe hurricane in 1876, but Simpson backed up his claim that it was the worst storm in a hundred years by his patient observations. In an article published in the *Miami Herald* he explained,

> I have been making it a point since I came to south Florida to examine the fallen trunks of our pines and wherever they were chopped or sawed off to count the rings of growth. These trees make a single growth a year during the warm season . . . and at this time a thin, dark ring is formed. Each of these . . . marks a year's growth and I have invariably found that the larger of our pines had from 90 odd to 125 such growth rings. This shows that a large proportion of our forest trees are a century old, that during that time they have withstood all storms, that they were not blown down in 1876 or any year since.[13]

While many historians wrote about the devastation this storm left behind—the dead and injured, the destroyed homes and commercial buildings, the loss of essential services—Simpson assessed the hurricane's impact on the environment. He described the effect of the shifting winds on trees. "Whenever there was a strong gust they were pushed far over and with any lull they moved back . . . so that . . . their roots were twisted and broken, they were lifted up and thrown down until they were well-nigh destroyed."[14]

Twenty-five large oaks in his hammock and many of his ornamental palms and exotic trees were toppled. Those still standing were stripped of their leaves, and their branches were broken. On the bayfront the giant mangroves were so torn up that most were either killed outright or so seriously injured that they died later. "In all my experience with hurricanes in Florida and the American tropics I have never seen a forest of mangroves seriously injured," he commented.[15]

Simpson recognized the deadly effect of airborne electrical charges on trees in such a storm. His studies of classical meteorology and his observations in the Florida Keys and the Caribbean islands of the aftermath of hurricanes led him to believe that many trees eventually died from these charges. "A vast amount of silent electricity passed from above into the earth during the progress of the hurricane and the trees acted as conductors for this until they were killed. Practically all the older pines in and around Lemon City were electrocuted without doubt. I am informed that during the night Biscayne Bay was covered with a great sheet of fire."[16]

Eight of the windows in Simpson's home blew in during the storm. Flora mopped up the water while Charles covered the openings as best he could. His house weathered the storm better than his plants did. "My roof, which is of shingles went thru with the least possible loss and did not leak and the damage to the whole building was not $25. . . . This house I planned and constructed with brain and hands and I am proud to tell you that every door and window fits perfectly since they have dried out and there is no sign of the building being racked."[17]

Six weeks after the storm he wrote Fairchild,

> It looks in the hammock and grounds as if a herd of colossal elephants had fought over it and then some Brobdingnagian had stirred up the whole with a stick. . . . [N]ot a fragment of boathouse or pavillion was left. I hear that pieces of them have been found just this side of Ocala. . . . I look for trees and am not sure where they were. Yesterday I saw a small Bauhinia three feet high covered with new leaves breaking out and it recalled the dove which bore to Noah an olive

> branch from a drowned world. . . . I see this morning other things are showing young foliage but there is so little left to grow. . . . Flora and I don't get time to weep.[18]

Simpson acknowledged the benefits of such storms.

> The hurricanes not only destroy but they build up. They wash away land in places and pile it up in others. . . . In the West Indies they break or uproot trees whose seeds are carried down streams, swept onward across the Gulf Stream, and are finally landed and planted on our shores. They carry birds, butterflies and other insects on their wings, . . . and the minute seeds of ferns and orchids and all are landed and established on our shores. They are ravaging destroyers but noble builders.[19]

A downside of the hurricane was its effect on real estate. The parties that had agreed to buy the Sentinels wanted the Simpsons to "throw off a large amount of the agreed price" because damage from the hurricane depreciated the value of the property. Simpson wrote Fairchild, "They have been backing and filling for quite a while, threatening to throw up the place if we didn't give them up a lot of their notes which we did, . . . finally giving it up just as a terrific tax was due."[20] Property values had hit bottom, but tax assessments were unchanged since boom times. Simpson had to borrow money for taxes just when he had drained his bank account to pay for the new edition of *Ornamental Gardening.*

The twin pines that towered over the Simpsons' home were another casualty of the hurricane. Six months after the storm he mourned their loss. "Both of the great Sentinels in front of our home are done, one being blown down by the hurricane and the other died so I got it down and rolled the two together and burned them up root and branch. It was a terrible ordeal for these brave trees had stood over and watched me for a quarter of a century. Without a doubt the salt spray did a lot of damage, but the main trouble was [that] the taller stuff was electrocuted."[21]

A dividend of the hurricane was the boost it gave to the Florida garden club movement. Restoring South Florida's image as "the land of flowers" became a patriotic duty. Miami Beach had been particularly hard hit, and, with the tourist season at hand, the chamber of commerce called on the Miami Beach Garden Club to spearhead a campaign to replant gardens destroyed by salt water. A task force of twenty-two women took to the streets to visit homeowners and advise them regarding what to plant and how to care for damaged trees and shrubs. Thousands of coconut palms and other tropical trees were planted along the streets, and ten thousand or more plants in paper pots were distributed door-to-door to provide a burst of color when the tourists arrived. In Miami, where the South Miami Garden Club had just been formed, its president, Mabel Dorn, was enlisted to join with the Junior Chamber of Commerce in a "beautification contest." New garden clubs springing up throughout South Florida embraced similar projects to rejuvenate the wind- and water-ravaged landscape.

At this time Simpson recalled entertaining a "cavalcade of women members of a garden club. . . . I gave them armloads of cuttings and seeds (for heavens sake don't tell the inspectors) and they were the happiest lot of ducks I ever saw," he wrote Fairchild.[22] In another correspondence he noted the change in attitude he found among the club members. "You know the women organized 17 garden clubs here and they are working like steam engines raising plants, experimenting, . . . giving in experience and exchanging plants. I think I have talked to garden clubs and otherwise fully 25 times since the first of the year, always to eagerly interested listeners who generally take notes and ask lots of questions."[23]

HAMMOCK RESTORATION HONORS SIMPSON

"Jungle Park" was the last publicly owned remnant of the original hammock that once clothed the entire bayfront of what was now Miami. It was home to several varieties of Florida tree snails and contained many plants of West Indian origin. Now the public was using it as a dump for derelict cars and rubbish of all kinds. Vagrants slept there at night, building campfires and trampling the vegetation. Simpson had talked to Gerry Curtis and the "boys" in the Miami Parks Department about this sorry situation and hoped something could be done about it. Curtis, looking for a fitting tribute to this old friend of the parks department, suggested to the city commission that the park be renamed.

> I respectfully request that the City Park located at South Miami Avenue and 15th Road be dedicated to Charles Torrey Simpson and that your Honorable Body pass the necessary resolution to call this public area Simpson Park.
>
> Your Honorable Body is familiar with the work that Mr. Simpson has done, not only in and around Miami but over the entire State. He has in the past been of valuable assistance to your park Superintendent and is always ready to give advice pertaining to our native and exotic flora. He has been especially interested in preserving for all time our

> native hammocks and with this in mind I feel that it would indeed be appropriate to dedicate the only public native hammock within the incorporated limits of a Florida city to Charles Torrey Simpson.

Subsequently the commission, by resolution, named the park in honor of Charles Torrey Simpson, "father of all south Florida naturalists and in recognition of the service he rendered this area."[24]

DOCTORAL ROBES

The University of Miami, chartered in 1926 by the state of Florida at the crest of the real estate boom, had opened its doors in Coral Gables, George Merrick's "city beautiful." Hardly had its first student been enrolled when the twin disasters of hurricane and the Depression engulfed southern Florida. Nonetheless, the fledgling school forged ahead, and, in 1927, as the first commencement approached, plans were made to present its first honorary doctorate. Then-president B. F. Ashe recalled that they "searched south Florida for the man who had made the most noteworthy contribution in science or letters, and the unanimous choice was [Charles Torrey Simpson]."[25]

Responding to a telegram from Dr. Ashe inviting him to join the academic procession, Simpson replied, "I will certainly be there and I cannot tell you how pleased and proud I will be to receive this recognition at your hands. For a good many years many have insisted on calling me "Doctor," a title to which I am not entitled and though I have explained that I had no such title, it is quite generally applied. If you are kind enough to give it to me then I shall feel that I am no longer sailing under false colors."[26]

Simpson's path to academic recognition had been a long one. Though he had distinguished himself in two divergent fields, malacology and horticulture, he felt keenly his lack of formal education, and his honorary doctorate of science raised his self-esteem and fulfilled his greatest expectation. John Gifford, associated with the University of Miami for many years as a professor of tropical forestry and conservation, commented, "He has often expressed to me his joy in receiving this degree from the University, representative of this region in which he had worked for so many years and which he knew and loved better than any other section on earth."[27]

Sharing the good news with Fairchild, Simpson wrote, "If you had heard Dr. Ashe talk to me as he put his hands on me you would have thought the old man had done something worthwhile. There was a fine

Simpson after receiving his honorary doctorate at University of Miami, 1927. Courtesy of the Historical Association of Southern Florida.

reception at the great hotel. I sneaked away, glad it was over for I don't like the limelight. Strangely enough, now nearly everyone calls me just plain 'mister!' "[28]

Shortly after the commencement ceremonies, Simpson wrote to Paul Bartsch about his paper on the Florida tree snails, enclosing a snapshot of himself in his academic robes. "The enclosed photo tells its own story. The University wanted to make me a Doctor of Science and I submitted. They made a big hurrah over it," he concluded.[29] Enclosed in the letter was another check for $750 to assist in the publication of Henderson's work.

The long-delayed second edition of *Ornamental Gardening* finally came out that summer. As he explained to Fairchild, "I think whoever was in charge this time was addicted to booze and there has been every kind of delay and bad work."[30] Self-published, it was dedicated "To the women of the Florida Garden Clubs who have faithfully, intelligently and effectively labored to beautify our State."

Fairchild was out of the country most of that year, but he returned to Coconut Grove long enough to celebrate Christmas and begin plans to build a new house at the Kampong. He wrote Simpson in response to a piece the latter had published in support of the beleaguered Miami area. "I am conscious of feeling proud to have known you and worked side by side with you for this great country of southern Florida. Marian tells me that you and Mrs. Simpson are invited to come and have a meal with us alone soon. I hope you can come. If you can't I will come to the mountain. I hope the mountain can come here, though."[31]

CHAPTER FIFTEEN

In Defense of the Everglades, 1927–1930

Man is merely a custodian of many things and when he passes on he leaves everything behind, even the ruins of what he destroyed.

John Clayton Gifford

A DRIVING FORCE

The need to preserve Florida's native landscape was the dominant message now in Simpson's writings and public appearances. His first suggestion that a part of lower Florida be set aside as a national park may have been in a talk he gave early on in that "cradle of Dade's culture," the Lemon City Library.[1] The theme was reiterated in his first book, *In Lower Florida Wilds,* published in 1920. Describing what he called "the south shore of the mainland" or "the great southwest wild," which included Flamingo, Cape Sable, and the Cuthbert Lake area, he commented, "This entire region . . . should be set apart by the federal government."[2] Florida historian Charlton Tebeau, tracing the origin of the park idea, said of Simpson's influence that "in time he went over nearly all of the ground of the proposed park, visiting the area as much as twice a year for thirty years and never ceasing his advocacy of a means to preserve remnants of the wild life he saw disappearing so rapidly."[3]

Gifford, Fairchild, Small, and other conservation-minded men also recognized the threat to this unique natural region and for some years had talked about setting it aside as a park. Then Ernest R. Coe, a landscape architect, arrived on the Miami scene in the late twenties and took hold of the idea, making the creation of a national park in the Everglades his top priority. One of the first doors he knocked on was Simpson's. He urged the old naturalist to throw his weight behind the cause and persuaded him to bring the plight of Florida's "Everglades Paradise" to the

public.

Simpson's voice carried authority. As a longtime resident of Florida, he had known the Glades before men and machines had altered the natural flow of water, changing historic weather patterns, and primeval habitats of wildlife. In a *Miami News* front-page article headlined "Everglades Paradise Wrecked," he wrote,

> In the good old days, say the beginning of the 20th century, the Everglades lay, a vast and beautiful sheet of swamp, covered, for the most part, with water and herbaceous vegetation. During the rainy season Okeechobee filled to overflowing, spilled its water over the surrounding region in every direction. . . .
>
> The growth was in many places rank, even magnificent; there was no trouble from fire; the rain which fell copiously during the wet season flooded everything. . . .
>
> It was a garden of flowers, with many species of surpassing beauty, the stately red lily, the queen of our wild plants, the matchless fragrant white swamp lily, and the spider lilies, the tall canna with its yellow blossoms and the taller purple flowered Thalias. Here were noble grasses, the great plume grass, the immense clusters of the world-wide rush . . . and everywhere cattails of three species. There was a host of lovely terrestrial orchids.
>
> . . . [T]here were many blue flowers, the lobelias, a Ruelia, a pickerel weed, a blue-eyed grass . . . and the splendid Florida bell flower whose dazzling indigo blossoms boldly faced the sun. . . .
>
> The entire region teemed with glorious animal life. Alligators haunted it and the crocodile and manatee were found around its southern and eastern borders. It was and still is the only spot in the United States inhabited by the West Indian land crab. Mink, otter, deer, the raccoon and a variety of small mammals were common. In its waters flourished that strange relic of perhaps 500,000,000 years ago, the gar pike, with its unequal tail, its flint-covered coat of armor and ball and socket vertebra. . . .
>
> It was the birds that gave color and glory to the whole. I cannot describe them, they covered the 'glades by millions, roseate spoonbills, the saintly herons and egrets, that dream of color the flamingo, a

host of ducks and pelicans and gulls. They filled the air, they crowded the water, this was their natural feeding ground as they made their annual migration to and from the tropics. Only a few are now left of the uncounted millions; they are mostly a lovely memory.[4]

That the Everglades were essential as a habitat for water birds, alligators, and other animals and served as a food depot for migratory birds was obvious to Simpson. What troubled him was what was unknown about the Everglades. "No one knew how much rain fell in a year or whether it could be gotten off the land in time to save crops. There was absolute ignorance about the soil, no one could tell what it would produce. As to the possibility that it could burn up, no one had ever thought of that."[5]

In what was described as a "light, quavering voice," Simpson gave frequent talks about the Everglades in person and on the radio. One evening he addressed several thousand people in Bayfront Park. "I gave the developers hell and have been petted a lot about it," he told Fairchild.[6]

To bring the plight of this region to the attention of the public and Congress, the Tropical Everglades National Park Association was formed, on December 12, 1928, with Fairchild as president and Ernest Coe as executive secretary. The genesis of the park was Royal Palm State Park, which had been established on Paradise Key by the Federation of Florida Women's Clubs twelve years before. Now the federation joined the movement and offered to add its approximately four thousand acres to the national park.

Writing to Pilsbry to say that tree snails had been found in hammocks south of the newly opened Tamiami Trail, Simpson commented, "We are making a tremendous effort to get the U.S. to set this region off for a National park and bird sanctuary and so far things seem to be favorable. The last estimate I have seen is to try for an area of about 2200 square miles and that would take in about everything not occupied south of the Trail, including most of the hammocks."[7]

SUMMING UP THE TREE SNAILS

Soon after writing to Pilsbry, Simpson's final scientific paper, "The Florida Tree Snails of the Genus *Liguus*," was published by the National Museum. Twenty-five pages long, it contained a map of lower Florida and the Keys and three color plates. In it he reiterated for the scientific community the theories he had expressed for the popular reader in *Out of Doors in Florida* and *In Lower Florida Wilds.* These included the concept that the Lower Keys, from Key West to Little Pine Key, were originally one large island; that the original *Liguus* had migrated from Cuba to the "one great island" sealed to seaborne branches and logs; and that plants and animals had traveled to the mainland over a land bridge that had existed from the region of the Matecumbe Keys across the Florida Bay to the mainland near Joe Kemp Keys.

> I have made a rather careful search in Florida having tramped the East Coast Railroad several times from Key Largo . . . to Key West at its terminus and back again. I have visited practically every one of these islands which have ever had *Liguus* and made collections on them. On the mainland I have been in nearly every locality in which these snails were found. . . . In all I have some kind of *Liguus* material from over 300 Floridian localities, most of which I have personally collected. For nearly 26 years I have had an opportunity to study these snails in my own hammock within a hundred feet of my door. Long before I began to collect (1882) man had wrought great destruction to the hammocks in which they live so that certain forms are on the verge of extinction and in some localities all evidence of them was obliterated, and at present the *Liguus* are almost exterminated in Florida. Great areas of forest have been recently cut in Cuba in order that sugar cane might be grown, and it is probable that it will be a short time only when these snails will be wiped out entirely in many localities in that island. Very much of the evidence necessary to the complete study of them is therefore missing.[8]

Simpson was not the only investigator of his time, but he was one of the earliest. He also investigated more territory, authoring in all seventeen of the then known fifty-two forms of *Liguus.*

A ZEST FOR LIFE

Publicly, Simpson vowed it was "time to quit," but privately his mind overflowed with plans for collecting trips, arrangements for speaking, and a new book—to be called *Florida Wild Life*—he had been asked to write for Macmillan. He often led parties from the garden clubs on jaunts to collect violets, ferns, wild orchids, and swamp plants. Helen Muir in *Miami U.S.A.* recalled one Saturday when he took nearly a hundred eager nature lovers on a wading trip to a cypress swamp, "wearing his faded khaki trousers, torn shirt, and canvas shoes, and carrying a stained bamboo staff. . . . At eighty-four his step was as light, his eye as sharp, and his kindliness as bright as ever."[9]

Though well into his eighties and a distinguished Florida personality,

Simpson kept to his old ways, maintaining his house and grounds with his own hands. In September 1929 a "slight" hurricane blew in, and, while the winds were no more than fifty miles an hour, the storm was a grim reminder of the earlier catastrophe. He wrote Fairchild,

> A good many people are discouraged; some have gone away and others are talking of leaving. . . . The women of the clubs, garden and otherwise, held a meeting in the University hall, Coral Gables, the other day and they sent for me to come and brace them up as some of them were pretty blue. I am generally scared when I stand up to talk in public but I was full of the burden of my subject and I think I never talked so well. Anyhow they cheered and cheered and when it was over there was an ovation.[10]

The Fairchilds' new house at the Kampong had been completed earlier in the year, and before Christmas Simpson wrote again to Fairchild, twitting him a bit about his new home and telling him about entertaining visiting "park executives."

> We lunched at your house and I carried off your chimney as a souvenir. I think that was all the damage we did. The park people couldn't believe that coconuts grew and bore good fruit, that mahogany, Silk cotton, Royal poincianas and Royal palms grew just as they do in the tropics. It especially doubled up the California crowd. Mr. Frank Shearer of Los Angeles kept saying they all grew in L.A. but finally when I asked how large they got to be he said "O, we raise them in tubs." . . . I want to assure you this park meeting did lots of good and the pack made about ten thousand pages of notes.[11]

An unpublished manuscript recovered from Simpson's house after his death tells about an overnight camping trip to Marco Channel with the Callahan sisters circa 1930. "The Callahans proceeded to make camp and Mrs. S. and the old man looked for driftwood for a fire. . . . With a closed car, side tent, double bed that extended over the seats plus two cots, an abundance of bedding, camp stools, wash basin, stove, full set of cooking utensils, even a mirror and face powder, all that was needed for a first class housekeeping establishment but a cat and a thermometer!"[12]

It was a far cry of the days of tramping with little more than a blanket, tin cup, and hunk of bologna carried in a gunnysack, but the joys of collecting were undimmed. "Mrs. Simpson and I wandered along the beach like a couple of happy children, picking up fine shells and watching the antics of the various marine crabs. . . . Again I felt the thrill of delight which it seems to me can only come to the man or woman who is turned loose among the natural history material in which he or she is so deeply interested."[13]

A newspaper columnist reports encountering Simpson at about this time on a Lake Okeechobee steamer.

> The lake was placid. Not a sail in sight. I turned from nature to man for diversion and . . . my eye finally rested upon a man sitting alone. A man of advanced years. . . . His outing costume might have been passed on to him by Kit Carson, so frayed and tattered was it. His hat was of the battered, nondescript variety and adorned with a few game fish flies. His face and hands were tanned to a chocolate brown. It was all too apparent that he had not had a shave for two weeks at least. . . . This wild man of Borneo or Florida proved to be none other than Dr. Charles Torrey Simpson, naturalist, world-famous conchologist; for years attached to the Smithsonian Institute at Washington; the greatest authority on the fauna and flora of Florida; author of "*In Lower Florida Wilds*" and other scientific works.[14]

CONGRESS INVESTIGATES THE PARK

The Everglades National Park project was being well received, and in February 1930 Congress authorized an investigation of the region proposed to be set aside. National park personnel and specialists in natural history descended on South Florida to survey the area by auto, houseboat, and even aloft in the Goodyear blimp. Simpson and John Gifford teamed up to guide the visitors on a boat trip in the Everglades, and Gifford later recalled their conversation.

> He always held that we are custodians of these wild creatures of all kinds both plant and animal and that it is our duty to deliver them to posterity in as good if not better condition than we found them. . . . He blamed many of the ills of today to speed. He always argued that the sense of saving time by speed depended upon the use to which the time thus saved was put and that speed destroyed the local concentration of business and tended to the development of big far distant centers of exchange. Perhaps he was right.[15]

In March, Simpson had surgery for the cataracts on his right eye, and his post office box overflowed with well-wishes. The deference accorded him in his declining years and his pleasure at working with the garden clubs had made him a happy man. "When they call the old man 'the daddy of the Garden clubs' it makes me think that life is worth while after all."[16] He admitted, however, to being fixed in his habits, irritated by small things such as a different spoon or fork at the table, or having his bed turned around. He was still inclined to be touchy and on one occasion took issue with Fairchild on the merits of the crotons, which Simpson described as "gorgeously colored plants . . . as much a part of the general scheme as are the bright feathers of parrots and peacocks or the noble leaves of palms."[17]

Fairchild wrote affectionately from his "Biological Nucleus" in Baddeck, Nova Scotia, to smooth Simpson's feathers. "Dear Friend; I didnt intend to hurt your feelings by my tirade against the crotons. I knew you would forgive me in the end though we might have a grand old scrap over them at first, but it was farthest from my thoughts to fletten you out as you say my sentences about them did."[18]

Simpson responded by return mail, picking up Fairchild's excuse that his preference was a matter of "taste" and expounding on the subject at length. The letter also brought the news that Elva Perrine, a sculptress who had also modeled Herbert Hoover, had asked Simpson to sit for a full-size clay bust. "It is a classic and I am so proud about it I have cut many of my old acquaintances."[19]

The Congressional junket to the Everglades had borne fruit, and later that year Representative Ruth Bryan Owen from Florida introduced a bill advocating the establishment of Everglades National Park. The hearing brought several days of testimony from national park service personnel, academic specialists in natural science, leaders of youth organizations, and the Audubon Society. Paul Bartsch spoke on the geology of the area, and Fairchild affirmed the region as unique to North America, comparing it to tropical regions he had visited throughout the world. Ernest Coe showed the congressional representatives lantern slides of Cape Sable's sandy beaches, roseate spoonbills, snowy egrets, giant turtles, and jungly hammocks, while Howard Kelly of Johns Hopkins University entertained the assembly with a live king snake and presented Ruth Bryan Owen with a collection of Florida tree snail shells. Seventy-eight pages of testimony in favor of making a vast nature preserve in lower Florida were recorded, and, as a result, it was approved as suitable for national park purposes. Simpson was overjoyed at the news, though he would not live to see the park dedicated seventeen years later, in ceremonies in the town of Everglades with President Harry S. Truman as the principal speaker.

CHAPTER SIXTEEN

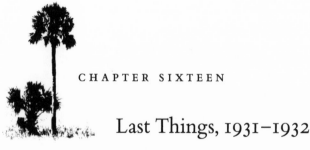

Last Things, 1931–1932

Dear Earth, place once of my abiding.

Ase in The Sojourner, *Marjorie Kinnan Rawlings*

AN INNER-CITY HAMMOCK

Soon after Jungle Park was renamed Simpson Park by the Miami City Commission in 1927, the Parks Department began restoration of Simpson Park. Trash was removed, plants replaced, and native trees planted. Simpson lent a hand with advice, provided plant materials, and contributed a bit of cash for extras.

In April 1931 about two hundred persons gathered in the new city park for its dedication. On the speaker's platform with the Simpsons were David Fairchild, the main speaker; the mayor of Miami; a representative from the garden clubs; and others who had been involved in the project. Simpson, uncomfortable in a stiff-wing collar, four-in-hand tie, and dress suit, claimed he would rather be "stood up and shot" than undergo such "flummery."

In his address to the group, Fairchild recognized the core of Simpson's studies—the old naturalist's lifelong pursuit of answers to questions about the origin of things: "We are facing today as never before in the history of the race, . . . an unsolved problem, a problem which man has not yet been brave enough or enthusiastic enough to solve—evolution. When you think of Dr. Charles Torrey Simpson working in his little laboratory for forty years, just remember that he had in the back of his mind always the problem of evolution, the change in things he saw about him."[1]

With the appreciation he was receiving from many quarters, the cynicism and bitterness that sometimes underlaid Simpson's thought in younger years fell away. Writing to thank Fairchild for his words at the dedication, Simpson commented, "I see a wonderful difference today in those who come from the packs that were here 15 years ago and it fills my heart with joy. So many are actually thirsting for knowledge that it makes me wish I was young and strong again."[2]

"The garden club folks" had asked Simpson to start a tree study club, and in preparing for it he inventoried the native and naturalized trees and large shrubs around his place. To his surprise, he found that they numbered about ninety! "So I am going to be a schoolmaster and I look forward to it with a lot of satisfaction," he told Fairchild.[3]

A VISIT FROM PILSBRY

Pilsbry had been in town just prior to the park dedication and mailed Simpson a packet of *Liguus* shells and a brief note to say how "keenly" he enjoyed his visit. "I hope that the park dedication went off smoothly. It sure was a trying ordeal for a modest naturalist," he commented. Simpson rejoined by acknowledging that he had "got through it with only the loss of a limb." Thanking Pilsbry for the ligs, he wrote wistfully, "Our visit seemed like old Davenport days and this made me young again; in fact my few gray hairs have become glossy black. I hope you may come again."[4]

The friendship between Simpson and Pilsbry was of long standing, dating back to the days of their youth. In fact, Pilsbry was his oldest living friend-colleague. Simpson's closest comrades had always been younger—Pilsbry by sixteen years, Reasoner by seventeen years, Fairchild by twenty-three years, and Henderson by twenty-five years. Simpson's diversified interests and ironic sense of humor gave him a youthful manner, and even in old age he retained the characteristic enthusiasm and eagerness that had endeared him to his friends.

The biographer encountered several stories about Simpson that suggest that he was a man of strong passions: the rumor that he joined the navy because of a "muss" with a young woman; his romantic involvement with his partner's wife in Bradenton; a remark that he was a "ladies' man"; and gossip that at seventy-five or eighty he had engaged in an affair with someone in the garden clubs. No doubt he enjoyed women, and it showed in the "sparkle" in his eye and the "spring" in his step. Those who knew him as mentor found no dried-up pedagogue spouting lifeless facts but a person who saw all of life as animated and, whether animal or vegetable, sharing the common goal of mating and reproducing.

Pilsbry sent Simpson some snapshots he had taken on his April visit to the Sentinels. "One of them looks as if you have just seen a large Liguus," he joked.[5] He also sent a group picture taken at a recent meeting of conchologists, which caused Simpson to fire off a postcard describing the bunch as "a wise looking lot of guys. . . . There is to be a big blowout here at our place June 3rd on the occasion of my 85th birthday. Come along and bring a jug of cider."[6]

EIGHTY-FIVE CANDLES

About one hundred guests came to the party, which was held on the lawn at the Sentinels. Fairchild had composed seventeen verses extolling the "great giant of the woods" and acknowledging his friend's understanding of "changes of kind and form and space, changes which he has always seen." Pilsbry was not able to be present, but he sent cordial greetings.

> In fact, I may be allowed to say, affectionate greetings. I don't know what you were up to in the first thirty-five years or so of your career, but I can testify that the last forty odd years have been full of strenuous labor in the cause of Science. I can congratulate you upon the recognition of the value of your work which has been given freely of late years, both in Europe and America. Wherever fresh water bivalves are studied, it is acknowledged that your work began a new era in that department, and outside of this you have been doing a full man's work, intellectual and physical, right along.[7]

This was high praise indeed from Pilsbry, who was acknowledged as the nation's most distinguished living malacologist.

A "MUST" FOR FLORIDA NATURE LOVERS

Macmillan brought out *Florida Wild Life: Observations on the Flora and Fauna of the State and the Influence of Climate and Environment on Their Development* in the spring of 1932 at a price of $2.50. The book, with more than 200 pages and 44 illustrations, was dedicated "To the women of the Miami region garden clubs, whose generosity has made possible its publication." *Florida Wild Life* contained new material on "The Work of Hurricanes" and "Florida Climate," including stories drawn from Simpson's personal experience and historical facts on frosts and freezes in southern Florida. These subjects were sidestepped by local publications because they were considered a deterrent to tourism and development interests, but Simpson met them head-on, concluding with a story about a woman who told her husband after a hurricane that she wanted to go somewhere else. He replied, "We have 360 days a year of the finest weather I ever saw and about five that are really bad. If you can tell me of any better place I will talk to you about moving."[8]

His new book covered a broad range of natural history topics: butterflies, tropical fish, Florida's golden spider, bird migration, frogs, crocodiles, alligators, song and water birds, even weeds and cockroaches. Seed dispersal, plant growth habits, protective coloration of fish and mollusks, how plants solve problems for survival, the evolution of leaves, and the dynamic nature of the universe all are touched on. One chapter was devoted to "A Naturalist Paradise," a description of his bayfront property. Here he expresses his innermost thoughts about nature.

> It is wonderfully quiet in the hammock; though the wind may roar outside yet in here one almost seems to be in a cellar; there is scarcely a breath of air stirring. At rare intervals one may hear the dropping of a twig or the chirr of some insect; a rabbit may run through the forest making a gentle pit-a-pat on the fallen leaves, but it is often possible to sit for an hour without hearing the slightest sound. . . .
>
> Into [this hammock] I can retire alone from the strife, the cares and worries of the world; here it seems to me, I can mingle with the very life of the forest; here I can come to confession, face to face with nature, and I am taken into the confidence of it all; here I become a part, however small, of the Great Scheme of Things.

Florida Wild Life introduced for the uninitiated the "great Southwest wild" being proposed for the new national tropical park, explaining its geological origin, its flat, rocky prairies, its shallow, brackish lakes, and the twisted labyrinths that conceal its innermost reaches from all but the most determined explorer. In a requiem for the Florida of old, Simpson warns of the consequences of wasting natural resources.

> Mankind seem to be almost crazy to destroy, claiming that what is done is necessary in order that food and the necessities of life may be produced and that money may be gained. Today the earth is glutted with wheat; we cannot dispose of our oranges, . . . there is sugar enough to sweeten all mankind excepting those who have it to sell; oil flows and gas blows from wells in a mad waste as if there was

enough for the supply of the world forever. Yet we are ready to destroy the forests, we will spend untold millions in draining swamps, in building great dams for irrigation in order that we may produce more. And when the land is impoverished, when the gas and oil have given out, . . . what then? Will the chemists, the electricians, the engineers supply our wants? Can they bring back the beautiful wild birds and animals that we have wantonly destroyed? All the skill, all the science in the world cannot revive a dead animal; they cannot restore a single species of plant that has been exterminated. . . .

They are gone, gone forever, these beautiful innocent wild birds and animals, the glorious forests, the wide untouched stretches of swamp, the peace and holiness of the Everglades. They are the victims of greed, of folly, of unbelievable brutishness and cruelty, of that strange desire in the heart of man to overrun, to trample out and mercilessly destroy. . . .

But let us not ring down the curtain in utter despair. . . . Within the last few years there has come an awakening. . . . And thanks to the splendid work of Ernest Coe, Dr. Fairchild and a few others, there is a good prospect that we may have a really great tropical park. . . . If this project carries, our children and children's children will have opportunity to see and possess at least a remnant of the wild life and natural beauty which has been so wantonly wasted and destroyed. Verily light is beginning to shine through the darkness.[9]

Florida Wild Life was received with delight by devotees of the natural world. The *New York Times* reviewer wrote, "One needs to read only a few pages to feel assured that here is a man who writes fascinatingly about the outdoors immediately around him because he loves and knows intimately every square foot of it, loves it so well that its growths of tree and plant become in his feeling almost human."[10] The *Boston Transcript* noted, "Out of his wide experience in research and investigation and his long residence in the State, Mr. Simpson reveals the many curious things done by wild growth under the influence of climate and environment."[11] Florida reviews hailed it as a "treasure-house of information," a must "for the library of every nature-lover who visits that region," and noted the author's untiring efforts to preserve the Everglades as a tropical national park.[12] Replying to a letter from John Small that cautiously praised the book, Simpson wrote, "The book seems to be received very favorably and from all I learn is selling quite well for such rotten financial conditions."[13]

In June 1932 Simpson was terminated from the U.S. Department of Agriculture. He broke the news to Fairchild, who also had been taken off the payroll. "I have been more or less prepared for dismissal as I saw in the *New York Times* that it was to have an overhauling and clear up all who could be spared. Mr. Ryerson wrote me a nice letter and I replied in kind for during all my connection with the department I have received only kindness and courtesy. It is going to make very hard sledding for us, but I hope we can keep out of the poorhouse. I never thought that you would be put out."

Pledging his loyalty to "Friend Fairchild," Simpson continued, "I can say in truth that you are one of three men who have come very close in my life. I never saw you but what I felt a thrill of unexplainable delight and I have only felt the same in the presence of Pliny Reasoner and John B. Henderson, two men who have stood by me through thick and thin."[14]

Gradually too, the signs were gathering of a dismissal of a more final sort. The old naturalist napped on the veranda more often. Loy Morrow, who lived in Simpson's neighborhood as a boy, recalled, "We liked to sneak under the porch and listen to him snore and when he did, it shook the whole house. It was up on stilts, you know." Morrow, who became superintendent of parks for Dade County, remembers Simpson as a kindly old man who told them about the tree snails and other things of interest in the hammock.[15] The final disposition of Simpson's scientific collections became of interest to academic circles. A letter from Charles Schuchert, curator emeritus of Yale University's Peabody Museum of Natural History, a colleague from Simpson's days at the U.S. National Museum, complimented Simpson on his natural history books and advised on the disposition of his shell collection: "I now have finished reading your three books on the natural history of southern Florida, and I enjoyed and profited much from them. . . . In one place I said out loud, 'And he has a collection of 20,000 species of molluscs!' Where is this gem to be landed for permanent keeping? Beware of the small institution, and most of the south that has not yet learned how to keep such treasures."[16] James Sturgis Pray, chairman of Harvard University's School of Landscape Architecture, wrote to suggest that Simpson might wish to entrust his "collection of works on ornamental gardening and plant materials" to Harvard, which he described as having "the third most important research library in the world." [17] These incidents and many other small things impressed on Simpson that his life was pulling up short.

Thoughts of death and the hereafter were evident in his last writings. If he had an image of hell, it was embodied in the giant mahoe tree whose roots and branches spread over nearly an acre of his lowlands. "Below this fine foliage and bloom all is darkness, death, dreariness and decay. Even to penetrate into such an uncanny growth in broad daylight almost gives one a feeling of fear. . . . The thought of becoming lost in such a place amid the maze of stems and decaying wood with rustling land crabs everywhere about one is terrible." [18] Regarding heaven, "I hope when I die I may go to some place where I can see the smooth, gray columns of royals, where I can gaze on their splendid, black-green leaves as they are tossed and shaken in the strong trade wind, where the wonderful leaflets of the coconuts dance and shimmer in the moonlight as they are gently moved by the soft, warm sea breeze." [19]

THE LAST GREAT ADVENTURE

Simpson called mid-winter Florida's "ebb tide . . . the time when the pendulum of life swings lowest." [20] On such a morning, December 17, 1932, he died. Though he had experienced recent attacks of angina and was being treated by Dr. Jay Filipse, his death was unexpected.

The day had begun like any other. He rose early and breakfasted with Flora. They were discussing the gathering of the North Miami Garden Club that had met at the Sentinels the day before. Soon he would rise and go into his study. As honorary chairman of the Florida Malacological Society, he was preparing a paper to be given to the group in January. Without warning, while seated in his chair, he toppled over onto the floor and died almost instantly from a heart attack.[21] Flora called to the neighbors to bring medical help, but nothing could be done. Just a fortnight before, when recuperating from chest pain, he had said to a friend, "When my time comes, I hope it will be quick. . . . My life has been active and I do not wish to linger on without possessing the necessary faculties to get about." [22]

The story of Simpson's death was carried on the front page of the *Miami News* evening edition of December 17. Describing him as "patriarch of the world of naturalists," the writer went on to remark that "for three score years, Dr. Simpson, whose enthusiasm for his work kept him sparkling with boyish exuberance up to the very hour of his death, had been an inspiration alike to co-workers in technical lines, and laymen just starting to browse on the outer fringe of Nature's glories."[23]

Friends were received at the funeral home chapel the day after his death, and the following day his open coffin, surrounded with floral tributes, was placed in the bamboo grove at the Sentinels, where hundreds of mourners gathered for the funeral. A violin solo played by a concealed musician was accompanied by the natural sounds of bamboo stems and palm fronds creaking and whispering in the offshore breeze, a last arboreal symphony for the fallen naturalist. Scriptures were read, prayers offered, and at the end a mile-long motorcar procession accompanied his body to Woodlawn Cemetery.

The *New York Times* noted the passing of this "prominent scientist" in their lead obituary, and the *Bureau County Republican* remembered him as one of the county's "most distinguished sons."[24] In Florida, the Miami press eulogized Simpson, calling him "one of the great men of Miami and America,"[25] citing his accomplishments in the fields of botany and malacology and comparing him to other noted regional naturalists such as John Burroughs, John Muir, and Henri Fabre. His humanity and humility, as well as his scientific achievements, were stressed in his obituaries, with the *Miami Herald* noting that "Dr. Simpson, although a noted personage, was of the benign temperament that wins the love of humbler folk. He was always accessible to the student of nature and gave freely of his time and knowledge to these." Regarding his personal traits, the *Herald* said, "He possessed a keen sense of humor and was never in any sense pedantic. His personal letters showed a flair that would indicate a youth rather than a serious scientist who was an octogenarian."[26] The *Miami Daily News*'s Sunday feature following his death recalled a tramp in the Everglades the article's author had taken with "Dr. Simpson" two years earlier.

> He said about natural science: "There's one thing about it—when a person grows older he has something that is ever new, a love that no one can take from him." And so, in his death, Science has lost a happy worker, and a man who really knew how to live has died. Nature, the immutable goddess who gives and takes in an endless cycle, and Dr. Charles Torrey Simpson, a votary who penetrated to the very heart of life, are one today—and thousands of friends and admirers are sorrowing over the death of the master.[27]

Fairchild was in the Bahamas the day of the funeral, and John Gifford was making his weekly radio broadcast. Gifford put aside his planned script and devoted his entire program to Simpson, concluding, "This country [South Florida] in its virgin state captured many rolling stones and of this varied collection none have accomplished more or served it better than Charles Torrey Simpson."[28]

A tribute of another sort was given many years later by Elsie Mettair Picot, who as a child had learned her first lessons about growing things from this gentle, kindly man. Still living in her pine cottage, with plants spilling out of her windows and porches, she recalled her old friend, saying, "I'm glad he took me under his wing. It meant learning things I would never have known otherwise. Without my plants and my study of plants there wouldn't be anything."[29] Elsie Picot was one of many whose lives were expanded by Charles Torrey Simpson's durable gift of the love of nature.

Epilogue

The Simpsons' friends rallied around Flora after the death of the "grand old man." The many loving tributes to her "dear husband" sustained her and, as she put it, "made me feel his presence very near."[1] David Fairchild flew home from Nassau when he heard of Simpson's death and called on Flora immediately to offer his condolences and any possible assistance.

SIMPSON'S ESTATE

In his will, Simpson had given specific instructions for the disposition of his library. With the exception of the volumes Flora wanted to keep, he directed that his papers and books on malacology be given to the University of Miami, those on botanical and horticultural matters to the plant introduction station at Chapman Field, and the remainder—general interest volumes—to the Flagler Memorial Library. To inventory his library was a major task for Flora, for when it was completed it contained 1,530 volumes. Among them were 468 travelogues, 153 books on conchology, 34 on geology, 256 on general science, 153 on botany and horticulture, 22 on entomology, 25 on anthropology, 38 poetry books, and 41 dictionaries.[2] Assessed at one dollar each in the estate, the actual value of this collection cannot be estimated because it included many rare, out-of-print books. Most had brown paper jackets with the cost and source of the book noted on the inside cover.

Some of Simpson's books can still be found in the stacks and on reserve in the University of Miami's Richter Library, such as the eleven-volume set by the French evolutionist Lamarck, *Histoire des Animaux sans Vertebres,* published in 1835. On the flyleaf is the notation, "Bought from Ruth Cook Smith. $14.25 for the set." Leafing through Lamarck's

Les Mollusques, one feels a sudden closeness to Simpson, who devoted so much of his life to the study of shelled animals. Within its pages are pressed the skeleton of a tiny, nearly transparent, spider, once a resident in Simpson's den, and the fragile, grassy-green silk ribbon that marked the reader's place.

Upon learning of Simpson's gift to Chapman Field, Fairchild wrote to Flora and offered his assistance in transferring the books to the field station. He also wrote to the Office of Foreign Plant Introduction in Washington, suggesting that a special letter of acceptance go to Flora from the secretary of agriculture. "I do not know anything about the red tape of such things, but suppose that there is any amount of it up there. I only hope that it is kept out of sight from Mrs. Simpson for her sensibilities are a consideration of the first order." Fairchild stressed that "the library is intended to be kept here and not taken to Washington and incorporated into the gigantic complex there where its identity would be lost."[3]

It was easy for Flora to pass Simpson's science books along to the University of Miami and the others to the Flagler Memorial Library, but she clung to the botanical and natural history books destined for Chapman Field, not only because of the information they contained but also because they embodied "the professor" himself—tangible evidence of what was lost. In her letter to Fairchild she asked for assurance that the books would be properly cared for. "It will be hard to see these dear familiar books, my husband's best companions, taken from the shelves. I'll try not to be selfish, but Professor gave me the right 'to reserve any books she wishes to.' . . . I know that you will agree with me that there must be a suitable place for housing the books. I would not like to have them packed away in boxes—they might better remain longer on my shelves."[4]

In addition to the books, Simpson's will, dated December 24, 1929, and witnessed by Andrew P. Fallesen and Louise F. Leybourne, included the house and nine remaining bayfront acres, his freshwater and marine shells, and mortgage bonds, fourteen promissory notes, and cash valued at some $18,958. Flora received two-thirds of his monetary estate, and Pliny received the remainder. The real estate passed directly to Flora, but when Pliny was killed in a work-related accident in 1933 she made his wife, Julia, the beneficiary of one-sixth of the proceeds of the sale of the property.[5]

Simpson's shell collection was split up, with the tropical western Atlantic marine shells going to the Rosenstiel Marine Laboratory of the University of Miami and the others shipped to the U.S. National Museum in Washington. The *Liguus* and other land and freshwater shells were given to the Biology Department of the University of Miami.

Five years after Simpson's death, the plot next to his was deeded by the Woodlawn Cemetery Association to the Garden Clubs of Miami, and the little stopper named for him by John Kunkel Small was planted there in his memory. Fairchild gave the dedication, and as he spoke a meadowlark lighted on the tree and sang.[6] Simpson once wrote, "To me, the notes of the meadow lark are more ravishingly sweet than any other."[7]

FLORA AND MARION

Flora continued the traditions of the revered professor. A newspaper feature in 1936 described her as "a scientist with a knowledge of tropical and semitropical plant life"[8] who was giving a series of lectures and leading the Tree Study Club, and another in 1940 described her at eighty as "of a rather retiring nature, she is inclined to deprecate her own accomplishments in the field of botany and horticulture. When you try to start talking about that she adroitly turns the subject to Dr. Simpson. 'His work was so much more important than mine, . . . All I ever did was just help him with some of the tiresome detail.' " The Simpson place was still "a riot of everything that grows and blooms in Florida."[9]

Fairchild extended to Flora the same affection and consideration he had given to Charles, interceding for her with the Veterans Administration in regard to her widow's pension and continuing his visits to the Sentinels. One year on the eve of Charles's birthday, an occasion that was often celebrated during his lifetime, he came to see her and gave her a copy of his book, *Exploring for Plants.* His inscription read: "As I sit and look out upon the palms and lianas and bamboos which the Professor planted in the early days of his sojourn here I seem to hear his joyous laughter again and see the sparkle in his face. It has never seemed the same here since he went and I have never ceased to miss his companionship."[10]

Flora lived to be eighty-four, and when she died Marion inherited the property, which then comprised nine acres, including the bayfront. The city of Miami studied a plan to buy it, but it was rejected, and Marion sold all but the one-acre homesite. Though she was unable to maintain the house, she would not budge from it. "They want to tear down the house because it is an eye-sore, but I have refused to sell at any price," she told *Miami Herald* writer Nixon Smiley.[11] Marion died intestate in 1963 at the age of sixty-seven, and during the lengthy litigation, regarding

the disposal of his estate, vandals broke into the house and destroyed Simpson's correspondence, papers, and photographs. Books were trashed, burned, and stolen. Windows were broken. The rains came in, and on several occasions fires were set in the house. Scavengers made off with what remained. Even Simpson's certificate for the honorary doctorate of science from the University of Miami and his Meyer Medal disappeared. The house was finally demolished as a neighborhood nuisance.[12] When the Palm Bay Club was built on the Simpson acreage, the lofty mangroves and sprawling mahoe that once grew on the waterfront were replaced with cement breakwalls and a marina for oceangoing yachts. A twenty-six story condominium now stands on what was the Simpsons' waterfront.

Nothing is left of the Sentinels for Simpson to haunt. Gone are the rows of black olive trees that lined the entrance road. No trace remains of the fern pool that once reflected graceful stands of bamboo, or the stone benches where he rested in contemplation of his "holy of holies." The bulldozers spared the giant West Indian silk cotton tree he had planted before 1912 from a seedling.[13] Its clawlike buttress roots extend for twenty-five feet at the base. Nearby an old ficus and a mango tree stand in close embrace—"whether kissing or biting I could not tell" was how Simpson described them.[14] Shading the asphalt parking lot of the Palm Bay Club is a gnarled, stunted oak, its trunk entwined with a prickly cactus, the beloved enemy of this great explorer of the Keys. More likely his spirit would be found in Watson Hammock on Big Pine Key, his habitual rendezvous, now part of the National Key Deer Preserve.

Simpson Park was expanded from its original five and one-half acres to eight and one-half acres when the city of Miami secured sixteen adjoining lots. In 1937 the Council of Garden Clubs raised funds for a community building in the park, where clubs and civic groups concerned with the environment meet. Faced with native limestone, it has offices, a botanical library, and an auditorium whose focal point is Henry Salem Hubbell's oil portrait of Simpson, which was painted from a photograph after his death. Simpson Park is still the target of vandals and vagrants, but a constant effort is being made by the city of Miami to protect and maintain this accessible bit of inner-city forest.

SIMPSON'S LEGACY

Simpson's name lives on in a park dedicated to him and in the scientific names of one or two trees and of numerous Florida tree snails and freshwater bivalves. It is often found in the bibliographies of scientific papers on naiads and mussels where the "Synopsis" and the *Catalogue* are cited. He is remembered as a folk hero by aficionados of Florida wildlife and wilderness areas, and his books are treasured by those fortunate enough to own them. The record they contain is an inventory of the plants and animals native to a Florida landscape that has been battered by hurricanes, challenged by droughts and changing weather patterns, and stifled by highways and buildings. His historic shell collections, partially gathered before the pollution of an industrial age, are a standard of comparison for biological diversity studies, and his geographical records of the original habitats of tree snails may still be useful to distribution studies. No small value can be placed on Simpson as a person: his frugal, humanistic behavior; his selfless devotion to his quest—very simply, as he often put it, "the discovery of nature's secrets"; and his determination to pass the torch of curiosity to others. He did not take himself seriously. His quest was a game, one that continually pulled him closer to his goal, like the "monster cottonwood" of his childhood that ever beckoned him on. Simpson embraced life as he embraced that cottonwood, and his infectious enthusiasm continues to draw others into his quest.

NOTES

In citing sources in the notes, short titles generally have been used. Frequently used sources are identified by the following abbreviations:

ANSP	Henry A. Pilsbry Papers, Library of the Academy of Natural Sciences, Philadelphia
BHL	Bryant Walker Papers, Bentley Historical Library, Michigan Historical Collections, University of Michigan, Ann Arbor
FTG	David Fairchild Papers, Special Collections, Fairchild Tropical Garden Library, Miami
HASF	Charles T. Simpson file, Charlton W. Tebeau Research Center, Historical Association of Southern Florida, Miami
NMNH	William H. Dall Papers, Division of Mollusks, National Museum of Natural History, Smithsonian Institution, Washington, D.C.
ORL	Charles T. Simpson file, Otto G. Richter Library, Archives and Special Collections, University of Miami
SIA	Smithsonian Institution Archives, Washington, D.C.
USDA	Agricultural Research Service, Information Staff, U.S. Department of Agriculture, Greenbelt, Maryland

Introduction

1. Charles T. Simpson, *In Lower Florida Wilds,* 114–15.

2. *Miami Daily News,* December 17, 1932.

3. Thomas Say to John F. Melsheimer, in Weiss, *Thomas Say: Early American Naturalist,* 58.

4. Charles T. Simpson, *Out of Doors in Florida,* 256.

5. Ibid., 136–37.

6. Charles T. Simpson, *In Lower Florida Wilds,* 328.

7. Charles T. Simpson to Roland M. Harper, February 12, 1910. W. S. Hoole Special Collections Library, University of Alabama.

8. Interview with author, March 1971.

9. *Science* 85 (1937): 333.

Chapter One: The Shaping of a Naturalist

1. Peattie, *Green Laurels,* 82.

2. Quoted from Nuttall, *Journal of a Journey into the Arkansas Territory,* preface, in Graustein, *Thomas Nuttall,* 1.

3. Charles T. Simpson, *Out of Doors in Florida,* 285.

4. Ibid.

5. In the nineteenth century, while the term *malacology* existed, the term *conchology,* meaning the study of shells, was most frequently used to describe that branch of zoology dealing with mollusks, because little was known about the soft-bodied animal within the shell. As the science advanced to include the life history of the animal, the term *malacologist* came to be applied. Though Simpson studied the animal as well as the shell, he referred to himself by the older term.

6. Charles T. Simpson, *Out of Doors in Florida,* 283.

7. Ibid., 286.

8. Charles T. Simpson to Helen A. Simpson, ca. 1926, in Helen A. Simpson, *Early Records,* 216–17.

9. Charles T. Simpson, *Out of Doors in Florida,* 282.

10. Joseph H. Simpson, Journal.

11. Charles T. Simpson, *Ornamental Gardening,* 39–40.

12. Charles T. Simpson, *Out of Doors in Florida,* 286.

13. Joseph H. Simpson, Journal.

14. Helen A. Simpson, *Early Records,* 216.

15. Ibid.

16. Ibid., 214–15.

17. Ibid., 215.

18. Ibid., 217.

19. Joseph H. Simpson, "Botanical Work, Etc."

20. *Miami News,* April 24, 1932.

21. Charles T. Simpson, *Out of Doors in Florida,* 288.

22. Helen A. Simpson, *Early Records,* 216.

23. Based on *Report of the Adjutant General of the State of Illinois* 4:66–73.

24. Charles T. Simpson, *Out of Doors in Florida,* 288.

25. Charles T. Simpson, *In Lower Florida Wilds,* 243.

26. Charles T. Simpson, *Out of Doors in Florida,* 256.

27. *Miami News,* April 24, 1932.

28. Charles T. Simpson to David Fairchild, August 21, 1930. FTG.

29. *Miami News,* April 24, 1932.

30. Ibid.

Chapter Two: Paradise Won

1. Charles T. Simpson, *Florida Wild Life,* 171.

2. Ibid., 157–58.

3. Ibid., 29–31.

4. Ibid., 156.

5. Ibid., 157.

6. Joseph H. Simpson, "Botanical Work, Etc."

7. *Taxpayers and Voters of Bureau Co., Ill.*

8. Charles T. Simpson, "Genus Making."

9. *Bureau County Republican* (Princeton, Ill). Newspaper undated, but Simpson dated his letter February 10, 1883. HASF.

10. Charles T. Simpson, *Florida Wild Life,* 183–84.

11. Charles T. Simpson, *Out of Doors in Florida,* 3.

12. Pinardi, *Plant Pioneers,* 31.

13. Simpson gives this date variously as 1883, 1884, and 1885, but most likely it was late winter (January–February) 1884.

14. Charles T. Simpson, *In Lower Florida Wilds,* 289–90.

15. Ibid.

16. Charles T. Simpson, *Out of Doors in Florida,* 294–95.

17. Ibid., 295–96.

18. Ibid., 296–97.

19. Charles T. Simpson, *In Lower Florida Wilds,* 150.

20. Pliny Reasoner to Mary W. Reasoner, December 28, 1884. Held by E. S. Reasoner, Oneco, Florida.

21. Pliny Reasoner to Mary W. Reasoner, January 8, 1885. Held by E. S. Reasoner.

22. A comprehensive account of these events is found in Matthews, *Edge of Wilderness,* and Grismer, *The Story of Sarasota.*

23. Grismer, *The Story of Sarasota.*

24. Pliny Reasoner to Mary W. Reasoner, December 28, 1884, held by E. S. Reasoner; Charles T. Simpson to William H. Dall, June 16, 1886, NMNH.

Chapter Three: Paradise Lost

1. Charles T. Simpson, *Out of Doors in Florida,* 2–3.

2. Pliny Reasoner to Mary W. Reasoner, May 12, 1885. Held by E. S. Reasoner.

3. Charles T. Simpson, *Out of Doors in Florida,* 7.

4. Pliny Reasoner to Mary W. Reasoner, May 3, 1885. Held by E. S. Reasoner.

5. Charles T. Simpson, *Out of Doors in Florida,* 11.

6. Ibid., 18.

7. Tebeau, *The Story of Chokoloskee Bay Country,* 12.

8. Charles T. Simpson, *Out of Doors in Florida,* 18.

9. Ibid., 22.

10. Ibid., 28.

11. Ibid., 31–32.

12. Ibid., 41–44.

13. Ibid., 45.

14. Ibid., 46–47.

15. Now Royal Palm Hammock is part of Collier Seminole State Park. Simpson describes their visit as having taken place in the early part of their voyage (*Out of Doors in Florida,* 19–21) but his article in *Plant World* ("A Visit to the Royal Palm Hammock") places it "on our return trip," as does Pliny Reasoner (Pinardi, *Plant Pioneers,* 50–53.). The palms would never have survived the long sea voyage to be planted at Reasoner's nursery.

16. Charles T. Simpson, "A Visit to the Royal Palm Hammock," 6.

17. Pinardi, *Plant Pioneers,* 52–53.

18. Pliny Reasoner to Mary W. Reasoner, November 12, 1885. Held by E. S. Reasoner.

19. Charles T. Simpson to William H. Dall, June 16, 1886. NMNH.

20. Charles T. Simpson, *Florida Wild Life,* 10, 40; Pinardi, *Plant Pioneers,* 54–57; Pliny Reasoner to Mary W. Reasoner, February 10, 1886, held by E. S. Reasoner.

21. Charles T. Simpson to William H. Dall, June 16, 1886.

22. Pliny Reasoner to Mary W. Reasoner, February 10, 1886. Held by E. S. Reasoner.

23. Ibid.

Chapter Four: The Midwestern Years

1. B. C. Couch. Excerpt from an unpublished family history.

2. Charles T. Simpson to William H. Dall, June 16, 1886. NMNH.

3. Charles T. Simpson to W. H. Pratt, December 10, 1886. Putnam Museum of History and Natural Science, Davenport, Iowa.

4. Ibid.

5. Charles T. Simpson, "Contributions to the Mollusca of Florida."

6. Charles T. Simpson to William H. Dall, January 10, 1888. NMNH.

7. Charles T. Simpson to William H. Dall, April 9, 1888. NMNH.

8. Charles T. Simpson, "Notes on the Unionidae of Florida," 406.

9. Charles T. Simpson to W. C. Pratt, July 8, 1889. Putnam Museum of History and Natural Science.

10. Charles T. Simpson to William H. Dall, January 9, 1889. NMNH.

11. Charles T. Simpson, "Genus Making."

12. Charles T. Simpson, *In Lower Florida Wilds,* 116.

13. Charles T. Simpson, "What Is a Species?" 79–80.

14. Charles T. Simpson to William H. Dall, June 2, 1889. NMNH.

15. William H. Dall to Charles T. Simpson, October 15, 1889. NMNH.

16. Charles T. Simpson to William H. Dall, October 23, 1889. NMNH.

17. Ibid.

18. W. H. Pratt to Henry A. Pilsbry, October 28, 1889. Putnam Museum of History and Natural Science.

19. Charles T. Simpson to William H. Dall, October 1889. NMNH.

20. William H. Dall to Charles T. Simpson, October 29, 1889. NMNH.

Chapter Five: Smithsonian Towers

1. Charles T. Simpson, "Collecting Notes," 38–39.

2. Charles T. Simpson, *In Lower Florida Wilds,* 343.

3. Charles T. Simpson, "Notes on Collecting Shells in Jamaica."

4. Charles T. Simpson, *Out of Doors in Florida,* 298–300.

5. Joseph H. Simpson to George Vasey, September 16, 1892. SIA.

6. Joseph H. Simpson to George Vasey, December 9, 1888. SIA.

7. Parker, *Synopsis and Classification,* 1124.

8. Charles T. Simpson, "A Review of von Ihering's Classification," 19.

9. Burch, *Freshwater Unionacean Clams,* 1.

10. Stansbery, "Eastern Freshwater Mollusks," 11.

11. Higgins, "A Catalogue of the Shell-bearing Species."

12. Madson, "Mississippi Shell Game."

13. Charles T. Simpson to Henry A. Pilsbry, November 21, 1891.

14. Charles T. Simpson, "Notes on *Unionidae,*" 86.

15. Charles T. Simpson, "On a Revision of the American *Unionidae,*" 78.

16. Simpson, "Notes on the *Unionidae* of Florida," 405.

17. A historical listing of all the published scientific names that have been used to describe one taxonomic group (such as a species) is called its synonymy.

18. Charles T. Simpson, "On a Revision of the American *Unionidae,*" 78.

19. Charles T. Simpson, "Synopsis of the Naiades," 512; Ortmann and Walker, "On the Nomenclature of Certain North American Naiades," 1–3.

20. Charles T. Simpson, "On a Revision of the American *Unionidae,*" 79.

21. Pilsbry, "Notes and Notices," 118–19.

22. Charles T. Simpson to William H. Dall, September 23, 1892. NMNH.

23. Charles T. Simpson, "A Reply to Professor Wheeler," 22–23.

24. Charles T. Simpson to William H. Dall, December 14, 1893. NMNH.

25. Charles T. Simpson to Henry A. Pilsbry, October 31, 1894. ANSP.

26. Charles T. Simpson to Bryant Walker, March 31, 1912. BHL.

27. Charles T. Simpson, "Paradise Key," 7.

28. Charles T. Simpson to William H. Dall, 1895. NMNH.

29. Charles T. Simpson, "Distribution of the Land and Fresh-water Mollusks."

30. Charles T. Simpson to Henry A. Pilsbry, March 13, 1895. ANSP.

31. Von Ihering, "Naiads from S. Paulo"; Charles T. Simpson, "A Review of von Ihering's Classification."

32. *Taxodont:* hinged teeth arranged in a row like a comb or file.

33. *Heterodont* (other or differing teeth): an arrangement of cardinal and lateral hinge teeth.

34. *Lasidium:* a three-segmented bivalve larva with a single shell that begins its life cycle free-swimming in the water.

35. Charles T. Simpson to Henry A. Pilsbry, March 13, 1895. ANSP.

36. Malacologists now have established a third group within the order Unionidae. These have a haustorium as a larvae and may be found in southern Asia, Africa, and South America.

37. Charles T. Simpson to William H. Dall, May 3, 1896. NMNH.

38. James A. Steed, assistant archivist, Smithsonian Institution, letter to author, November 12, 1973.

39. Charles T. Simpson to William H. Dall, September 13, 1898. NMNH.

40. Charles T. Simpson to William H. Dall, December 27, 1898. NMNH.

41. Charles T. Simpson to Henry A. Pilsbry, August 18, 1899. ANSP.

42. Charles T. Simpson, "Synopsis of the Naiades," 502.

43. Charles T. Simpson to Bryant Walker, December 10, 1910. BHL.

44. Pilsbry, "Arnold Edward Ortmann" [obituary], *Nautilus* 40, no. 4 (April 1927): 109–11.

45. *Miami Daily News,* April 24, 1932.

46. von Ihering, "The Unionidae of North America," 39.

47. Charles T. Simpson, "On the Classification of the Unionidae."

48. "Publications Received," review of Simpson's "Synopsis," *Nautilus* 14, no. 10 (March 1901): 130–31.

49. Ferris, "A New Lampsilis from Arkansas," 39.

50. Charles T. Simpson to Bryant Walker, December 5, 1910. BHL.

51. Graham Bell Fairchild, letter to author, November 19, 1973.

52. *Miami Daily News,* undated newspaper clipping. HASF.

Chapter Six: The Sentinels

1. Peters, *Lemon City,* 252.

2. Joseph H. Simpson to Charles T. Simpson, May 21, 1902. ORL.

3. Charles T. Simpson, *Florida Wild Life,* 119–21.

4. *Miami Daily News,* April 24, 1932.

5. Charles T. Simpson to David Fairchild, September 26, 1926. FTG.

6. Charles T. Simpson to William H. Dall, April 20, 1903. NMNH.

7. Ibid., March 21, 1907.

8. Charles T. Simpson, *Ornamental Gardening,* 15; Marion Roper, quoted in in Smiley, "Strange Home Built by Noted Naturalist."

9. Charles T. Simpson, *Florida Wild Life,* 118–19.

10. Charles T. Simpson, *Ornamental Gardening,* 21.

11. Charles T. Simpson, "In the Hammock," 12–13.

12. Charles T. Simpson, *Ornamental Gardening,* 3–4.

13. Elsie M. Picot, interview with author, March 31, 1971, October 3, 1972.

14. *Miami Herald,* April 9, 1922.

15. Charles T. Simpson, *Ornamental Gardening,* 17–18.

16. Roper, "Building Pools."

17. *Miami Herald,* July 30, 1950.

18. Charles T. Simpson to William H. Dall, October 20, 1908. NMNH.

19. Charles T. Simpson, *In Lower Florida Wilds,* 130.

20. Small, "Royal Palm Hammock," 170.

21. Charles T. Simpson, *In Lower Florida Wilds,* 131–32.

22. Charles T. Simpson, "The Florida Keys and the Southern Mainland," 10.

23. Charles T. Simpson, *In Lower Florida Wilds,* 133–34.

Chapter Seven: Tropical Plant Distribution

1. Fairchild, *The World Was My Garden,* 113.

2. Gifford, *Ten Trustworthy Tropical Trees,* 67–68.

3. *Miami Weekly Metropolis,* April 4, 1913.

4. Charles Brookfield, interview with author, 1972.

5. Charles T. Simpson, *In Lower Florida Wilds,* 362.

6. Gertrude Peterson, interview with author, February 1973.

7. Charles T. Simpson, *In Lower Florida Wilds,* 353–72.

8. Charles T. Simpson to William H. Dall, 1908. NMNH.

9. Fairchild, *The World Was My Garden,* 401.

10. Graham Bell Fairchild, letter to author, November 23, 1973.

11. Dorn, *Tropical Gardening for South Florida,* 9–13.

12. Marjory S. Douglas, letter to author, March 20, 1990.

Chapter Eight: Revival of the Catalogue

1. *Miami Daily News,* December 17, 1932.

2. Charles T. Simpson to William H. Dall, October 20, 1908. NMNH.

3. Charles T. Simpson, *In Lower Florida Wilds,* 321–28.

4. Ibid., 315–16.

5. John B. Henderson, Jr., to Andrew Carnegie, January 26, 1904. SIA.

6. Charles T. Simpson to Bryant Walker, June 11, 1910. BHL.

7. Abbott, ed., *American Malacologists.*

8. Goodrich, "Bryant Walker."

9. Charles T. Simpson to Bryant Walker, June 11, 1910. BHL.

10. Charles T. Simpson to Bryant Walker, December 5, 1910. BHL.

11. Charles T. Simpson to Bryant Walker, February 9, 1912. BHL.

12. Charles T. Simpson to Bryant Walker, March 3, 1912. BHL.

13. Charles T. Simpson to Bryant Walker, March 16, 1912. BHL.

14. Ibid.

15. Charles T. Simpson to Bryant Walker, March 31, 1912. BHL.

16. Ortmann and Walker, "On the Nomenclature of Certain North American Naiades," 1–3.

17. Arnold Ortmann to Bryant Walker, April 19, 1920, in van der Schalie, "An Old Problem," 96.

18. Charles T. Simpson to Bryant Walker, March 3, 1912.
19. Charles T. Simpson to Bryant Walker, April 2, 1913.
20. Charles T. Simpson to Bryant Walker, August 4, 1914. BHL.
21. "Publications Received."

Chapter Nine: The Naturalists' Cruise to Cuba

1. Henderson, *Cruise of the Tomás Barrera,* 1.
2. Barbour, *A Naturalist in Cuba.*
3. Henderson, *Cruise of the Tomás Barrera,* 2–3.
4. Ibid.
5. Ibid., 3.
6. Charles T. Simpson, "In Old-World America," 22.
7. Henderson, *Cruise of the Tomás Barrera,* 22–23.
8. Ibid.
9. Ibid., 30.
10. Ibid., 41–42.
11. Henderson, *Log Book of the Tomás Barrera.*
12. Ibid.
13. Ibid.
14. Ibid.
15. Ibid.
16. Ibid.

Chapter Ten: Tramping in the Keys

1. Pilsbry, *Land Mollusca of North America,* 51.
2. Charles T. Simpson, *Out of Doors in Florida,* 346–47.
3. Ibid., v.
4. Charles T. Simpson, *In Lower Florida Wilds,* 76–77.
5. Ibid, 50.
6. Charles T. Simpson, *Out of Doors in Florida,* 335.
7. Ibid., 373–75.
8. Charles T. Simpson, *In Lower Florida Wilds,* 50–51.
9. Vignoles, "Observations upon the Floridas," in Pilsbry, "Variation and Zoogeography of *Liguus,*" 441.
10. Charles T. Simpson to William H. Dall, October 20, 1908. NMNH.
11. Charles T. Simpson, *In Lower Florida Wilds,* 47–48.
12. Charles T. Simpson, *Out of Doors in Florida,* 369.
13. Watson's Hammock is now part of the Key Deer Preserve.
14. Charles T. Simpson, *Out of Doors in Florida,* 369.
15. Ibid., 328–29.
16. Nicolas Winkleman, interview with author, June 12, 1974.
17. Charles T. Simpson, *In Lower Florida Wilds,* 55–56.
18. Ibid., 347.

19. Ibid., 347–48.

20. Ibid., 350–51.

21. Even when designated as a state park, Paradise Key could not be protected against fire once the draining of the Everglades reduced its historic water barrier. Wildfires burned out much of Paradise Key several times until, in 1947, the Key became part of the Everglades National Park and federal funds were available to provide firefighting equipment. See Tebeau, *They Lived in the Park,* 134–35, and Douglas, *The Everglades,* 374–76.

22. Charles T. Simpson, *Out of Doors in Florida,* 243–46.

23. Charles T. Simpson. "Paradise Key."

Chapter Eleven: Field Trips with John Kunkel Small

1. Harold H. Hume, "John Kunkel Small—An Appreciation."

2. Information on the Deering estate came from a series of undated articles by Eleanor Bisbee in the *Miami Daily Metropolis* ca. 1917. HASF.

3. Charles T. Simpson, *In Lower Florida Wilds,* 110–11.

4. Ibid., 111.

5. Ibid., 112. Cuthbert Lake and the entire area covered by this expedition this day are now within the Everglades National Park.

6. Charles T. Simpson, *In Lower Florida Wilds,* 113.

7. Small, "A Cruise to the Cape Sable Region, 192.

8. Ibid., 193.

9. Charles T. Simpson, *In Lower Florida Wilds,* 170–73.

10. Charles T. Simpson, *Florida Wild Life,* 150.

11. The preceding four excerpts are from Charles T. Simpson to Roland M. Harper, April 20, 1915. W. S. Hoole Special Collections Library, University of Alabama.

12. Fairchild, *The World Grows Round My Door,* 213–14.

13. Charles T. Simpson, *Ornamental Gardening,* 8.

14. Ibid., 9–10.

15. Charles T. Simpson, *In Lower Florida Wilds,* 49.

16. Charles T. Simpson, *Ornamental Gardening,* 10.

17. Ibid., 22.

18. Ibid., 50.

19. *Miami Metropolis,* June 17, 1916. HASF.

20. Fairchild, *The World Grows Round My Door,* 28–34.

21. Charles T. Simpson to David Fairchild, February 27, 1916. FTG.

22. Charles T. Simpson, *Ornamental Gardening,* 73.

23. Charles T. Simpson to John K. Small, November 5, 1921. Loaned to the author by George K. Small.

24. Charles T. Simpson to David Fairchild, April 17, 1917. FTG.

25. Charles T. Simpson, *Out of Doors in Florida,* 173.

26. Ibid., 172.

27. Charles T. Simpson to John K. Small, June 25, 1917. Loaned to the author by George K. Small.

28. Charles T. Simpson to John K. Small, postcard, September 2, 1918. Loaned to the author by George K. Small.

29. Joseph H. Simpson to E. N. Rose, February 15, 1898. SIA, Record Unit 221, Division of Plants, box 21, J. H. Simpson, folder 5.

30. Lillie B. McDuffie, *The Lure of the Manatee,* 289–90.

31. Helen A. Simpson, *Early Records,* 217.

32. Charles T. Simpson to Roland M. Harper, February 12, 1910.

33. Helen A. Simpson, *Early Records,* 217.

34. Dorn, *Tropical Gardening for South Florida,* 40.

Chapter Twelve: A Passion for Knowing

1. Charles T. Simpson, *In Lower Florida Wilds,* 35–38.

2. Ibid., 12–13.

3. Ibid., 16.

4. Ibid., 14. At Matheson Hammock State Park in Coral Gables at low tide, bathers can wade in the shallow waters of the bay half a mile from shore.

5. Barbour, *That Vanishing Eden,* 200–201.

6. "Books Old and New," unidentified newspaper article. HASF.

7. *Booklist* 17 (October 1920): 28.

8. *Geographical Review,* 11, no. 4 (October 1921).

9. *New York Times,* December 26, 1920, 18.

10. *Early Records,* 216.

11. Charles T. Simpson, *Out of Doors in Florida,* 83.

12. Ibid., 70.

13. Tebeau, *Florida's Last Frontier,* 45.

14. In 1949 the Collier Corporation moved the entire community of Caxambas to Goodland, another site on Marco Island, to facilitate their plans for a housing development.

15. The story of Simpson and Mercer's "pilgrimage" to Deep Lake is taken from *Out of Doors in Florida,* 76–90.

Chapter Thirteen: An Icon for Nature

1. Charles T. Simpson to David Fairchild, June 9, 1925. FTG.

2. Charles T. Simpson to David Fairchild, January 28, 1924. FTG. Simpson's avenue of poincianas can be seen in bloom in early June on South Miami Avenue leading to Simpson Park.

3. *Miami Herald,* October 22, 1922.

4. Charles T. Simpson to David Fairchild, January 28, 1924. FTG.

5. Charles T. Simpson, "The Criminal Driver against the Public," *Miami Daily News,* August 16, 1924.

6. Charles T. Simpson, *Out of Doors in Florida,* 323.

7. Ibid., 318.

8. Ibid., 394.

9. *Miami Herald,* April 9, 1922.

10. Charles T. Simpson to David Fairchild, August 31, 1924. FTG.

11. John B. Henderson to G. P. Putnam's Sons, April 12, 1922. ORL.

12. *Washington Star,* undated article, ca. January 11, 1923. HASF.

13. Letter and list of his introductions are found in the National Programs Staff files, Agricultural Research Service, U.S. Department of Agriculture.

14. Charles T. Simpson to David Fairchild, March 2, 1923. FTG.

15. David Fairchild, excerpt from Douglas, "American Genetic Assn. Honors South Florida Botanist-Philosopher."

16. Healey, *The Plant Hunters,* 176–78; also Fairchild, "Foreign Plant Introduction Medal." While in the early 1900s Meyer never heard the terms *germplasm* or *gene pool,* the *USDA Bulletin,* describing the nominating procedure for the Meyer Medal, noted that he searched for "the rudimentary and long-forgotten parent stock or the as yet unused wild plant that may be adapted to man's profit by cultivation." Currently, the Meyer Medal is given by the Crop Science Society of America for "Plant Genetic Resources" to those who exemplify Meyer's "ideal of service to humanity through collecting, conserving, or evaluating earth's plant genetic resources."

17. (1) Barbour Lathrop; (2) Louis Trabut Algerian; (3) E. M. Fenzi, Tripoli; (4) CTS. Douglas's article (*Miami Herald,* April 1, 1923) erroneously lists Simpson as the fifth recipient. Corrected in memo from the USDA Agricultural Research Service, New Programs Files, February 1, 1994.

18. Charles T. Simpson to David Fairchild, March 30, 1923. FTG.

19. Douglas, "American Genetic Association Honors South Florida Botanist-Philosopher."

20. Fairchild, "Foreign Plant Introduction Medal."

21. Douglas, "American Genetic Association Honors South Florida Botanist-Philosopher"; Douglas, *Adventures in a Green World,* 57; Marjory S. Douglas, interview with author, June 7, 1974.

22. Charles T. Simpson to Theodore Spicer-Simson, July 3, 1923. FTG.

23. Charles T. Simpson to David Fairchild, March 2, 1923. FTG.

24. Barbara Fairchild Muller, interview with author, February 9, 1973.

25. Charles T. Simpson, *Out of Doors in Florida,* 94–95.

26. Unidentified article, probably from a Miami newspaper. HASF.

27. *Miami Herald,* n.d. HASF.

28. *Jacksonville Times,* n.d. HASF.

29. *Miami Daily News,* Sunday garden section, n.d., 8. HASF.

30. Charles T. Simpson to David Fairchild, January 28, 1924. FTG.

31. Charles T. Simpson to David Fairchild, March 18, 1924. FTG.

32. Charles T. Simpson to David Fairchild, August 31, 1924. FTG.

33. Graham Fairchild, letter to author, November 23, 1973.

34. Charles T. Simpson to David Fairchild, March 18, 1824. FTG.

35. *Miami Herald,* editorial, June 26, 1923.

36. Charles T. Simpson to David Fairchild, August 31, 1924. FTG.

37. Charles T. Simpson to David Fairchild, February 18, 1925, FTG; Charles T. Simpson, "Notes on *Gongora galeata.*"

38. Charles T. Simpson to David Fairchild, June 9, 1925. FTG.

39. Chapman Field continued as a USDA Agricultural Research Service until 1995, when it was closed as a consequence of President Clinton's budget cuts. In recent years the emphasis has shifted from a testing center for tropical plants to collecting germ plasm of essential plants. *Miami Herald,* February 12, 1994, B1.

40. Charles T. Simpson to David Fairchild, June 9, 1925. FTG.

41. Charles T. Simpson to Paul Bartsch, November 29, 1925. NMNH.

42. Charles T. Simpson to Paul Bartsch, August 29, 1925. NMNH.

43. Paul Bartsch to Charles T. Simpson, September 10, 1925. NMNH.

44. Charles T. Simpson to Paul Bartsch, November 29, 1925. NMNH.

45. Henderson's personal papers in the Smithsonian contain a handwritten catalog of the *Testacellide,* one of the sluglike families of Cuban land snails.

Chapter Fourteen: Ups and Downs

1. Elsie M. Picot, interview with author, March 31, 1971.

2. Charles T. Simpson to David Fairchild, February 21, 1926. FTG.

3. Ibid.

4. These unscrupulous real estate agents took out options, or "binders," on property for a small sum, with the first payment due in one month. In the meantime, the options were resold at a profit several times, which escalated prices.

5. Charles T. Simpson to David Fairchild, February 21, 1926. FTG.

6. Ibid.

7. Fairchild, *The World Was My Garden,* 419.

8. Charles T. Simpson, *Florida Wild Life,* 127.

9. Charles T. Simpson, "In the Hammock."

10. Charles T. Simpson to Paul Bartsch, May 10, 1926. NMNH.

11. Charles T. Simpson to David Fairchild, September 26, 1926. FTG.

12. Simpson's assertion so impressed Donald C. Gaby, a meteorologist formerly employed by the National Hurricane Center and the National Environmental Satellite Service in Miami, that he went on a fifteen-year quest to track Simpson's hypothetical hurricane. By researching nineteenth-century weather records he discovered evidence of a great storm and determined that it would have hit Miami with great force on September 14, 1824. Gaby, "1824 Storm Search Is Rewarding."

13. Charles T. Simpson, "The Worst Hurricane," *Miami Herald,* November 14, 1926.

14. Charles T. Simpson, *Florida Wild Life,* 142.

15. Ibid., 142–44.

16. Ibid., 142–43.

17. Charles T. Simpson to Orange Averill, October 16, 1926.

18. Charles T. Simpson to David Fairchild, September 26, 1926.

19. Charles T. Simpson, *Florida Wild Life,* 153.

20. Charles T. Simpson to David Fairchild, April 20, 1927. FTG.

21. Ibid.

22. Charles T. Simpson to David Fairchild, July 12, 1927. FTG.

23. Charles T. Simpson to David Fairchild, August 27, 1928. FTG.

24. Gerry Curtis to Miami City Commissioners, January 23, 1927.

25. Bowman F. Ashe to Flora Simpson, December 26, 1932.

26. Charles T. Simpson to Bowman F. Ashe, June 1, 1927.

27. Gifford, "A Tribute to Simpson."

28. Charles T. Simpson to David Fairchild, July 12, 1927. FTG.

29. Charles T. Simpson to Paul Bartsch, July 6, 1927. NMNH.

30. Charles T. Simpson to David Fairchild, April 20, 1927.

31. David Fairchild to Charles T. Simpson, December 19, 1927. ORL.

Chapter Fifteen: In Defense of the Everglades

1. *Miami Herald,* April 3, 1955.

2. Charles T. Simpson, *In Lower Florida Wilds,* 112.

3. Tebeau, *They Lived in the Park,* 130–31.

4. Charles T. Simpson, "Everglades Paradise Wrecked by Blunders," *Miami News,* 1928, 1.

5. Ibid.

6. Charles T. Simpson to David Fairchild, September 27, 1928. FTG.

7. Charles T. Simpson to Henry A. Pilsbry, March 8, 1929. ANSP.

8. Charles T. Simpson, "The Florida Tree Snails," 1.

9. Muir, *Miami USA,* 186–87.

10. Charles T. Simpson to David Fairchild, October 21, 1929. FTG.

11. Charles T. Simpson to David Fairchild, December 13, 1929. FTG.

12. Charles T. Simpson, unpublished manuscript, probably 1930 (Simpson refers to the trip in a letter to David Fairchild, August 21, 1930). ORL.

13. Ibid.

14. Unidentified newspaper article by Edgar O. Achorn. HASF.

15. Gifford, "A Tribute to Simpson." ORL.

16. Charles T. Simpson to David Fairchild, August 21, 1930. FTG.

17. Charles T. Simpson, *Ornamental Gardening,* 43–45.

18. David Fairchild to Charles T. Simpson, August 13, 1930. ORL.

19. Charles T. Simpson to David Fairchild, August 21, 1930. FTG.

Chapter Sixteen: Last Things

1. *Miami Daily News,* April 1, 1931.

2. Charles T. Simpson to David Fairchild, April 4, 1931. FTG.

3. Ibid.

4. Henry A. Pilsbry to Charles T. Simpson, April 8, 1931; Charles T. Simpson to Henry A. Pilsbry, April 14, 1931. ANSP.

5. Henry A. Pilsbry to Charles T. SImpson, May 22, 1931. ANSP.

6. Charles T. Simpson to Henry A. Pilsbry, May 28, 1931. ANSP.

7. Henry A. Pilsbry to Charles T. Simpson, June 1, 1931. ANSP.

8. Charles T. Simpson, *Florida Wild Life,* 167.

9. Ibid., 126–27; 193–95.

10. *New York Times,* March 13, 1932.

11. *Boston Transcript,* July 16, 1932.

12. T. S. McNicol, "Wild Life in Florida," *Hollywood Herald,* May 13, 1932, and Samuel Scoville in undated, unidentified review, in Simpson file, HASF. Also *Miami Herald,* March 6, 1932.

13. Charles T. Simpson to John K. Small, May 25, 1932. Loaned to the author by George K. Small.

14. Charles T. Simpson to David Fairchild, July 1, 1932.

15. Loy Morrow, interview with author, 1973.

16. Charles Schuchert to Charles T. Simpson, October 10, 1932. ORL.

17. James Sturgis Pray to Charles T. Simpson, November 29, 1927.

18. Charles T. Simpson, *Florida Wild Life,* 7.

19. Ibid., 57.

20. Ibid., 171.

21. His certificate of death listed the cause as "Coronary sclerosis, Angina pectoris. Sudden death, probably coronary occlusion." Florida Bureau of Statistics, registration no. 1319, December 17, 1932.

22. Henry G. Frampton, *Miami Daily News,* December 18, 1932.

23. Henry G. Frampton, *Miami Daily News,* December 17, 1932.

24. *New York Times,* December 18, 1932; *Bureau County (Ill.) Republican,* January 5, 1933.

25. *Miami Herald* editorial, December 18, 1932.

26. *Miami Herald,* December 18, 1932.

27. *Miami Daily News,* December 18, 1932.

28. Gifford, "A Tribute to Simpson." ORL.

29. Elsie M. Picot, interview with author, March 31, 1971.

Epilogue

1. Flora Simpson to David Fairchild, January 22, 1933. FTG.

2. *Miami News,* February 12, 1933.

3. David Fairchild to Knowles Ryerson, January 7, 1933 (erroneously dated 1932). FTG.

4. Flora Simpson to David Fairchild, January 11, 1933. FTG.

5. R. C. Houser, trustee and executor of Flora Simpson's estate, interview with author, 1974.

6. Mrs. Alice Swinson, daughter of Charles Mosier, first caretaker of Royal Palm State Park, interview with author, January 15, 1974.

7. Charles T. Simpson, *Florida Wild Life,* 179, and *Out of Doors in Florida,* 367.

8. Unidentified newpaper article, 1936. HASF.

9. *Miami Daily News,* Farm News section, 1940. HASF.

10. Quoted in an undated letter from John Echoff, bookseller, to Barbara Fairchild Muller. FTG.

11. *Miami Herald,* July 30, 1950.

12. R. C. Houser to David Alexander, former Historical Museum of Southern Florida director, February 23, 1966, HASF.

13. Charles T. Simpson, *Ornamental Gardening,* 147.

14. Charles T. Simpson to David Fairchild, September 26, 1926.

BIBLIOGRAPHY

Selected Publications of Charles Torrey Simpson

MOLLUSKS AND CLASSIFICATION

"Contributions to the Mollusca of Florida." *Proceedings of the Davenport Academy of Sciences* 5 (1886): 45–72.

"Notes on Some Indian Territory Land and Fresh-Water Snails." *Proceedings of the U.S. National Museum* (1888): 449–54.

"Genus Making." *Nautilus* 3, no. 1 (January 1889): 5–8.

"What Is a Species?" *Nautilus* 3, no. 7 (November 1889): 78–80; 3, no. 8 (December 1889): 88–90.

"On the Means of Distribution of the *Unionidae* in the Southeastern United States." *Nautilus* 5, no. 2 (June 1891): 15–17.

"Notes on *Unionidae*." *Nautilus* 5, no. 8 (December 1891): 86–88.

"On a Revision of the American *Unionidae*." *Nautilus* 6, no. 7 (July 1892): 78–80.

"Collecting Notes." *Nautilus* 6, no. 4 (August 1892): 37.

"Notes on the *Unionidae* of Florida and the Southeastern States." *Proceedings of the U.S. National Museum* 15, no. 911 (1892): 405–36.

"A Reply to Professor Wheeler." *Nautilus* 7, no. 2 (June 1893): 22–23.

"A Review of von Ihering's Classification of the *Unionidae* and *Mutelidae*." *Nautilus* 7, no. 2 (June 1893): 17–21.

"Distribution of the Land and Fresh-Water Mollusks and Fossil Shells of the West Indian Region and Their Evidence with Regard to Past Changes of Land and Sea." *Proceedings of the U.S. National Museum* 17, no. 1011 (1894): 423–50.

"Notes on Collecting Shells in Jamaica." *Nautilus* 7, no. 10 (February 1894): 110–13.

"Notes on the Classification of the Unios." *Nautilus* 11, no.2 (June 1897): 18–23.

"Synopsis of the Naiades, or Pearly Freshwater Mussels." *Proceedings of the U.S. National Museum* 22, no. 1205 (1900): 501–1044.

"On the Classification of the *Unionidae.*" *Nautilus* 15, no. 8 (November 1901): 77–82.

"A New Land Operculate from Haiti." With John B. Henderson. *Nautilus* 15, no. 7 (1901): 73–74.

A Descriptive Catalogue of the Naiades or Pearly Fresh Water Mussels. Detroit: Bryant Walker, 1914.

"New Floridian Subspecies of the Genus *Liguus.*" *Proceedings of the Biological Society of Washington* 33 (1920): 121–26.

"The Florida Tree Snails of the Genus *Liguus.*" *Proceedings of the U.S. National Museum* 73 (1929): 1–25.

FLORIDA NATURAL HISTORY AND FIELD TRIPS

"A Visit to the Royal Palm Hammock of Florida." *Plant World* 5, (1902): 4–7.

"Effects on Vegetation of the Hurricane in Florida." *Plant World* 6 (1903): 284–85.

"Collecting in the Everglades." *Fern Bulletin* 17 (1909): 38–41.

"Native and Exotic Plants of Dade County, Florida." *Proceedings of the Florida Horticultural Society* (1912): 44–46.

"In the Hammock." *Tropic* 1, no. 2 (May 1914): 11–15.

"In Old-World America, Being the Random Notes of a Naturalist in Cuba." *Tropic* 1, no. 6 (September 1914): 21–26; 1, no. 7 (October 1914): 24–26.

"The Florida Keys and Southern Mainland: A Trip to Paradise Key." *Tropic,* 1, no. 10 (January 1915): 7–10; 1, nos. 11–12 (February–March 1915): 9–12.

"A Summer Morning at 'The Sentinels.'" *Tropic* 3, no. 1 (October 1915): 30–35.

"Paradise Key." *Tropic* 4, no. 1 (April 1916): 5–9.

"An Old Tramp in the Florida Keys." *Natural History* 19, no. 6 (December 1919): 657–64.

"Notes on *Gongora galeata.*" *Journal of Heredity* 16 (March 1925): 39–93.

"Bamboos and Grasses." *Hollywood Magazine* 1, no. 6 (April 1925): 28–31.

"Swamp Plants of Florida." *Beautiful Florida* 5, no. 9 (May 1929):

"Keys of a Wonderland." *Nature Magazine* 15, no. 6 (January 1930): 33–36.

"Epiphytes or Air Plants." *National Horticultural Magazine* 10 (July 1931): 181–85.

BOOKS ON NATURAL HISTORY AND HORTICULTURE

Ornamental Gardening in Florida: A Treatise on the Native and Exotic Decorative Plants Adapted to Florida and Their Cultivation, with Suggestions for the Ornamentation of Our Homes and Gardens. Little River, Fla.: Published by the author. First edition, 1916; second edition, 1926.

In Lower Florida Wilds: A Naturalist's Observations on the Life, Physical Geography, and Geology of the More Tropical Part of the State. New York: G. P. Putnam's Sons, 1920.

Out of Doors in Florida: The Adventures of a Naturalist Together with Essays on the Wild Life and the Geology of the State. Miami: E. B. Douglas, 1923.

Florida Wild Life: Observations on the Flora and Fauna of the State and the Influence of Climate and Environment on Their Development. New York: Macmillan, 1932.

Secondary Sources

Abbott, R. Tucker. *Compendium of Landshells: A Color Guide to more than 2,000 of the World's Terrestrial Shells.* Melbourne, Fla.: American Malacologists, 1989.

———, ed. *American Malacologists.* Falls Church, Va.: American Malacologists, 1973.

Barbour, Thomas. *A Naturalist in Cuba.* Boston: Little, Brown, 1945.

———. *That Vanishing Eden.* Boston: Little, Brown, 1945.

Bartsch, Paul. "Mollusks." In *Shelled Invertebrates of the Past and Present,* by Ray S. Bassler, Charles E. Resser, Waldo L. Schmitt, and Bartsch. Washington, D.C.: Smithsonian Institution, 1934. Reprint, New York: Dover, 1968.

Bayer, Frederick M. "Charles T. Simpson's Types in the Molluscan Genus *Liguus* in Florida." *Smithsonian Miscellaneous Collections* 107, no. 16 (1948): 1–8.

Blatchley, Willis Stanley. "Willis S. Blatchley Visits C. T. Simpson, March 1911." In his *In Days Agone,* 123–41. Indianapolis: Nature Publishing Co., 1932.

Brookfield, Charles M., and Oliver Griswold. *They All Called it Tropical.* Miami: Data Press, 1964.

Brent, Peter. *Charles Darwin: A Man of Enlarged Curiosity.* New York: Harper and Row, 1981.

Burch, John B. *Freshwater Unionacean Clams (Mollusca:Pelecypoda) of North America.* Hamburg, Mich.: Malacological Publications, 1975.

Clarke, James Mitchell. *The Life and Adventures of John Muir.* San Francisco: Sierra Club Books, 1980.

Clench, William J., and G. B. Fairchild. "The Classification of Florida *Liguus.*" *Proceedings of the New England Zoological Club* 17: 77–86.

Cunningham, Isabel Shipley. *Frank N. Meyer, Plant Hunter in Asia.* Ames: Iowa State University Press, 1984.

Dall, William H. "On a Collection of Shells Sent from Florida by Mr. Henry Hemphill." *Proceedings of the U.S. National Museum* 6, no. 1 (June 1883): 318.

Darwin, Charles. *The Origin of Species by Means of Natural Selection.* London: John Murray, 1859. Facsimile of first edition, New York: Penguin, 1982.

Davidson, Treat. "Tree Snails, Gems of the Everglades." *National Geographic* 127, no. 3 (March 1965): 372–87.

Dorn, Mabel. *Tropical Gardening for South Florida.* South Miami: South Florida Publishing Co., 1952.

Dorn, Mabel White, and Marjory Stoneman Douglas. *The Book of Twelve for South Florida Gardens.* South Miami: South Florida Publishing Co., 1928.

Douglas, Marjory Stoneman. *Adventures in a Green World: The Story of David Fairchild and Barbour Lathrop.* Coconut Grove, Fla.: Field Research Projects, 1973.

———. "American Genetic Assn. Honors South Florida Botanist-Philosopher." *Miami Herald,* April 1, 1923.

———. *The Everglades: River of Grass.* Revised edition. Miami: Banyan Books, 1977.

Ewan, Joseph. "A History of Botanical Collecting in Southern Florida." In *A Flora of Tropical Florida,* by Robert W. Long. Coral Gables, Fla.: University of Miami Press, 1971.

Fairchild, David. "Foreign Plant Introduction Medal." *Journal of Heredity* 11, no. 4 (April 1920): 169–70.

———. *The World Grows Round My Door.* New York: Scribners, 1947.

Fairchild, David, with Elizabeth Kay and Alfred Kay. *The World Was My Garden: Travels of a Plant Explorer.* New York: Scribners, 1938. Reprint, Miami: Banyan Books for the Fairchild Tropical Garden, 1982.

Ferris, James H. "A New Lampsilis from Arkansas." *Nautilus* 14, no. 4 (August 1900).

Frierson, L. S. *A Classified and Annotated Check List of the North American Naiades.* Waco, Tex.: Baylor University Press, 1927.

Fuller, Samuel, and Inga Brynildson. *Freshwater Mussels of the Upper Mississippi River.* Madison: Wisconsin Department of Natural Resources, 1985. Based on a poster by the same name published by the U.S. Fish and Wildlife Service and the U.S. Army Corps of Engineers.

Gaby, Donald C. "1824 Storm Search Is Rewarding." *Update* (Historical Association of Southern Florida) (November 1984): 7–10.

Gifford, John C. *On Preserving Tropical Florida.* Compiled and with a biographical sketch by Elizabeth Ogren Rothra. Coral Gables, Fla.: University of Miami Press, 1972.

———. *Ten Trustworthy Tropical Trees.* Emmaus, Penn.: Gardeners' Book Club, 1946.

———. "A Tribute to Simpson." WIOD radio broadcast, Coral Gables, Florida, December 19, 1932. University of Miami Special Collections.

Goodrich, Calvin. "Bryant Walker 1856–1936." *Nautilus* 50, no.2 (October 1936): 59–64.

Graustein, Jeannette E. *Thomas Nuttall, Naturalist: Explorations in America, 1808–1841.* Cambridge, Mass.: Harvard University Press, 1967.

Grismer, Karl. "In the Days of the Vigilantes." In his *The Story of Sarasota,* 79–92. Sarasota, Fla.: M. E. Russell, 1946.

———. *The Story of Sarasota: The History of the City and County of Sarasota, Florida.* Sarasota: M. E. Russell, 1946.

Haas, Fritz. *Superfamilia Unionacea.* Berlin: De Gruyter, 1969.

Healey, B. J. *The Plant Hunters.* New York: Scribners, 1975.

Heard, William H., and Richard H. Guckert. "A Re-evaluation of the Recent

Unionacea (Pelecypoda) of North America." *Malacologia* 10, no. 2 (1970): 333–55.

Henderson, John B., Jr. "Collecting in Haiti." *Nautilus* 15, no. 2 (June 1901): 13–16.

———. *The Cruise of the Tomás Barrera.* New York and London: G. P. Putnam and Sons, 1916.

———. *Log Book of the Tomás Barrera.* Handwritten log of the Cuban expedition to the Colorado Reefs, May–June 1914. John B. Henderson Papers, Smithsonian Institution, Washington, D.C.

Higgins, Frank. "A Catalogue of the Shell-bearing Species, Inhabiting the Vicinity of Columbus, Ohio with Some Remarks Thereon." Twelfth Annual Report, Ohio State Board of Agriculture, 1857, 548–55.

Hoffmeister, John Edward. *Land from the Sea.* Coral Gables, Fla.: University of Miami Press, 1974.

Hume, H. Harold. "John Kunkel Small—An Appreciation." In *Ferns of the Southeastern States,* by John Kunkel Small. New York: Hafner, 1964.

Jobling, Mary Elizabeth Simpson. "Reminiscences of Pioneer Days." *Tiskilwa Chief* (Ill). Ca. 1914. University of Miami Special Collections.

Kay, Elizabeth D. "David Fairchild—A Recollection," and George H. M. Lawrence, "A Bibliography of the Writings of David Fairchild." Reprinted from *Huntia* 1:71–102. Hunt Botanical Library, Carnegie Institute of Technology, Pittsburgh, 1964.

Lanier, Sidney. *Florida: Its Scenery, Climate, and History.* Philadelphia: Lippincott, 1876.

Madson, John. "Mississippi Shell Game." *Audubon* 87, no. 2 (March 1985): 46–68.

Matthews, Janet Snyder. *Edge of Wilderness: A Settlement History of Manatee River and Sarasota Bay. 1528–1885.* Tulsa, Okla.: Caprine Press, 1983.

McDuffee, Lillie B. *The Lures of the Manatee: A True Story of South Florida's Glamorous Past.* Manatee, Fla.: Published by the author, 1933. Reprint, Bradenton, Fla.: Oliver K. Fletcher, Jr., 1967.

Miller, Hugh. *The Testimony of the Rocks, or Geology in Its Bearings on Two Theologies, Natural and Revealed.* Edited by Stephen J. Gould. Salem, N.H.: Ayer, 1980.

Muir, Helen. *Miami U.S.A.* Coconut Grove, Fla.: Hurricane House, 1953.

Official Directory of the City of Miami and Nearby Towns. 1904. Reprint and Facsimile Series, Historical Museum of Southern Florida, 1974.

Ortmann, Arnold Edward. "A Monograph of the Naiads of Pennsylvania." *Mem. Carnegie Museum* 4 (1911): 279–347.

———. "A New System of the Unionidae." *Nautilus* 23, no. 9 (February 1910): 114–20.

Ortmann, Arnold Edward, and Bryant Walker. "On the Nomenclature of Certain North American Naiades." *Occasional Papers of the Museum of Zoology* (University of Michigan), no. 112 (July 1, 1922): 1–75.

Parker, Sybil P. *Synopsis and Classification of Living Organisms.* New York: McGraw-Hill, 1982.

Parks, Arva Moore. *The Forgotten Frontier.* Miami: Banyan Books, 1977.

Peattie, Donald Culross. *Green Laurels.* New York: Simon and Schuster, 1936.

Peters, Thelma. *Lemon City: Pioneering on Biscayne Bay, 1850–1925.* Miami: Banyan Books, 1976.

———. *Miami 1909 with Excerpts from Fannie Clemons' Diary.* Miami: Banyan Books, 1984.

Pierce, Charles William. "The Cruise of the Bonton." *Tequesta: Journal of the Historical Museum of Southern Florida* 22 (1962): 3–77.

Pilsbry, H. A. *Land Mollusca of North America.* Vol. 2, pt. 1. Academy of Natural Sciences of Philadelphia Monographs, no. 3 (1946): 37–102.

———. "Notes and Notices." *Nautilus* 6, no. 10 (February 1893): 118–19.

———. "A Study of the Variation and Zoogeography of *Liguus* in Florida." *Journal of the Academy of Natural Sciences of Philadelphia,* Series 2, 15 (1912): 429–71.

Pinardi, Norman J. *The Plant Pioneers.* Torrington, Conn.: Rainbow Press, 1980.

Proby, Kathryn Hall. *Audubon in Florida.* Coral Gables, Fla.: University of Miami Press, 1974.

"Publications Received." Review of Simpson's *Descriptive Catalogue. Nautilus* 28, no. 5 (September 1914): 59–60.

Reasoner, Pliny. "The Condition of Tropical and Semi-tropical Fruits in the United States." U.S. Department of Agriculture, Division of Pomology. *Bulletin* 1 (1887): 1–100.

Report of the Adjutant General of the State of Illinois, containing reports for the years 1861–66. Vol. 4. Springfield, Ill.: Phillips Brothers, 1901.

Roper, Marion. "Building Pools." Unpublished manuscript, 1935.

Safford, W. E., "Natural History of Paradise Key and the Nearby Everglades of Florida." *Smithsonian Report for 1917,* 377–434. Washington, D.C.: U.S. Government Printing Office, 1919.

Simpson, Helen A. *Early Records of the Simpson Families in Scotland, North Ireland, and Eastern United States.* Philadelphia: Lippincott, 1927.

Simpson, Joseph Herman. "Botanical Work, Etc." Unpublished manuscript, 1917. Joseph H. Simpson files, Eaton Florida History Room, Manatee County Public Library System, Bradenton, Florida.

———. Journal. Vols. 1 and 2. Unpublished manuscript, ca. 1916. Bureau County Historical Society, Princeton, Ill.

———. "Pioneer Chapters in the History of Bureau County." *Bureau County Republican* (Ill.), 1916. Reprint, 1928.

Small, John Kunkel. "A Cruise to the Cape Sable Region of Florida." *Journal of the New York Botanical Garden* 17 (November 1916): 189–202.

———. *Ferns of the Southwestern States.* New York: Hafner, 1964.

———. *From Eden to Sahara: Florida's Tragedy.* Lancaster, Pa.: Science Press Printing Co., 1929.

———. "Narrative of a Cruise to Lake Okeechobee." *American Museum Journal* 18 (December 1918): 684–700.

———. "Royal Palm Hammock." *Journal of the New York Botanical Garden* 17 (October 1916): 165–72.

Smiley, Nixon. "Strange Home Built by Noted Naturalist." *Miami Herald*, July 30, 1950.

Stansbery, David H. "Eastern Freshwater Mollusks (I): The Mississippi and St. Lawrence River Systems." From the American Malacological Union symposium, Rare and Endangered Mollusks. *Malacologia* 10, no. 1 (1970): 9–22.

———. "Rare and Endangered Freshwater Mollusks in Eastern United States." *Proceedings of a Symposium on Rare and Endangered Mollusks (Naiads) of the United States*, 5–18. Columbus: Ohio State University Center for Tomorrow, 1971.

Stein, Carol. "Naiad Life Cycles: Their Significance in the Conservation of the Fauna." In *Proceedings of a Symposium on Rare and Endangered Mollusks (Naiads) of the United States*, 19–25. Columbus: Ohio State University Center for Tomorrow, 1971.

Sterki, Victor. "Notes on the Unionidae and Their Classification." *American Naturalist* 37 (1903): 103–13.

Stroud, Patricia Tyson. *Thomas Say, New World Naturalist*. Philadelphia: University of Pennsylvania Press, 1992.

Taxpayers and Voters of Bureau Co., Ill. Illinois. Bureau County Archives, 1877.

Teale, Edwin Way, comp. *Green Treasury: A Journey through the World's Great Nature Writing*. New York: Dodd, Mead, 1952.

Tebeau, Charlton W. *Florida's Last Frontier*. Coral Gables, Fla.: University of Miami Press, 1966.

———. *A History of Florida*. Coral Gables, Fla.: University of Miami Press, 1971.

———. *The Story of the Chokoloskee Bay Country with the Reminiscences of Pioneer C. S. "Ted" Smallwood*. Coral Gables, Fla.: University of Miami Press, 1955. Reprint, Miami: Banyan Books, 1976.

———. *They Lived in the Park: The Story of Man in the Everglades National Park*. Coral Gables, Fla.: Everglades Natural History Association and University of Miami Press, 1963.

University of Michigan Catalogue of Graduates, Non-graduates, Officers, and Members of the Faculties. Ann Arbor: University of Michigan Press, 1923.

van der Schalie, Henry. "An Old Problem in Naiad Nomenclature." *Nautilus* 65, no. 3 (January 1952): 93–99.

von Ihering, Hermann. "The Unionidae of North America," Parts 1–2. *Nautilus* 15, no. 4 (August 1901): 37–39; 15, no. 5 (September 1901): 51–53.

von Jhering [Ihering], Hermann. "Naiads from S. Paulo and the Geographic Distribution of the Freshwater Fauna of South America." *Arch. Naturg.* 59, no. 1 (1893): 45–140.

Weiss, Harry B. *Thomas Say: Early American Naturalist*. Springfield, Ill., and Baltimore: C. C. Thomas. Reprint, New York: Arno, 1978.

White, Gilbert. *The Natural History of Selbourne*. Vols. 1 and 2. New York: Appleton, 1895.

INDEX

Page numbers in italic indicate illustrations.